Tellers and Listeners

by the same author

The Novels of George Eliot

The Appropriate Form:
An Essay on the Novel

The Moral Art of Dickens

The Exposure of Luxury:
Radical Themes in Thackeray
(Peter Owen)

The Advantage of Lyric:
An Essay on Feeling in Poetry

Tellers and Listeners

The Narrative Imagination

by

BARBARA HARDY

UNIVERSITY OF LONDON
THE ATHLONE PRESS
1975

Published by
THE ATHLONE PRESS
UNIVERSITY OF LONDON
at 4 *Gower Street London* WC1

Distributed by Tiptree Book Services Ltd
Tiptree, Essex

© *Barbara Hardy* 1975

ISBN 0 485 11153 5

Printed in Great Britain by
WESTERN PRINTING SERVICES LTD
Bristol

To Julia and Bob

Preface

Nature, not art, makes us all story-tellers. Daily and nightly we devise fictions and chronicles, calling some of them daydreams or dreams, some of them nightmares, some of them truths, records, reports, and plans. Some of them we call, or refuse to call, lies. Narrative imagination is a common human possession, differentiating us, as Isocrates insisted, from the animals, and enabling us to 'come together and found cities and make laws and invent arts'.[1] Isocrates is aware that we narrate to each other, and to ourselves. A different kind of book might dwell on the primary imagination, taking its illustrations from psychologists' casebooks, diaries, letters, and tapes. The disadvantage of such materials is that they are informal, but still literary, and I have preferred to take for granted the evidences of observation and introspection. The object of this book is to look at these natural narrative forms and themes, which have been neglected by critics but recognized by narrative artists.

Narrative artists have avoided the common heresy of supposing narrative to be an exclusively literary form. They have usually, moreover, shown an implicit sense of its ordinariness. Michel Butor has observed that 'narrative...extends considerably beyond the scope of literature',[2] but has emphasized the existence of our common narrative activity chiefly in order to define the need and purpose of formal experiment in what he calls the unverifiable forms of art. His distinction is challenging but strange. Most of the novelists who have written about the narrative activity of everyday life have been alert to its unverifiable and unreliable nature. Their interest, analysis, and judgement, being implicit, is often buried in their forms and themes, and

---

[1] Isocrates, *Antidosis*, trans. George Norlin (London, 1929), ii, p. 327.

[2] 'Le roman est une forme particulière du récit. Celui-ci est un phénomène qui dépasse considérablement le domaine de la littérature; il est un des constituants essentiels de notre appréhension de la réalité.' Michel Butor, *Essais sur le Roman* (Paris, 1969), p. 7.

needs some unearthing. I have tried, therefore, to use literary criticism in order to argue the limits and limitations of literature.

The narratives within formal narrative can be regarded in many ways. We can see them as aspects of form, action, and character. We can observe their psychological and biographical expressiveness; it is of some interest and significance to see which novelists are drawn to the analysis of truths and lies, to gossip and slander, to memory, and to reticence. We can also observe the significance for genre, period, and culture. Internal narrative often occupies a prominent place within short stories because it is a useful aid to compression. It is important in epic and the picaresque novel as carrying a large part of the narrative burden, as well as introducing social, psychological, and formal variety. Its place in epic and picaresque narrative also points the social variations. The importance of oral story-telling in a culture will be reflected in the literature. Our own age of the camera and the tape-recorder displaces and fragments narration, introducing an element of first-hand reporting into social narratives, such as news-casting and documentary film, as well as into the novel, drama, and cinema. I want to bypass social interests in order to focus attention on narrative artists' moral and psychological analysis of our common discourse.

Most story-tellers have been more pessimistic about narrative than Isocrates or Butor. If it is an aspect of creation and love, it is a source of delusion and a means of hostility. If it attempts truths, it refuses and perverts candour. If it can instruct, delight, solace, and invent, it can also parade, seduce, discourage, and destroy. But its activities often defy such clear categories. We postulate pasts for those we meet and surmise futures for them and ourselves. We extrapolate the living into phantoms of as yet unconfirmed or unrealized potentiality. We live in narrative phantasmagorias as we live in countries and climates. Such energies are necessary and necessarily open to abuses. Narrative artists have been concerned with the non-aesthetic forms of narrative because of their awareness of such imaginative action.

Epic, romance, ballad, histories, novels, and tales of all kinds illustrate the moral play of narrative imagination. Homer, Rabelais, Cervantes, Swift, Fielding, Flaubert, and Jane Austen are all wary of books, but their criticism stretches beyond mere professional in-fighting, and even beyond a warning against literacy, to alert us to the dangers of creativity and impressionability as tellers and listeners.

The books celebrate unbookishness. Don Quixote and Sancho

Panza know that their author can't write their sequel without them. Odysseus is praised for telling stories as well as a professional bard. Lockwood recognizes the eloquence and leisurely particulars of Nelly Dean's story. Joyce values Leopold and Molly Bloom's story-telling as well as Stephen's. And the dangers of the real story-telling are appreciated too, in con-men, liars, slanderers, bad gossips, and flatterers. The use and abuse of narrative are perennial and central themes of literary stories. There is of course a danger in laying such stress on literary revelations of non-literary powers. It is obviously impossible to explain away literature's interest in the non-literary as comic or realistic sleight-of-hand, but the great tellers of tales and writers of novels are using their skills of expression, invention, and synthesis in order to appreciate and analyse the story-telling of everyday life, and so may be the last people to show this telling as it really is. It is hard for talent to refine itself out of existence, but that is precisely what it sometimes attempts. Observation and attentive listening may anticipate or endorse the novelist's insistence that the informal or amateur narratives, public or private, can also be express-ive, inventive, and synthetic. The man in the street who says that he could write a novel if only he had the time isn't necessarily a laughing-stock. Like everyone else, he is telling stories and scraps of stories every day of his life, assembling and revising the stories of his days into an informal autobiography. It wouldn't necessarily be a readable narrative, let alone a best-seller or a work of genius, and it might be too inarticulate, unformed, and uninventive to be interesting even as a tape-recording of the mind, a type of *récit verité*. But even if we take the dimmest view of the narrative powers of the dimmest mind, story-telling doesn't have to be brilliant in order to perform its good or bad functions. It is characteristic of great story-tellers to warn us not only off books, but also off brilliance. Homer's *Odyssey*, Jane Austen's *Emma*, and Twain's *Huckleberry Finn* sheer away from an excessive admiration for genius and too easy a contempt for stammer-ings and silence. It would be a mistake to dismiss such warnings as either ironically amusing or haplessly patronizing.

The professional story-teller goes beyond the amateur in his analysis of what he is doing, and that analysis helps us to look more closely at the acts and arts of narrative. To do so is to be brought to its limit and verge, as it lapses and relapses into the moans, murmurs, and babble which precede all narrative, as it turns into laughter and crying, as it hopelessly or wisely turns to silence or music. It takes an appreciation of narration to recognize these limits. Homer, Mark Twain, and James Joyce speak with experienced voices to challenge our susceptibility to narrative virtuosity, Thomas Hardy reminds us of the secrecy and evasion of human lovers as they listen to a nightingale, Shakespeare insists that some forms of eloquence can invoke silence as the only resort of wisdom, decency, and grace, Wordsworth tells us that some stories can't be told, and Beckett shows that the choice of one story involves the suppression of others, and refuses to claim reliability for memory or art.

To look closely at narrative is to recognize its collaboration with other powers of imagination. In literature, as outside it, we speak in a mixture of modes. To tell a story is often to perform, as we can see in the public narrations of Odysseus, Jingle, Huckleberry Finn, and the Confidence Man, and the private narrations of Molly and Leopold Bloom. To tell a story is often to make images, as we can see in the parables of Christ, the flattery of Satan, the slander of Iago, the reminiscences of Hardy's Woodlanders, and the remorse of Stephen Dedalus. It may be to exclaim, to rhapsodize, or to brood darkly, like Mrs Gamp, Proust's Marcel, Lawrence's Mellors, or Beckett's paralytics and travellers. It may be to generalize and animate story through symbol, as in Dorothea Brooke's attempts to relate past and present, or in the metaphors offered by Henry James's characters in *The Wings of the Dove* and *The Golden Bowl*. Story-telling may be dramatic, imagistic, lyrical, and mythopoeic, but it always narrates, retails a sequence of events. Most of my illustrations come from stories, usually though not always from prose fiction, and although I have necessarily isolated their concern with narrative, they will almost always yield other significances. Narrative is hardly ever, if at all, simply and solely narrative.

What I am suggesting about narrative applies more broadly to all artistic forms which may at times imitate, or appear to imitate, aspects of experience outside art, but are not using exclusively aesthetic forms and powers. Although most literary forms are mixed and analyse the mixture of forms in experience outside art, there is a certain tendency to specialize in the analysis of form and theme. The dramatist will be particularly drawn to the dramatic modes of performance and presentation, the film director to problems of vision and image. I have drawn on literary narrative in order to bring out its affinity with the forms of everyday life, dream and fantasy, lies and slander, bad and good gossip, affectionate telling, and reticence, but these topics are of course very far from exclusive, and the list could be greatly extended. I have tried to extend it a little, approaching the subject from another angle by a detailed analysis of the narrative themes of three authors, Dickens, Hardy, and Joyce. I had originally thought that a discussion of narrative was something to be found only in certain novelists and narrative poets, but I have come to realize that narrative is a common theme of narrative. Since any narrative artist will yield illustration, I have to admit an arbitrariness in my choice of novelists, but they are all profound and far-reaching analysts of narrative structures and values. Dickens's themes of narrative performance and joke, Hardy's themes of parish history and naïve story, Joyce's themes of secret, surmise, disclosure, confession, and sexual narrative, are all topics which could have found a place in the more general section of my book. But I have found it useful to place these topics in the context of individual writers.

The approach through theme and the approach through the author evade an historical approach. There are histories of narrative and their writers and readers will be able to use any aspects of my discussion which seem relevant. A chronological account would not only have involved a massive analysis of epic, romance, fiction, and drama, but would have blurred the outlines of my argument. There are certain narrative devices proper to certain genres and certain genres typical of certain periods, but I have wanted to emphasize those forms which all narratives have in common. Although the self-conscious analysis of narrative appears prominently in eighteenth-century novelists such as Swift, Fielding, Sterne, and Diderot, and recurs in our own century with Joyce, Proust, Mann, Gide, Beckett, and Nabokov, the sophisticated reflexive forms explore the same moral and psychological narrative themes as the less artistically introspective novels of the nineteenth century. The great realistic novelists of England, France, and Russia tend to look first at life and let artistic significance filter through as secondary implication, while the self-analysing novels are often explicit about narrative technique and response in order to imply a deeper moral significance. Many narrative writers, of all periods, mix the modes and vary the implications, using professional analysis and parody to accompany or play against a broader concern. The blend of form and theme can be seen in Homer, Jane Austen, Thackeray, and

Joyce, and its implications seem to override differences of time, culture, and technique to reveal a continuity of interest in the common humanity of narrative.

The approach through individual writers raises, if faintly, a bio-graphical significance. To encounter such questions head-on would also be to write a different kind of book and to blur the simplicities of my present argument. It is impossible not to observe Dickens's recurrent interest in an urgent story told to a half-comprehending but satisfied listener, or Joyce's interest in sexual fantasy and the specula-tions of jealousy and secrecy, but I have made no attempt to develop such promptings.

From the *Arabian Nights* to Beckett's trilogy, prose narrative has delighted in the presentation of individual narrators. Socrates explains in the *Republic* that Homer is telling a story all the time, but 'where he is delivering a speech in character, he tries to make his manner resemble that of the person he has introduced as speaker'.[3] Narration has been thoroughly motivated by the professional narrators, who have never been content with an artistic inspiration and impetus. Accordingly, narrators can be much more than animated narrative devices or author's disguise. Narrators include barely individualized spokesmen, whose point of view gives a starting-point but is scarcely crucial, like George Eliot's male narrator in *Scenes of Clerical Life*, characters who give a marvellous excuse for story but recede into the background like Scheherazade or the narrator of *The Golden Ass*, conspicuous narrator-figures in the foreground of the novel, like Jane Eyre, David Copperfield and Esther Summerson, and more subtle figures like Emily Brontë's Lockwood and Nelly Dean, Conrad's Marlow, Scott Fitzgerald's Nick Carraway, Ford Madox Ford's Dowell, or the hero of Glenway Wescott's neglected *Pilgrim Hawk*, who form part of a narrative *trompe l'œil*, in which they fluctuate from background to foreground. But novelists are implicitly, if not explicitly, aware of the totality and persistency of narrators. I have, therefore, not included a separate discussion of the prominent narrators who bear the main burden of narrative, though they have of course made their presence felt.

This book goes back to May 1959, when James Britton and Nancy Martin asked me to talk about the nature and functions of narrative at a meeting of the London Association for the Teaching of English. I have since profited from their work, particularly from James Britton's

[3] F. M. Cornford, trans., *The Republic of Plato* (Oxford, 1941), p. 79.

Language and Learning. Other past and present members of L.A.T.E. have been encouraging, including John Dixon, always heartening in his belief that a book would eventually be extricated from the phantoms that kept presenting and effacing themselves. To all these friends who are teachers and educationalists I am deeply grateful; without them the book would probably not exist, though they are not responsible for any of its shortcomings. I hope they will not be disappointed by my conventionally literary illustration.

In February 1968 a version of my talk was published in *Novel*, as a contribution to the symposium, 'Towards a Poetics of Fiction', whose very title is a useful reminder of the neglect of narrative. My essay 'An Approach through Narrative' made tentative claims which I have now extended in this book. I am grateful to the editors for their original invitation and for permission to make some use of this essay in the second chapter 'Fantasy and Dream'. Chapter VI, on 'Dickens', appeared in *The Dickensian* in May 1973. Chapters I and VIII, on 'Narrative Imagination' and 'Joyce', formed the basis of the Ewing Lectures which I gave at University College of California at Los Angeles in April 1974. I am grateful to Ada Nisbet and to my other sponsors and friends in Los Angeles.

I am indebted in many ways to friends, colleagues and students. Jean Elliott gave invaluable assistance and the following helped with ideas, references, and illustrations: William Barber, Michel Blanc, John Edge, Barbara Glenn, Peter Mudford and Rita Richards.

B.H.

Contents

PART ONE

Forms and Themes

I

Narrative Imagination

Well, you know or don't you kennet or haven't I told you
every telling has a taling and that's the he and the she of it.
(James Joyce, *Finnegans Wake*)

Imagination's image-making has engrossed critics of fiction, as they
have followed the lead of critics of poetry and drama. Imagination's
narrative constructions have been less successful in soliciting attention.
We have of course looked hard at total narrative forms like epics,
novels, and stories, but much less closely at the narratives within those
forms. A metaphor represents and realizes on its tiny scale, as the
poem or play or novel of which it forms a part represents and realizes.
Similarly, the narratives within narratives reflect the nature and
structure of their totality, 'organs', as Coleridge said of Shakespeare's
dramatic characters, 'to the whole'. The narrative within the narrative
is intent on revealing and forming its meanings through telling, and also
through not telling, through listening, and not listening. Form, character, theme, authorial individuality and values cannot be properly analysed unless we sharpen, deepen and broaden our concepts of narrative.

Sharpening them, we look harder at the network of narratives of
which all novels are made. (Not only novels, but they are a good place
to begin, just as poetry was a good place to begin work on imagery.)
Deepening them, we may break down the distinction between experience which is aesthetic and experience which is not aesthetic.
(This can also be done through other literary genres and other arts,
but it is simpler to begin with the examples one knows best.) Broadening
them, we may look beyond the novel to these other forms of literature
where narrative is also important—epic, drama, poetry, history,
biography, essay—and beyond them to the larger life of which art
forms a part rather than an imitation. In that larger life, the shared and
secret life of all our days and nights, narrative plays an important part.
Narrative, like drama, lyric, or dance, cannot be regarded simply as an
aesthetic invention used by artists in order to control, manipulate,

order and investigate the experiences of that life we tend to separate from art, but must be seen as a primary act of mind transferred to art from life. The novel does not invent its structures but heightens, isolates and proceeds to analyse the narrative forms, methods, and motions of perception and communication. Sometimes explicitly, always implicitly, the novel is concerned to analyse the narrative forms of ordinary life.

We cannot take a step in life or literature without using an image. It is hard to take more than a step without narrating. Before we sleep each night we tell over to ourselves what we may also have told to others, the story of the past day. We mingle truths and falsehoods, not always quite knowing where one blends into the other. As we sleep we dream dreams from which we wake to remember, half-remember and almost remember, in forms that may be dislocated, dilapidated or deviant but are recognizably narrative. We begin the day by narrating to ourselves and probably to others our expectations, plans, desires, fantasies and intentions. The action in which the day is passed coexists with a reverie composed of the narrative revision and rehearsals of past and future, and in this narrative too it is usually hard to make the distinction between realism and fantasy which we make confidently in our judgements of literary narratives. We meet our colleagues, family, friends, intimates, acquaintances, strangers, and exchange stories, overtly and covertly. We may try to tell all, in true confession, or tell half-truths or lies, or refuse to do more than tell the story of the weather, the car, or the food. We may exchange speaking silences or marvellous jokes. And all the time the environment beckons and assaults with its narratives. Walls, papers, mass-media, vehicles, entertainments, libraries, talks, slogans, politicians, prophets and Job's comforters persuade, encourage, depress, solicit, comfort and commiserate in narrative forms. Even when we try to escape narrative, as when we listen to music or do mathematics, we tend to lapse. Even logicians tell stories. Humankind cannot bear very much abstraction or discursive reasoning. The stories of our days and the stories in our days are joined in that autobiography we are all engaged in making and remaking, as long as we live, which we never complete, though we all know how it is going to end.

The novel uses and analyses these forms of narrative which are essential and crucial aspects of our experience of ourselves, of each other, and of the larger world. Through the forms of literary narrative, large and small, macrocosmic and microcosmic, we may elucidate these fundamental narrative processes. The narrative artists have been, unsurprisingly, interested in the nature of their own medium and form, and, surprisingly, have perceived what psychologists and critics have neglected. The analysis of narrative by the professional novelists and story-tellers is implicit and explicit. If we look at the cells of narrative, instead of the whole body, we will see the reflections of our own storytelling. We will also see more fully the nature of literary narrative.

If we look closely even at the imagery of prose discourse it seems inclined to narrative energies. The Sermon on the Mount, for instance, is rich in images of everyday or domestic objects, like salt, candles and pearls. But I cannot hope to invoke their power without doing more than merely name the images. They are not statically pictorial or emblematic but involve narrative. The salt has lost its savour and cannot do its job of seasoning food, the candle has been absurdly put under a bushel instead of being put in a candlestick, the pearls are madly cast before swine. Not only does each image tell its singular story, but that story invokes another. The strange but illustrative treatment of the salt, the light, and the pearls is only appreciated when it is easily and implicitly referred to our memory of the normal way of treating salt, light and pearls. The memory of accumulated ordinary experience joins with the narrator's brilliantly bizarre invention to create the whole narrative in which salt, light, pearls and many other images are activated to instruct a humble and desperate audience in the ways of blessed righteousness and godliness.

Mr Casaubon enters *Middlemarch* uttering an image which enthralls Dorothea Brooke: 'My mind', he observes, 'is something like the ghost of an ancient, wandering about the world and trying mentally to reconstruct it as it used to be, in spite of ruin and confusing changes' (ch. ii). The image of the archaeological ghost may be misleadingly enticing but it is a most suitable emblem for Mr Casaubon, though even the reader does not see how suitable it is for some time. (Its source is the proem to *Romola*, from which it is transferred to *Middlemarch* with considerable irony.) It is very quickly answered by an image proffered by Dorothea, the appropriate emblem for her bright dream of ancillary function, that of 'a lamp-holder'. Each of these images forms part of a little story. Mr Casaubon's is told politely, publicly, even perhaps with a gleam of his very wintry humour, though we can't be sure of that. Dorothea's is told rashly, privately, and certainly without any humour.

She reconstructs his story of reconstruction to include herself and to join his story with her very different story of ardour, aspiration and a longing for knowledge of the past to help in the present. The autobiographies of these two people are disparate but they have to be joined. Dorothea performs that act of imaginative grafting familiar to us all. She thinks over what he has just said, 'To reconstruct a past world', and here she is still attending to Casaubon's story. But she adds, 'doubtless with a view to the highest purposes of truth', and here she is telling his story in the way she needs and wishes it to be. This little phrase is the link her imagination forges to join the stories, and join their lives.

The cellular structure of internal narrative grows through many such joins. The process of creating character, relationships, plot and formal continuity is often managed through the characters' making, remaking, listening and half-listening to each other's stories. This is how Homer does it in the *Odyssey*. The first speaker is Helen who has put an anodyne into the wine to free reminiscence from pain. She is speaking in public, in her husband's presence, about her stay in Troy. She ends:

> 'The other women of Troy were loud in their lamentations, but I rejoiced, for I was already longing to go home again. I had suffered a change of heart, repenting the infatuation with which Aphrodite blinded me when she lured me to Troy from my own dear country and made me forsake my daughter, my bridal chamber, and a husband who had all one could wish for in the way of brains and good looks.'

> 'My dear,' said the red-haired Menelaus, 'your tale was well and truly told. I have wandered far in this world, I have looked into many hearts and heard the counsels of the great, but never have I set eyes on a man of such daring as the indomitable Odysseus. What he did in the Wooden Horse is another example of the man's pluck and resolution. I remember sitting inside it with the pick of the Argive army, waiting to bring havoc and slaughter on the Trojans, when you appeared on the scene, prompted, I can only suppose, by some god who wished to give the victory to Troy, for Prince Deiphobus came with you.' (bk. v)[1]

And he goes on with the story of Helen's mimicry of the voices of the wives of the Argive warriors, a stratagem which failed.

[1] The translation used is that of E. V. Rieu in the Penguin edition.

This pair of narratives glance delicately, diplomatically, but decidedly towards the listeners and the tellers. They provide the answer to a question which must have passed through many readers' minds: how did Menelaus and Helen deal with the story of their past? The telling makes a definite contribution to the characters of two of the most important persons in the story of Troy, but the character of these story-tellers is here allowed to enter only briefly. The main business is the telling of the story to Telemachus about his father. Homer always allows his stories to be shaped and coloured by tellers and listeners, but the shaping and colouring is controlled and subordinated. This narrative episode is also an example of the main medium in this epic poem, where action is almost entirely related, indirectly and dramatically, in a chain of telling in which the characters participate. It is necessary that Odysseus should be a great story-teller for it is on his narrative skill (compared by Alcinous to that of a professional bard, like Demodocus) that the telling of the *Odyssey* largely rests. But the telling is varied. It moves from one character to another in a continuous but diversified telling. Homer never forgets who is telling, to whom, what, where, and when.

The stories told by the story-tellers of Homer, the Gospels, and George Eliot have individuality, not only in language but in their narrative theme and form. Homer is particularly interested in lies and narrative deviation, Christ in parables, George Eliot in inner fantasy. Novelists must have a very wide range of narrative, which is bound to include the major modes of fantasy, memory, narrative exchange, and will probably also include lies, truths, boasts, gossip, confessions, confidences, secrets, jokes, not to mention romances and novels. From this storehouse of narrative each narrative artist makes his biassed choice. Virgil, Milton, Samuel Richardson, Dickens and Mark Twain are, like Homer, fascinated by lies, though also by truths. George Eliot, D. H. Lawrence and Aldous Huxley are interested in the anatomy of gossip, though as they exploit its powers they like also to analyse its shortcomings, by explicit commentary and implicit comparison with the nature of full and truthful narrative. Wordsworth and Joyce are exceptionally good at telling the story of the development of the artist's narrative and imagistic imagination, but are also very good at the unsophisticated story of unanalytic minds; sometimes they set the one against the other.

The interest in narrative often strikes us as a particularly professional interest, but it is seldom merely professional. Despite the popularity of artist-novels, novels have a tendency not to be narrowly or directly about novelists. What every novelist knows most about is writing novels, but the analysis of narrative imagination is usually two-headed. It looks towards art, and towards life. We cannot always tell which is primary, the professional or the unprofessional concern, just as we cannot know whether the interest in the life-narrative started off the novelist's career or developed with the writing. In Jane Austen's *Emma*, for instance, the author obviously has some personal and professional interest in describing a heroine who is 'an imaginist, on fire with zeal and speculation'. But Jane Austen never writes a novel about a novelist. Emma's are the temptations of a human being possessed of a fertile narrative imagination and they are also the temptations of a lazy, rich, clever young woman living in a small village, brought up by weak and amiable people who have let her have things her own way. When Jane Austen wrote *Emma* she seems to have been writing about the strengths and weaknesses of human imagination from a sensibility alerted by professional experience. Perhaps more striking than the major events of the plot is the occasional account of Emma's mind. On one occasion it is revealed when idling and off-duty. She expects little and sees little. Both expectation and actuality show the characteristic working of her mind:

> ... Emma went to the door for amusement.—Much could not be hoped from the traffic of even the busiest part of Highbury;—Mr. Perry walking hastily by, Mr. William Cox letting himself in at the office door; Mr. Cole's carriage horses returning from exercise, or a stray letter-boy on an obstinate mule, were the liveliest objects she could presume to expect; and when her eyes fell only on the builder with his tray, a tidy old woman travelling homewards from shop with her full basket, two curs quarrelling over a dirty bone and a string of dawdling children round the baker's little bow-window eyeing the gingerbread, she knew she had no reason to complain, and was amused enough; quite enough still to stand at the door. A mind lively and at ease, can do with seeing nothing, and can see nothing that does not answer. (ch. xxvii)

Of course being Emma, the heroine of *Emma*, she doesn't see nothing for long. Her author is busy providing her with material, as novelists must, and in a minute two people come down the road to feed her imagination with more nourishing viands. But that one moment of relaxed energy shows Jane Austen's feeling for the easy strength of Emma's mind and shows it the more plainly in a rare disengagement from its favourite materials. The absence of action lays bare the mind's delight in its own powers. Jane Austen's heroine is on the look-out for narrative material, her mind is ready, vigorous, untroubled, and can exercise itself pleasurably on remarkably little. This is Emma's power and her danger. Emma's author must have experienced such power, danger, and pleasure, in art as well as in life.

Sometimes, however, the case is reversed, and what looks like a highly professional and self-conscious reflection turns out to have a broadly humane relevance. Everyone's list of sophisticated and self-analytic novelists must include Cervantes, Fielding, Sterne, Diderot, Joyce, Beckett and Nabokov. They are great comic novelists who are sufficiently assured of their virtuosity to be able to fool about with it, brilliant clowns who feign clumsiness, naïveté, uncertainty or ineptness in order to tease and in order to make quite certain that we don't mistake something that looks easy for something that is easy. Such expert pretences and teases are the conceits and witticisms of the narrative imagination. Amongst them we might include the conversation between Don Quixote and Sancho Panza about their author's dependence on their actions for his novel, Sterne's peremptory command to his lady reader to go back and re-read the previous chapter, and the game of shuffled contingencies played so gaily by Diderot and so gloomily by Beckett. Each of these examples presents the common narrative conceit of internal telling and listening. Story-tellers and their good or bad listeners are important in all novels, but in this group of narrative gamesmen we find the figure presented with a subtle and dazzling comic virtuosity.

In Cervantes's *Don Quixote*, the travellers, Don Quixote and Sancho Panza, are passing a frightening and uncomfortable night, terrified by a fearful roar, and waiting nervously for what the morning may bring. Good reasons for telling stories include trying to keep your head on your shoulders, passing the time in inns, on the road, and on your death-bed, making sense out of confusion, covering up the naked truth, introducing yourself, or soothing your child. On this occasion, Don Quixote, who is often the teller, has asked Sancho to tell a story, to distract them both from fear and noise. Even though he has asked for it, he is an impatient listener:

Don Quixote then thought fit to claim his promise, and desired him to tell some of his stories to help to pass away the time. 'Sir,' quoth Sancho, 'I am woefully frightened, and have no heart to tell stories; however, I will do my best; and now I think on it, there is one come into my head, which, if I can but hit on it right, and nothing happen to put me out, is the best story you ever heard in your life; therefore listen, for I am going to begin. In the days of yore, when it was as it was, good betide us all, and evil to him that evil seeks. And here, sir, you are to take notice that they of old did not begin their tales in an ordinary way; for it was a saying of a wise man whom they called Cato, the Roman Tonsor, that said, "Evil to him that evil seeks," which is as pat for your purpose as a ring for the finger, that you may neither meddle nor make, nor seek evil and mischief for the worse, but rather get out of harm's way; for nobody forces us to run into the mouth of all the devils in hell that wait for us yonder.' 'Go on with thy story, Sancho,' cried Don Quixote, 'and leave the rest to my discretion.' 'I say then,' quoth Sancho, 'that in a country town in Estremadura, there lived a certain shepherd, goatherd I should have said; which goatherd, as the story has it, was called Lope Ruiz; and this Lope Ruiz was in love with a shepherdess, whose name was Toralva, the which shepherdess, whose name was Toralva, was the daughter of a wealthy grazier, and this wealthy grazier—.' 'If thou goest on at this rate,' cried Don Quixote, 'and makest so many needless repetitions, thou wilt not have told thy story these two days. Pray thee tell it concisely, and like a man of sense, or let it alone.' 'I tell it you,' quoth Sancho, 'as all stories are told in our country, and I cannot for the blood of me tell it any other way, nor is it fit I should alter the custom.' 'Why then, tell it how thou wilt,' replied Don Quixote, 'since my ill fortune forces me to stay and hear thee.' 'Well then, dear sir,' quoth Sancho, 'as I was saying, this same shepherd, goatherd I should have said, was extremely in love with that same shepherdess, Toralva, who was a well-trussed, round, crummy strapping wench, coy and froppish, and somewhat like a man, for she had a kind of beard on her upper lip; methinks I see her now standing before me.' 'Then I suppose thou knewest her,' said Don Quixote. 'Not I,' answered Sancho, 'I never set eyes on her in my life; but he that told me the story said this was so true, that I might vouch it for a real truth, and even swear I had seen it all myself. Well—but, as you know, days go and come, and time and

straw make medlars ripe; so it happened, that after several days
coming and going, the Devil, who seldom lies dead in a ditch, but
will have a finger in every pie, so brought it about, that the shepherd
fell out with his sweetheart, insomuch that the love he bore her
turned into dudgeon and ill-will; and the cause was, by report of
some mischievous tale-carriers that bore no good-will to either
party, for that the shepherd thought her no better than she should be,
a little loose in the hilts, and free of her hips. Thereupon, being
grievous in the dumps about it, and now bitterly hating her, he even
resolved to leave that country to get out of her sight: for now, as
every dog has his day, the wench perceiving he came no longer
a-suitoring her, but rather tossed his nose at her, and shunned her,
she began to love him, and doat upon him like anything.' 'That is the
nature of women,' cried Don Quixote, 'not to love when we love
them, and to love when we love them not. But go on.' 'The shepherd
then gave her the slip,' continued Sancho, 'and driving his goats
before him, went trudging through Estremadura, in his way to
Portugal. But Toralva, having a long nose, soon smelt his design;
and then what does she do, think ye, but comes after him bare-foot
and bare-legged, with a pilgrim's staff in her hand, and a wallet at
her back, wherein they say she carried a piece of looking-glass, half
a comb, a broken pot with paint, and I do not know what other
trinkums-trankums, to prink herself up. But let her carry what she
would, it is no bread and butter of mine; the short and the long is,
that they say the shepherd with his goats got at last to the river
Guadiana, which happened to be overflowed at that time, and, what
is worse than ill luck, there was neither boat nor bark to ferry him
over; which vexed him the more, because he perceived Toralva at
his heels, and he feared to be teased and plagued with her weeping
and wailing. At last he spied a fisherman in a little boat, but so little
it was, that it would carry but one man and one goat at a time. Well,
for all that he called to the fisherman, and agreed with him to carry
him and his three hundred goats, over the water. The bargain being
struck, the fisherman came with his boat, and carried over one goat;
then he rowed back and fetched another goat, and after that another
goat. Pray sir,' quoth Sancho, 'be sure you keep a good account
how many goats the fisherman ferries over; for if you happen to
miss one, my tale is at an end, and the devil a word have I more to
say. Well then, whereabout was I?—Ho! I have it.—Now the

landing-place on the other side was very muddy and slippery, which made the fisherman be a long while in going and coming; yet for all that he took heart of grace, and made shift to carry over one goat, then another, and then another.' 'Come,' said Don Quixote, 'we will suppose he has landed them all on the other side of the river; for, as thou goest on one by one, we shall not have done these twelve months.' 'Pray let me go on in my own way,' quoth Sancho. 'How many goats are got over already?' 'Nay, how the devil can I tell!' replied Don Quixote. 'There it is!' quoth Sancho: 'did I not bid you keep count? On my word the tale is at an end, and now you may go whistle for the rest.' 'Ridiculous!' cried Don Quixote: 'pray thee is there no going on with the story unless I know exactly how many goats are wafted over?' 'No, Mary is there not!' quoth Sancho, 'for as soon as you answered, that you could not tell, the rest of the story quite and clean slipped out of my head; and in truth, it is a thousand pities, for it was a special one.' 'So then,' cried Don Quixote, 'the story is ended.' 'Ah, marry is it!' quoth Sancho, 'it is no more to be fetched to life than my dead mother.' (vol. I, bk. iii, ch. vi)[2]

Novels are full of bad listeners, just as plays are full of bad audiences. Like Fielding or Sterne attacking the neo-classical pedantry of the Hypercritick, or Beckett praising the conveniently impenetrable paper of the *Times Literary Supplement*, Cervantes takes great pleasure in writing about an impatient and unregulated response to a rambling and digressive narrative. The pleasant self-indulgence of needling or disarming one's unsympathetic readers is infrequently resisted. Cervantes subtly draws our attention, in the gentlest possible way, to the need to suspend disbelief and preconceptions. Don Quixote is the master, instructor, teller. But as he has ordered a story from his squire he should stop asserting himself. Fielding makes Partridge unable to listen quietly while the more polite, educable and sensitive Tom Jones responds to the Man of the Hill's story. Cervantes shows more democratically that masters as well as servants can be bad listeners and the don is rebuked. The moral is plain. You must be attentive and you must accept the conventions of the story-teller. If you need his story, then let him have it his way. Otherwise, the story will stop.

[2] The translation used is that of P. Motteux (1701–3), which is reprinted in the Everyman edition.

This listening test with its narrative nemesis has larger implications. Cervantes is joking about the rationalism of his mad don, but he is seriously showing that Don Quixote must learn to listen to Sancho. He may be mad but he responds to experience, and the well-known process of osmosis in which this famous pair come to partake of each other's qualities largely depends on their telling and their listening.

In Diderot's great comic novel, *Jacques le Fataliste*, Diderot's Jacques is engaged, like Tristram Shandy, in telling the much interrupted story of a love-life. His master, who is usually the listener within the novel, is constantly tantalized by the interruptions, and bitterly complains. The reader also constantly heckles and pesters the author with his complaints and questions, which are given a dramatic entry to the novel. The reader's participation provides the peremptory author, a show-off god writing his novel about fatalism, with plenty of opportunities to put the reader in his place. It is evident that the characters are being determined and the chief narrative conceit of the novel turns on the appropriateness of a fictional character being a fatalist. Jacques feels that everything they do 'down here' for good or for ill, is written 'up on high'. The inferiority of life on the page is made wittily plain but not allowed to promote feelings of superiority in the reader. The reader's curiosity and impatience is a major source of interruption and when on one occasion he typically insists on halting the often-halted narrative to ask many questions about Jacques's master the author tells him:

> He was a man. A man with strong passions like you, reader; curious like you, reader, importunate like you, reader, asking questions like you, reader.—And why did he ask questions?—A good question! He asked questions to learn and to tell again, like you, reader.[3]

The question 'And why did he ask questions?' is one of Diderot's best narrative jokes. But the comic juggling suddenly drops into a solemn truth about telling and listening, and takes us from the self-conscious conceit about novels to the larger human condition: 'He asked questions to learn and to tell again, like you, reader.'

[3] Il était homme.—Homme passionné comme vous, lecteur; homme curieux comme vous, lecteur; homme importun comme vous, lecteur; homme questionneur comme vous, lecteur.—Et pourquoi questionnait-il?—Belle question! Il questionnait pour apprendre et pour redire comme vous, lecteur...

Sometimes the novelist is interested in truthfulness, a subject we may be glad to find of more importance than that of realism. Homer sympathized with narrative zeal. While his Odysseus depends on his narrative arts to get back home, the habitual manipulation of many different listeners has a certain corrupting effect on his imagination, like writing advertising copy. He needs to be rebuked and the rebuke comes most appropriately from Pallas Athene for the compulsive and redundant act of telling a lie to her:

> 'What a cunning knave it would take', she said, 'to beat you at your tricks! Even a god would be hard put to it.
>
> And so my cunning friend, Odysseus the arch-deceiver, with his craving for intrigue, does not propose even in his own country to drop his sharp practice and the lying tales that he loves from the bottom of his heart. But no more of this: we are both adepts in chicane. For in the world of men you have no rival as a statesman and orator, while I am pre-eminent among the gods for invention and resource.' (bk. xiii)

It has occurred to Odysseus to tell the truth now he is in Ithaca but he refrains, 'loyal as ever to his own crafty nature'. The liar is lying to a superior liar, but he is not at a loss for an answer and excuses himself. She is so clever in disguise that it is hard for a man to know whom he is talking to. It is on the occasion of this failure to keep up his story (as he manages to do so successfully with other women, mortal and immortal, Calypso, Circe, Nausicaa, Arete, and Penelope, often with Athene's help) that the goddess admires his wariness and recommends that policy of silence which Joyce may have remembered in *A Portrait of the Artist as a Young Man*, where his hero contemplates silence, and in *Ulysses*, where his hero practises it constantly.

Homer tells us that there are those we cannot lie to. Mark Twain tells us that there are those we should not lie to. Surely remembering Homer, Twain makes Huckleberry Finn begin the novel he narrates by explaining that his author has told the truth in the main but has included some 'stretchers', like most people. Like his author and like his ancestors, Don Quixote, Sancho Panza and Odysseus, Huck also has to get by with telling stories. Like the stories of Odysseus, they are fictional autobiographies, adapted for each new occasion and each new listener, told and acted with great zest and often marked by creative overkill. Like Odysseus, Huck also has to be steadied and kept in touch with truthfulness. His Athene is Jim, who is himself not above telling good lies. Huck cons Jim into believing that a whole night's adventures didn't really happen but were all part of a dream and as soon as Jim amazedly and reluctantly accepts the story, as 'the power-fulest dream I ever see', Huck points to the evidence that it did really happen after all, the leaves, rubbish and smashed oar, which are revealed as the light suitably and symbolically clears. Jim's reply is a necessary reproach, because up to now Huck's stories have been told in their joint interests. They are on the same raft, running for their lives, and they are distinguished from the really aggressive liars, the Duke and the King, by having each other to whom they do tell the truth. Jim is doubly outraged since Huck has persuaded him to re-tell the story of what he has been duped into believing is a dream, and has 'painted it up considerable'. Mark Twain's playful juggling with lies is comic but serious and Jim's indignation inspires him to seize the trash as the right symbol for Huck, 'trash is what people is dat puts dirt on de head er dey fren's en makes 'em shamed'. Huck has to learn that you must have someone to whom you don't tell lies. There is a limit to the fertility of the narrative imagination. It is not good to lie to friends, just as it is no good to lie to gods.

Mark Twain reminds us that the novelist is particularly alive to the morality of narrative. This is of course not to say that he will not take great pleasure in the impersonation of narrative abuse. D. H. Lawrence was eloquent on the subject of gossip, distinguishing its superficiality, antagonism, and moral condescension, from the novel's probing, re-spectful, loving imagination. His story is concerned to make implicit this sympathy, as it tells the most private story in the most private lan-guage and contrasts it with the crude and moralistic, self-flattering rejections of public gossip. But Lawrence threw himself with great gusto into Mrs Bolton's rattling and animated narrative. As Clifford Chatterley observes, she has come to live a posthumous life, taking her oxygen from air that had passed through other people's lungs. It is certainly burnt up with great energy:

'That's all they care about, clothes. They think nothing of giving seven or eight guineas for a winter coat—colliers' daughters, mind you—and two guineas for a child's summer hat. And then they go to the Primitive Chapel in their two-guinea hat, girls as would have been proud of a three-and-sixpenny one in my day. I heard that at the Primitive Methodist anniversary this year, when they have a built-up platform for the Sunday School children, like a grandstand going almost up to th' ceiling, I heard Miss Thompson, who has the first class of girls in the Sunday School, say there'd be over a thousand pounds in new Sunday clothes sitting on that platform! And times are what they are! But you can't stop them. They're mad for clothes. And boys the same. The lads spend every penny on themselves, clothes, smoking, drinking in the Miners' Welfare, jaunting off to Sheffield two or three times a week. Why, it's another world. And they fear nothing, and they respect nothing, the young don't. The older men are that patient and good, really, they let the women take everything. And this is what it leads to. The women are positive demons. But the lads aren't like their dads. They're sacrificing nothing, they aren't: they're all for self. If you tell them they ought to be putting a bit by, for a home, they say: That'll keep, that will, I'm goin' t' enjoy mysen while I can. Owt else'll keep! Oh, they're rough an' selfish, if you like. Everything falls on the older men, an' it's a bad outlook all round.' (*Lady Chatterley's Lover*, ch. ix)

The opposition between a good and a bad narrative, superficial and profound, as in *Lady Chatterley's Lover*, or truthful and untruthful, as in *Paradise Lost* or *Othello*, is a frequent foundation for the structure of novels or epics. Its importance as a self-conscious structural principle reflects its larger importance for action and value. Narrative is crucial, in life and in literature. Our ordinary and our extraordinary day depend on the stories we hear. One piece of news, a change of intention, even a revision of memory, a secret, a disclosure, a piece of gossip may change our lives. The writer of Genesis does not err when he makes the fall of Man depend on a lie and a slander, and Homer does not exaggerate when he makes Troy's fall depend not just on a wooden horse but on Sinon's lie, the story that persuaded the Trojans to tear down their walls rather than *not* take in the horse. Wordsworth was fully aware of the crucial narrative, though what he tries to do in *Lyrical Ballads* is to underplay excitement and drama and stress the importance of events that may not seem of great interest to the listener who wants sensational stories. So he insists, in an appropriately lame and earnest manner, in 'Simon Lee':

> O reader! had you in your mind
> Such stores as silent thought can bring,
> O gentle reader! you would find
> A tale in every thing.
>
> What more I have to say is short,
> I hope you'll kindly take it;
> It is no tale; but should you think,
> Perhaps a tale you'll make it.

Wordsworth's narrators are occasionally in danger of adopting a tone that is *faux-naif*, as in 'The Thorn', where the narrator's particularity becomes too obtrusively and ludicrously garrulous and fussy, but some of his simple story-tellers are brilliantly determined to stick to their story. The heroine of 'We are Seven' wins the battle between two narratives: her loving pragmatism refuses to mourn the deaths that seem so companionable and defeats the adult's rational and religious attempt to correct her and impose his story.

Another victory of simplicity over rational experience comes in 'Anecdote for Fathers', where one of his best story-tellers, the boy Edward, may recall Cordelia in his illustration of the dangers of urging someone to tell a story. Father-like, the father tries to elicit the full story of Edward's preference for Kilve over Liswyn:

> 'For, here are woods and green-hills warm;
> There surely must some reason be
> Why you would change sweet Liswyn farm
> For Kilve by the green sea.'
>
> At this, my boy, so fair and slim,
> Hung down his head, nor made reply;
> And five times did I say to him,
> 'Why? Edward, tell me why?'
>
> His head he raised—there was in sight,
> It caught his eye, he saw it plain—
> Upon the house-top, glittering bright,
> A broad and gilded vane.
>
> Then did the boy his tongue unlock,
> And thus to me he made reply;
> 'At Kilve there was no weather-cock,
> And that's the reason why.'

Oh dearest, dearest boy! my heart
For better lore would seldom yearn,
Could I but teach the hundredth part
Of what from thee I learn.

Wordsworth's own liking for moral anecdote is splendidly varied and criticized by the tellers inside his tales. *Lyrical Ballads* recognizes that everyone has a story in them, that narrative genius is not always in the ascendent, and that narratives are not always forthcoming and must not be commanded. Listeners must respect silence as well as stories.

2
Fantasy and Dream

I forgave Don Quixote all for his admission in the cart.
(W. H. Auden, 'Memorial for the City', *Nones*)

A tale my imagination created, and narrated continuously. . .
(Charlotte Brontë, *Jane Eyre*)

We can distinguish the extremes of indulgent fantasy and faithful document but the many intermediate states blur the distinction. The element of dream can be sterile and dangerously inward looking; it can also penetrate and accept a wide range of disturbing, irrational experience that cannot easily be accepted, ordered, understood or reconstructed. Dream can debilitate but its subversive discontents are vital for personal and social development. It can provide escape or a look at the unwished-for worst. It lends imagination to the otherwise limited motions of faithful memory and rational planning. It acts on the future, joining it with past. It creates, maintains and transforms our relationships: we come to know each other by telling, untelling, believing and disbelieving stories about each other's pasts, futures and identities. Dream probes and questions what can be static and too rational stories about past, future and identity, and in the process is itself steadied and rationally eroded. We tell stories in order to escape from the stubbornness of identity. As Randall Jarrell reminds us in 'Children Selecting Books in a Library',

> What some escape to, some escape: if we find Swann's
> Way better than our own, and trudge on at the back
> Of the north wind to—to—somewhere east
> Of the sun, west of the moon, it is because we live
>
> By trading another's sorrow for our own; another's
> Impossibilities, still unbelieved in, for our own...
> 'I am myself still?' For a little while, forget:
> The world's selves cure that short disease, myself,
> And we see bending to us, dewy-eyed, the great
> CHANGE, dear to all things not to themselves endeared.

He propounds the paradox that to be mature involves escape, or rehearses a disengagement from self which is perfected in death. Thus we may be engaged in telling ourselves stories in a constant attempt to exchange identity and history, though many of us stay sufficiently self-attached to rewrite the other stories for our own purposes. But 'escaping' and 'escaping to' form only a part of narrative activity and function. We tell stories in order to change, remaking the past in a constant and not always barren *esprit d'escalier*. The polarity between fantasy and reality is another instance of convenient fiction: we look back to go forward or to stay in a past-centred obsession. Like most works of fiction, personal history is made up of fantasy and realism, productivity and idling. Fantasy-life does not come to an end at eighteen but goes on working together with the more life-orientated modes of planning, faithful remembering and rational appraisal.

Henry James likes to show the working of sensibility and intelligence in the present happening, but since he so often centres the interest in a spectator he can show and exploit a slight but subtle and important gap between happening and interpretation: the narrative contains a narrative of what happens counterpointed on a narrative of what seems to be happening, or what the spectator tells himself is happening. The gap is also present—on an enormous scale and with vast irony—in *Tom Jones* and *Wuthering Heights*. One of James's great achievements is to narrow the gap so that some readers never see it at all and the rest have to work uncomfortably hard to see it. Amongst his major themes is the relation between what occurred and what was reported, expected, believed, dreamed and falsified. The self-contemplating narrative of fiction is nowhere subtler and more explicit than in *The Ambassadors*.

Let us begin with the *locus classicus*, Strether by the river:

What he saw was exactly the right thing—a boat advancing round the bend and containing a man who held the paddles and a lady, at the stern, with a pink parasol. It was suddenly as if these figures, or something like them, had been wanted in the picture, had been wanted more or less all day, and had now drifted into sight, with the slow current, on purpose to fill up the measure. They came down slowly, floating down, evidently directed to the landing-place near their spectator and presenting themselves to him not less clearly as the two persons for whom his hostess was already preparing a meal. For two very happy persons he found himself straightway taking them—a young man in shirt-sleeves, a young woman easy and fair, who had pulled pleasantly up from some other place, and being acquainted with the neighborhood, had known what this particular retreat could offer them. The air quite thickened, at their approach, with further intimations; the intimation that they were expert, familiar, frequent—that this wouldn't at all events be the first time. (bk. xi, pt. iv)

David Lodge, in *The Language of Fiction*, quotes Wittgenstein's saying, 'The limits of my language are the limits of my world'. Mediated through the limits of James's language are the limits of his narrative, but he is explicitly aware of such limitations and they form at least a major part of his subject. Our narratives are of course limited by our sensibility, inhibitions, language, history, intelligence, inclinations to wish, hope, believe, dream. *The Ambassadors*, like most great novels, is concerned with the powers and limitations of narrative and so Strether is shown here, as elsewhere, seeing and telling. He has been seeing these same characters and telling himself stories about them for a long time and here he is seeing them for the first time with the truly alienated vision of the stranger. He is therefore made to show his sensibilities as narrator. We are about to see—not for the last time indeed in this novel that goes on moving—a climactic collision between what he wants to tell and what he has to see. We see his impulse to order and his impulse to praise, first in the pure form of a vision of people who mean nothing to him. The imagery is pictorial and even impressionistic, deriving as it does from the generalized imagery of painters, painting and aesthetic vision, and from the localized context of the remembered unbought painting by Lambinet. But James's is the kind of picture most impressionists did not paint, the kind that tells a full story. Like Lawrence, he seems often to write about artists so that he may and yet need not be writing about novelists. Here the implications, for all the trembling visual delicacy and radiance, are plainly narrative. The figures are 'as if' wanted in the picture but they come to break down the picture's static composition and will not stay, like figures cut through by the frame, on the edge of the impressionist landscape. They continue to move, to come nearer and loom larger, they cease to be compositionally appropriate to the picture and become people.

The stories Strether tells are elegant configurations, and who should know more than Strether's creator about the special temptations of aesthetic arrangement in narrative? But Strether is also moved to tell stories out of curiosity: he does not know enough, he is kept guessing, there are secrets and mysteries. He is lied to by little Bilham and left by Maria Gostrey, who runs away rather than lie or stop telling the story. Maria says at the end that Strether has been vague. He has also, of course, been benevolent. He is more like a Dickens than a James, trying to see the best in people, wanting his characters to be moral as well as dashing. James's method is to show the special bent of Strether's vague and curious benevolence in a routine act of consciousness. What is there in this passage that is coloured by the viewpoint of Strether and his story-telling? He straightway takes the couple for 'very happy persons' on the slight evidence of their dress, their youth, the day, the boating, and nothing else. He sees them as having pulled 'pleasantly' from somewhere else. But much of what he says and thinks is rightly inferred from what is before him. Strether is not a narrator like Emma, who projects her wishful fantasies and interpretations on to highly intransigent materials. Strether needs more malleable stuff to work in. Just as Jane Austen tells us, as well as shows us, that Emma is an imaginist, so James gives us many explicit clues long after we might have ceased to need them. Here he tells us that Strether's inventiveness is active: 'the air quite thickened, at their approach, with further intimations'. The scene is of course created for a narrator by a narrator and the last stroke of irony is that the air was indeed quite right to thicken.

Strether is not the only narrator, only the chief one. Most novels concerned with the nature of narrative—that is, most novels—create tensions between narrators. In *To the Lighthouse* we have Mr Ramsay, the realist who will not use fantasy and lies even to comfort a child, and Mrs Ramsay who will, but who also tells James the terrible fairy-story of 'The Fisherman's Wife', thus making it clear that she is no mere sentimental protector of the child. In *The Mill on the Floss* we have the narrow, moralizing realism of Tom Tulliver, the narrow, powerful fantasy of Stephen's desire, and the strengths and weaknesses of dream, moral scheme and shaping passion in Maggie. In *The Ambassadors* Strether's benevolently-coloured vagueness is contrasted with Maria's truth-telling, little Bilham's kind lies and Chad's dazzling evasions and omissions which reveal a master of the kind of narrative that will make for success in advertising.

We also have within single characters the attempt to attend to what really happens and the desire to apply the distorting pressure of wish and faith. Distortion often takes the most subtle form of the benevolent story: Strether, like Isabel Archer in *The Portrait of a Lady* or Dorothea Brooke in *Middlemarch*, does not move from selfish fantasies towards life as it really is but from self-abnegatory fantasies towards a different story. There is a conflict between the story such characters tell themselves—about marrying Casaubon, helping society, marrying Gilbert Osmond, not marrying Lord Warburton, living hard no matter how, and so forth—and the harder, more realistic story their author has written for them. Yet in a sense the story these heroic characters try to live does shape their lives too. The ironies are blurred and complex. Dreams are productive when they lead to productive conflicts. Stories need not be just lies.

But there are novelists who show a larger discrepancy between the inner narrative and the novel. Gissing and Hardy write about characters very like the heroic figures in James and George Eliot—but characters who do not succeed in making their fantasy in any sense productive, who indeed fail most bitterly in the imaginative attempt to tell the story of life as they wish to lead it. Tess is a passive instance, involved and manipulated by her family's narrative, in all its socially significant and pathetic crudeness, rather than by her own energies. Jude is the classical instance of failure of imagination, since the tale he tells himself can have no substance and would have been better untold. Gissing's heroes are often like Hardy's. In *Born in Exile* the hero creates an enterprising narrative and role, feigning religious belief and intelligently attempting to give society what it wants in order to take what he wants. Gissing shows the social impulse to lie in the extreme inventiveness of the man who is essentially a novelist's creation, who researches for his lie, dresses for it, moves into the right environment and acts it out, right to the point of collapse. He shows here, as in *New Grub Street*, the failure to impose and sustain a certain kind of story, though in *Born in Exile* the breakdown is weak, coming out of accidental, though probable, discovery, rather than out of socially and psychologically expressive action. Gissing diverts the interest and misses a fine opportunity, failing to finish his story properly like his hero. Indeed, the two failures may be related. Gissing may fail because he cannot carry through a story about a man who lives a lie—or rather, about a man of such imagination and humanity. His novels are full of more simplified minor characters, like some of the successful writers in *New Grub Street*, who lie successfully by finding the right formula and telling the right story to themselves and others in the right place at the right time and in the right style.

Some novelists and novels are more optimistic about the stories people tell. They show the productiveness of fantasy. Joyce and Beckett exhibit the healing power or the sheer survival-value of myth-making, of telling stories about past and future and identity, even in the face of a dislocation of time and identity. The nostalgias and unrealities and comfort of the dream of youth, love and past happiness, for instance, are set against Molly Bloom's sexually-obsessed repetitions —another narrative novelists did not invent—and against the harshness of infidelity and impotence and the grander nostalgias of the *Odyssey*. Beckett's human beings tell stories in the least promising circumstances, in the mud, dragging the sacks, jabbed and jabbing: they tell the incoherent story of life as they feel its pressures, with the odd sweet flash of what seems to be memory. The novels of Beckett are about the incorrigibility of narrative. Indeed the pessimistic novelist who wrote a story in which narrative as an act of mind had collapsed would clearly be telling lies about the relation of his own creativity to his own pessimism. Novelists are expected to show the story going on. But in Beckett the production of story, joke, memory or dream is strenuous, spasmodic, often absurd. Narrative survives, no more.

There are novelists who are less clearly in command of the relation between the story-telling of their characters and the novel in which the stories are told and discussed. Jane Austen creates novels in which characters learn to imagine scrupulously and feel correctly in response to the sense of probability. Her novels might be said to describe the difference between writing a Gothic novel and a Jane Austen novel. They broach, in order to overcome, the errors of promiscuous or pretentious story-telling. Mrs Gaskell, Dickens, and George Eliot write novels of a different kind: they set out to show a similar process of learning how to dispense with fantasy, but one which in the end succumbs to fantasy after all. And here too, as in Gissing, is a kind of understandable inconsistency: they are attempting what they know, even if they fail.

In Mrs Gaskell's *North and South* Margaret Hale tells herself a story, a fable about North and South. The novel tests, corrects and dispels this story and others. The narrative is full of supporting cases, not just of blatant and apparently deliberate instances of differences between North and South, but of people telling stories. Bessy Higgins tells the common story of Heaven which her father sees as the sustaining fantasy she needs. Mr Hale tells himself a story about leading a new life in the North. Mrs Thornton tells a story about North and South too, and a more interesting and personally-coloured story about her son and the marriage he may make. Margaret also tells other stories. One is about saving her brother's reputation and bringing about a family reunion. Whenever character comes up against character there is an immediate narrative reaction and the marked social and regional contrast encourages social fable, though the significant narratives that are tried and dispelled are moral and psychological. Mrs Gaskell is often said to be a rather mechanical and sensational plot-maker but I have been struck by the way the heavily-plotted parts of this novel (almost like sensation-novels in capsule form) eventually have the effect of showing up the falsity and sensationalism of the stories the characters tell. The story about Margaret's brother brings out not only her fantasy of rescue and reunion but also the lie that Thornton has told himself about her moral nature. Mrs Gaskell was clearly interested in the way we tell high moral tales about ourselves and each other. This novel takes us and the characters through the complex process of rejecting untrue stories.

Yet it ends with the reconciliation of Margaret and Thornton which subsidizes his new liberalized attitudes and activities, with the fabulous story of the financial failure and the legacy. The novel which criticizes sensational narrative ends by constituting its own palinode— it offers allegiance to what it has pretended to disdain. We run up against a concluding fable after all, one which resembles the stories that have been tested and found wanting, in its falsity and its ready usableness.

Such a self-division is not a weakness peculiar to Mrs Gaskell. We find it, as I remarked, in Dickens and George Eliot too. They write novels about growing away from romantic day-dream into realistic acceptance, but most of their novels—except perhaps *Middlemarch*— end with a dream-conclusion and wish-fulfillment. *David Copperfield* tells the story of a novelist who learns to discipline his heart and though there is an interesting lack of connection between his development as a novelist and his development as a man he certainly thinks he learns to stop dreaming by finding in other people's stories the traps and dangers of his own. The novel does not proceed single-mindedly to this goal. Its brilliant parodies of calf-love are anticipations, both literary and psychological, of David's blindness. We eventually follow him into the 'real' world. Unfortunately, neither the Wordsworthian imitation of natural sublimities in Switzerland nor the saintly and rocklike qualities of Agnes clear the heady air and the final harmony of his financial, professional, moral and domestic successes seems more dreamlike and unreal than anything that has gone before. Not only do we find a criticism of the dangers of dreaming but Dickens moves further and further away from the real world, salvaging fantasy by plot and idealized invocation. *David Copperfield* is Dickens's most divided novel, I believe, but a similar self-destructiveness and contradiction exist in many of his other books.

Dickens's attempt to criticize fantasy may often fail because he depended much on sexual fantasy and because he was caught in a fairly common Victorian dilemma—antagonism between faith in the individual and despair of society. Almost the reverse might be said of George Eliot but she too illustrates the attempt to supplant fantasy by realism and uncontrolled reversion to fantasy. As in Dickens, her characters tell stories to each other, to themselves, try to impose the stories, try to live by them, try to 'escape or escape to'. She puts an enormous energy of imagination and intelligence into a critical analysis of the stories we tell about life. There is no doubt that she sees the purgation of fantasy as her end. She speaks of gradually forgoing poetry and accepting prose and all her novels explore the moral consequences of sterile dreaming and productive realism. She shows the interpenetration of many narrative modes more fully than in earlier English novels: the social myth, the literary fantasy, the sustained and culture-fed fantasy, the imaginative fantasy (Maggie's), the ethically noble fantasy (Dorothea's), the banal but still potent fantasy (Hetty's), and the tempting nightmare (Gwendolen's). As an analyst of such illusions she ranks with Stendhal and Flaubert. But in *The Mill on the Floss* she too succumbs as Mrs Gaskell and Dickens succumb.

I neither want nor need to trace Maggie Tulliver's story in order to bring out the clash between analysis and dénouement. We follow Maggie's progress through the dreamworld of a child's fantasy-life, responding to varied deprivations, sufficiently individualized and sufficiently common. We follow her through the solicitations and failure of the fantasies of literature, myth, music, religion, and sexual desire. George Eliot not only analyses the individual qualities of the different stories Maggie listens to and tells herself, she most subtly shows their mutual influence, correction, tension, and interpenetration. Maggie's fantasies are not knocked down like ninepins but leave their traces even when they have been explicitly discarded: we see her giving up the nourishing fantasies of wishfulfilling childish story, Romantic poetry, Scott and Thomas à Kempis, but eventually each is shown to exert a lingering influence, both for good and evil. At the end, after a searching and scrupulous analysis, after escorting her heroine into a solitude few Victorian fictional characters ever know, George Eliot too falls back into fantasy: the answer to prayer, the healing flood, the return to the past, forgiveness, the brother's embrace, and—most subtle illusion—forgiveness and understanding newborn in Tom's eyes. The novel disavows the prose realities and saves its heroine from the pains of fresh starts and conflicts by invoking the very narrative consolation it has been concerned to analyse and deny.

Charlotte Brontë did rather better than George Eliot in showing the posthumous life of the dreamer whose dream has been utterly dispelled. She lets Jane Eyre and even Caroline Helstone end with a greater measure of human happiness than Maggie Tulliver, but in *Villette* and *Shirley* she shows a rare ability to create the emptiness that the dreamer can feel on waking. Lucy Snowe experiences low expectations, breakdown, then a period of disciplined higher hopes and dreams after she meets Graham Bretton. Throughout their friendship her fantasy is controlled with a steely grip and the pathetically tense dialogue between Hope and Reason represents the inner life of such rational dreaming. Loss and recovery follow, wryly expected and accepted, and then an exceedingly brief period of congenial love. The tiny margin of content probably shows Charlotte Brontë's own reduced expectations even when she gets so close to her personal fantasy as in the love of Lucy (a version of herself) for M. Paul Emanuel (a version of M. Héger). The dream is itself cut terribly short and in the ending to *Villette*, as in all its narrative tones, there is the sense of a long hard survival, like that dreamed of so bitterly by Isabel Archer as she travels from Italy to England to see Ralph before his death. Lucy is thoroughly and harshly rehearsed in the dreamless life and survives on her own. There is no rescue or companionship, only a professional success and self-reliance both admirable and sour. It is the kind of ending we rather wish George Eliot had been able to give just one of her heroines, but they, like their author, are all sustained by something more than a dream of love. Their development and achievement in moral vision is the dream she allows to them and to herself. Bleakness and boredom are conditions admitted into George Eliot's works only as evidence of moral and imaginative incapacity.

Charlotte Brontë's contribution to the analysis of fantasy is her ability to show post-oneiric survival. Thomas Hardy, like Charlotte Brontë, is very good on survival but his survivors tend to be people who have never expected much, whose imagination has never soared: an Elizabeth-Jane, whose hopes have always been so muted that even when they are realized she refuses to step up the expectation of happiness, or a Marty South, whose love for Giles Winterborne is never shown as involving passionate fantasy, only a wry recognition of a deep moral congeniality. These rational survivors acknowledge from a limited experience that dream is debilitating and dangerous. Charlotte Brontë makes her dreamers experience the danger, letting dream's frantic passions flow about so that we appreciate the strength of intelligence that controls and subdues it:

> ...at eighteen the true narrative of life is yet to be commenced. Before that time we sit listening to a tale—a marvellous fiction— delightful sometimes, and sad sometimes, almost always unreal. Before that time our world is heroic; its inhabitants half-divine or semi-demon; its scenes are dream scenes: darker woods and stranger hills; brighter skies, more dangerous waters; sweeter flowers, more tempting fruits: wider plains, drearier deserts, sunnier fields than are found in nature, overspread our enchanted globe. What a moon we gaze on before that time! How the trembling of our hearts at her aspect bears witness to its unutterable beauty! As to our sun, it is a burning heaven—the world of gods.
>
> At that time—at eighteen, drawing near the confines of illusive, void dreams, Elf-land behind us, the shores of Reality rise in front. These shores are yet distant; they look so blue, soft, gentle, we long to reach them. In sunshine we see a greenness beneath the azure, as of spring meadows; we catch glimpses of silver lines, and imagine the roll of living waters. (*Shirley*, ch. vii)

Jane Eyre, Caroline Helstone, Lucy Snowe, and St John Rivers submit briefly to the power of fantasy but are not overwhelmed by it.

Although the structures and images which suggest its lures derive from the elusive, void and febrile dreams of Gondal and Angria, the characters in Charlotte Brontë's novels are nothing if not rational fantasists. When Caroline Helstone contemplates her dream of love it is certainly not in the spirit of anyone listening to a marvellous and unreal fiction. We are told that she trusts her eighteen-year-old visions without suspecting delusion because 'the foundations on which they rested appeared solid'. As she tells herself that story of the future which is compounded of knowledge and fantasy, she is cool, controlled and rational. She argues sensibly, 'When people love, the next step is, they marry', and carefully checks untoward or exaggerated words, even in warm recollection and hopeful imagining: 'his love-making (friendship I mean; of course I don't yet account him my lover...)'. She does not confuse life and literature: 'his love-making...is not like what we read of in books—it is far better—original, quiet, manly, sincere'. Her enthusiasm has the true ring of internal restrained Brontë feeling: 'I *do* like him!'; and in the imagined future there is a little space for some telling of her husband's faults, 'for he has a few faults'. This is restraint, not fever. Her distinction between the stories we read and her story of the future is confirmed when she imputes to Robert the quality of originality in making love. Literary dreamers like Don Quixote, Emma Bovary, Catherine Morland and Lord Jim are often blind to particulars, seduced by the ideal, by all that is stereotyped and vague. But her cautious and intelligent checking of the dream of a desired future does not save Caroline, any more than Lucy Snowe's control saves her. Jane Austen is also very good at showing this kind of verification in *Emma*, as a characteristic of emotional coolness, and it is Emma's life-line. She is not in love with Frank Churchill, though she has to create and look at a very detailed narrative of various proposals of marriage before realizing in the processes of critical analysis that all the stories end with significant refusal on her part, and then making the sane inference. Where Charlotte Brontë excels is in showing a powerful but temporary unleashing of fantasy still basically subjected to check and control. St John Rivers is moved by Jane to make an uncharacteristic confession of his feeling for Rosamond Oliver but grimly measures out the time he can spend on fantasy, with a watch: 'And he actually took out his watch and laid it upon the table to measure the time' (*Jane Eyre*, ch. xxxii). There follows a typical dialogue of fantasies. Jane persuasively imputes to him an immediate imagining of obstacles, 'some iron blow of contradiction...a fresh chain to fetter your heart', but St John denies this, inviting her to fancy his submissive and indulgent but temporary fantasy:

> 'Fancy me yielding and melting, as I am doing: human love rising like a freshly opened fountain in my mind and overflowing with sweet inundation all the field I have so carefully and with such labour prepared—so assiduously sown with the seeds of good intentions, of self-denying plans. And now it is deluged with a nectarous flood—the young germs swamped—delicious poison cankering them: now I see myself stretched on an ottoman in the drawing-room at Vale Hall at my bride Rosamond Oliver's feet: she is talking to me with her sweet voice—gazing down on me with those eyes your skilful hand has copied so well—smiling at me with those coral lips. She is mine—I am hers—this present life and passing world suffice to me. Hush! say nothing—my heart is full of delight—my senses are entranced—let the time I marked pass in peace.' (ch. xxxii)

They are silent, to let us hear St John breathing 'fast and low' while the watch ticks. When the allotted quarter of an hour is past, he dismisses the fantasy, 'that little space...given to delirium and delusion'. He explains to Jane that his fantasy of a future with Rosamond is compounded of sense as well as desire; it includes his knowledge of unsuitability and future regret, the 'calm, unwarped consciousness' that is unimpaired by the dream. Like Caroline, St John is an intelligent dreamer, reasoning as well as longing, keeping his head. What saves him from folly is what saves Jane from self-destruction and Lucy Snowe from final disintegration: this ability to imagine extremity, but to correct, restrain and eventually give it up. Common sense may slow and cool the story of the future, as it does with Caroline, or permit it a small licensed performance before dismissing it entirely, as with St John, or keep it as a perpetual constituent of the dream, as with Jane Eyre. But it cannot save these rational fantasists from distress.

The characters in Charlotte Brontë tend to share their author's combination of coolness and fever, calm and fret. Their wild flights of fancy leave and return to a common earth. She generally creates people who tell themselves her sort of story, of course, but constructive capacity, passion and outcome vary from character to character. Where the plots turn on expectation and disappointment, or anticipation and reversal, the presentation of fantasy is crucial. But whatever the events of the plot, fantasy is an invariable part of psychological presentation. Jane Eyre longs for new horizons, always finds and strains against new limits, and makes it absolutely plain that her frustrations are peculiarly those of Victorian woman:

> Anybody may blame me who likes, when I add further, that, now and then, when...I climbed the three staircases, raised the trapdoor of the attic, and having reached the leads, looked out afar over sequestered field and hill, and along dim skyline—that then I longed for a power of vision which might overpass that limit; which might reach the busy world, towns, regions full of life I had heard of but never seen; that then I desired more of practical experience than I possessed; more of intercourse with my kind, of acquaintance with variety of character, than was here within my reach. I valued what was good in Mrs Fairfax, and what was good in Adèle; but I believed in the existence of other and more vivid kinds of goodness, and what I believed in I wished to behold.
>
> Who blames me? Many, no doubt; and I shall be called discontented. I could not help it; the restlessness was in my nature; it agitated me to pain sometimes. Then my sole relief was to walk along the corridor of the third story, backwards and forwards, safe in the silence and solitude of the spot, and allow my mind's eye to dwell on whatever bright visions rose before it—and, certainly, they were many and glowing; to let my heart be heaved by the exultant movement, which, while it swelled it in trouble, expanded it with life; and, best of all, to open my inward ear to a tale that was never ended—a tale my imagination created, and narrated continuously; quickened with all of incident, life, fire, feeling, that I desired and had not in my actual existence.
>
> It is vain to say human beings ought to be satisfied with tranquillity: they must have action; and they will make it if they cannot find it. Millions are condemned to a stiller doom than mine, and millions are in silent revolt against their lot. Nobody knows how many rebellions besides political rebellions ferment in the masses of life which people earth. Women are supposed to be very calm generally: but women feel just as men feel...(ch. xii)

Jane's powerful longings are urgent and demanding, for real companionship, for more knowledge and excitement, physical, intellectual, and moral, for more vivid kinds of goodness. She only longs for what her author is going to provide but she is always alert to the likelihood that nothing will be provided. Such a sense of having to live without getting all you can imagine makes Charlotte Brontë's characters melancholy stoics. The sense of reality is the result of a self-consciousness about fantasy in the presence of an inclination for dreaming.

The power to imagine and to observe her own imaginative act is to stand Jane in good stead when she has to fight, with her vivid goodness, against Rochester's arguments, needs and desires. Her temptations and her powers are those of the imaginative life and the forms created and explored by her imagination are specifically narrative forms. Like her author, Jane has the solace and pain of an inner core of reverie. She never ceases to tell herself stories until they are overtaken by the actual story of her own love and conscience, moving her out of the role of listener and fantasist into that of participant. Her solitude needed private reverie but it stops when she can talk and listen to Rochester. She comes to love through knowing, and knows through the exchange of story. The conversation of their narratives is an unbalanced exchange of truths and lies, reticences and admissions, divulgences, reserve and demand, realism and fantasy. When Rochester tells her the story of his love-life, her sheer nerve as listener seems to derive from her own inner habituation to fantastic guilts and judgements. Like the other heroines, she has passion enough to need a forceful, rational inner monitor, intelligence enough to shape the story of a possible future with care and probability, and detachment enough to observe and to judge her own passions and imagined happenings. She even comes to recognize the strongest and subtlest of all her temptations, the temptation to live in Rochester's falsifying dream. The habit of responding to fantasy is bound up with a habit of wariness and no story passes without the severest scrutiny. If Charlotte Brontë creates her fictions from Angrian abandon and fever, from intensities and unrealities, it is not without submitting them to the rigours of critical self-consciousness. The awareness of story-telling is essential to the stories of renunciation and stoicism which these novels tell.

The presence of watchful intelligence makes the essential distinction between dream and day-dream, between the passive submission to fantasy and the fully imaginative narrative which looks before and after, which is self-analytic as well as wishfully inventive. When Emma

Woodhouse weaves her stories she sometimes stops to look at them, to draw inferences and conclusions from their content, style, and tendencies. When Stephen Dedalus considers becoming a Jesuit he imagines the possible future, tells himself the story, puts in the day-to-day specific detail of place and time, habits and companions, but then finds that the story won't bear scrutiny because it lacks probability and is uncharacteristic of what he knows of himself. These dreamers stop dreaming, separate themselves from their fantasies, analyse, judge, and are accordingly made wise.

Dreams in novels are images which express the waking lives of the dreamers more lucidly and rationally than the real dreams of our sleeping lives outside fiction. They are acts with consequences. Both Jane Eyre and Stephen Dedalus are shown dreaming real dreams as well as day-dreams, though such dreams are attached with conspicuous relevance to the themes of the novel; Stephen's are dreams of appeals and calls and Jane's are dreams of deprivation and distress. The most interesting dreams, in life and literature, are day-dreams, those active inventions which we create and can control, and the great dreamers of fiction, Alice and Kafka's K., are to all intents and purposes day-dreamers, with some active say in what they dream, even while they sleep. While literary critics and pedagogues pass judgements and even construct syllabuses on the assumption that there is a hard and fast line drawn between the indulgent dream and the clear directing vision of real life, the day-dreamers in the novel know better.

This verification of fantasy, familiar in all lives, resembles and reflects the artist's need to ground and shape a likely story, which must be controlled by credibility and pattern. It also resembles the reader's pre-critical and critical experience. Such scruples even crop up in Beckett, where one of the narrators in *Texts for Nothing* wonders if he has come back from the dead, but wryly decides that it's not like him to do a thing like that. Beckett's recessions and permutations are warmed by the humour and controlled by the reasonableness of such knowing self-contemplation. In Lewis Carroll's two scientific fantasies, *Alice in Wonderland* and *Through the Looking-Glass*, the same combination of extreme fantasy, urgent feeling, and rational inspection has its characteristic form. Lewis Carroll dramatizes a child's common and uncommon sense. He takes care to make Alice very common-sensical, as her attitudes to language make clear. She is least imaginative, most literal-minded and pedantic when she scrutinizes the language of the Looking-Glass people. The White Knight complains that the messenger's loud whisper goes through his head 'like an earthquake', and she thinks that it would have to be a very tiny earthquake. She is scientist to Humpty Dumpty's poet, mean-mindedly objecting to his glorious use of the word 'glory'. She corrects the White Knight's splendid simile 'as fast as lightening', telling him that he's thinking of another kind of fastness. He defeats her with a crafty shift into hyperbole, 'it was all kinds of fastness with me', but Alice remains unconvinced, her feet firmly planted on whatever firm ground is provided by the chessboard of Looking-Glass-Land.

Though unimaginative about language, she is sufficiently won over by Humpty Dumpty's practical criticism of Jabberwocky to respond intelligently, thus spotting the hardest bit of the portmanteau language-game, 'wabe is the grass plot round the sundial'. She also puns, though inadvertently, while bemused by the Mouse's tail as she listens to his tale. But for the most part her language is resolutely plain or rational. Her most conspicuous similes, those of a telescope and a candle, are matter-of-fact and scientific in content and in form, as far removed as possible from the poetic conceit. As she sighs for the unattainable garden glimpsed through the little door, she seizes scientifically on the need to shut up like a telescope, wonders if there may be a book on the table with rules for such a telescoping, and eventually compares her enlargement to the opening out of the largest telescope there ever was. What appeals to her is not hyperbole, extravagance, or magic, but science, controlling speculation and shaping language. The simile of the telescope is more than a typically scientific and rational image; it is also an example of her creative decisiveness. It is Alice who first thinks of the possibility of shifting her size, for she is more than merely adaptable. She is a jump ahead of the wonders that she meets and having recognized that the old laws don't apply she thinks in terms of new laws. She learns the workings and possibilities of Wonderland, but makes the decision for herself. First comes her idea about getting smaller, *then* the little bottle marked 'Drink me'. Alice is making up her story, or her dream, as she goes along. She attends to causality. She usually expects power to come from books.

This creative energy is shown even more clearly at the beginning of *Through the Looking-Glass*. In *Alice in Wonderland* Alice falls asleep because she is bored by the book which has no pictures and conversations. So she makes up her own story which is rich in everything her sister's book lacks in conversation and illustration. *Through the Looking-Glass* describes her as being half-asleep in her chair but we are alerted to her powers of fancy and invention in her favourite game of 'let's pretend' and her reasoning and inventiveness are far from sleepy. Once more her taste is contrasted with that of her more 'exact' sister, who has objected that they can't pretend to be 'kings and queens' as Alice suggests, because there are only two of them. Just as the story of Wonderland counters and escapes from her sister's adult literary preference, so the Looking-Glass world defiantly carries out the intention to play at being 'kings and queens'. The intention doesn't flout science but uses it, starting with Alice's decision, fully detailed and explanatory, to go through the looking-glass. The fantasy is introduced by the *fiat* of the creative artist but the planning is rational:

> 'Oh, Kitty! how nice it would be if we could only get through into Looking-glass House! I'm sure it's got, oh! such beautiful things in it! Let's pretend there's a way of getting through into it, somehow, Kitty. Let's pretend the glass has got all soft like gauze, so that we can get through. Why, it's turning into a sort of mist now, I declare! It'll be easy enough to get through—' She was up on the chimney-piece while she said this, though she hardly knew how she had got there. And certainly the glass was beginning to melt away, just like a bright silvery mist. (ch. i)

Although this premeditated and deliberate trip is a dream, it is clearly presented as a product of Alice's alert and wakeful imagination. She decides what she would like to do and her 'let's pretend' bridges the speculation and the action of fantasy. Carroll ends, but does not begin, the stories by emphasizing their status of dream, so producing an exciting initiation of wonders, conferring on them a vivid reality unblurred by admissions and recognitions of dreaming. He is also imitating the sensations of real dreaming, with Alice falling into the dreams in good faith and not knowing that she is dreaming until just before she wakes up. And at the beginning he emphasizes the creative decision to create, the essential preliminary invocation which is so often used as a beginning in works of literature from the Bible to Beckett.

What Alice decides is complicated. What she dreams of in *Alice in Wonderland* is a book of rules and her analogy for the size-change is a telescope. What she dreams of in *Through the Looking-Glass* is a world where reversals are to be expected: 'First, there's the room you can see through the glass—that's just the same as our drawing-room, only the things go the other way.' She knows too that the words in the books go the wrong way. Each fantasy is composed of magic and science. Fantasy begins only where science ends: Alice refuses to take the part for the whole and will not be taken in by what may turn out to be mere smoke-screens:

> 'I want so much to know whether they've a fire in the winter: you never *can* tell, you know, unless our fire smokes, and then smoke comes up in that room too—but that may be only pretence, just to make it look as if they had a fire.' (ch. i)

We must of course distinguish between Carroll's science and Alice's. He didn't underrate the scientific reasoning of children, as is demonstrated by the story of Alice Raikes's solution to the puzzle about the reflection of the girl holding her orange in the left hand: 'Supposing I was on the *other* side of the glass, wouldn't the orange still be in my right hand?' The complex teasing of the child listener or reader and the complicity of the adult listener or reader[1] depend on the ironies of combining nonsense and science, like shifting the base of arithmetical notation to make it look like arithmetical nonsense:

> 'Let me see: four times five is twelve, and four times six is thirteen, and four times seven is—oh dear! I shall never get to twenty at that rate!' (*Alice in Wonderland*, ch. ii)

Speculations about time-telling at the centre of the earth can join with the madness of the Mad Hatter's tea-party, with a little joke about the ambiguities of metaphor thrown in:

> Alice had been looking over his shoulder with some curiosity. 'What a funny watch!' she remarked. 'It tells the day of the month, and doesn't tell what o'clock it is!'
>
> 'Why should it?' muttered the Hatter. 'Does *your* watch tell you what year it is?'
>
> 'Of course not,' Alice replied very readily: 'but that's because it stays the same year for such a long time together.'
>
> 'Which is just the case with *mine*,' said the Hatter.

---

[1] It should be remembered, too, that there was another adult besides Carroll in the boat, and so his story was not for the children alone. See A. L. Taylor, *The White Knight* (Edinburgh and London, 1952), p. 45.

Alice felt dreadfully puzzled. The Hatter's remark seemed to have no sort of meaning in it, and yet it was certainly English...

Alice sighed wearily. 'I think you might do something better with the time,' she said, 'than waste it in asking riddles that have no answers.'

'If you knew Time as well as I do,' said the Hatter, 'you wouldn't talk about wasting *it*. It's *him*.'

'I don't know what you mean,' said Alice.

'Of course you don't!' the Hatter said, tossing his head contemptuously. 'I dare say you never even spoke to Time!'

'Perhaps not,' Alice cautiously replied: 'but I know I have to beat time when I learn music.'

'Ah! that accounts for it,' said the Hatter. 'He won't stand beating. Now, if you only kept on good terms with him, he'd do almost anything you liked with the clock.' (ibid., ch. vii)

Henry James would speak of 'viewpoint', but even in less formidable language, Carroll is wrestling with complex problems of narrative. Of course the author knows more than Alice, but like other successful creators of character, he can project her dramatized viewpoint apart from his own, finding appropriate child-versions or Wonderland-versions for his arithmetic, his physics, his logic, and his rhetoric. Alice is unlike him in childish ignorance but sufficiently like him in mind and temper to be able to tell his kind of story within the story he tells about her. So her 'let's pretend' is a speculation combining knowledge, reason and fancy. Alice's sturdy common sense weaves through all her fantasies, though they are often started off by the gusto of inventiveness. Once in Wonderland she not only conforms very quickly to the extraordinary new conditions, learning by experiment that certain old limits are transcended, but enjoys wondering at the wonders. She dislikes wild language but is at home with wild situations, like being drowned in a pool of her own tears, being ordered about by animals when she goes back to the upper world, and being cut off from her feet. It doesn't require much for her to take off into fantasy, though it does require something. It requires the prompting of what is extraordinary and not 'normal', like the pool of tears, the role-reversals of humans and animals, and the change of size which also changes her relation to parts of her own body. The fantasy acts to control her, to facilitate her survival and to diminish the feelings of fear, panic and desolation which afflict her from time to time, and are, of course, actually responsible for the pool of tears. Alice's sense of fantasy, like Carroll's, is evidence of her sense of humour and keeps her going. She hangs on to humour as she hangs on to science and social probability. The fantasy is sometimes ironic. Seeing the funny side of drowning in your own tears involves some measure of detachment, both from grief and from death.[2] The project of writing a letter to your foot makes fun of the horrors and disability of size- and shape-changing. It is a practical project, though, and this is important. Many of the fantasies take the form of bizarre but usefully sensible solutions to difficulties, scientific attempts to play the game of real life within the dream. They also touch on certain experiences of actual dreaming, where the sense of incredulity is sometimes amusingly or pathetically strong when it attempts to apply inapplicable rules. Alice sees only one way out as she contemplates the future relationship with her feet. To that extent, her imagination is scientific and concerned with problem-solving. She is also recognizing the need to placate and ingratiate, another lesson she seems to confirm rather than learn in the ferocious underworld. She had better be nice to her feet or they won't carry her where she wants to go, and while she uses the social conventions of her waking world in which people are pleased and propitiated by presents, she sensibly realizes that a shoe is one of the few presents you can give to a foot. She is also aware—like her companion dreamers in grander novels—of what she is doing. With Alice, just as with Caroline Helstone, Emma, and Stephen Dedalus, fantasy is subjected to realistic scrutiny. And even as she enjoys what she's doing, like all artists, she is also aware that it's very peculiar:

> 'I almost wish I hadn't gone down that rabbit-hole—and yet—and yet—it's rather curious, you know, this sort of life! I do wonder what *can* have happened to me! When I used to read fairy-tales, I fancied that kind of thing never happened, and now here I am in the middle of one! There ought to be a book written about me, that there ought! And when I grow up, I'll write one—but I'm grown up now,' she added in a sorrowful tone; 'at least there's no room to grow up any more *here*.' (ch. iv)

> 'I shall be punished for it now, I suppose, by being drowned in my

[2] William Empson's amusing essay in *Some Versions of Pastoral* seems to me to exaggerate greatly the morbidity of the Alice books.

own tears! That *will* be a queer thing, to be sure! However, everything is queer to-day.' (ch. ii)

'How queer it seems,' Alice said to herself, 'to be going messages for a rabbit! I suppose Dinah'll be sending me on messages next!' And she began fancying the sort of thing that would happen: ' "Miss Alice! Come here directly, and get ready for your walk!" "Coming in a minute, nurse! But I've got to watch this mouse-hole till Dinah comes back, and see that the mouse doesn't get out." Only I don't think,' Alice went on, 'that they'd let Dinah stop in the house if it began ordering people about like that!' (ch. iv)

'...—but I must be kind to them,' thought Alice, 'or perhaps they won't walk the way I want to go! Let me see: I'll give them a new pair of boots every Christmas.'

And she went on planning to herself how she would manage it. 'They must go by the carrier,' she thought; 'and how funny it'll seem, sending presents to one's own feet! And how odd the directions will look!

Alice's Right Foot, Esq.

Hearthrug,

near the Fender,

(with Alice's love).

Oh dear, what nonsense I'm talking!' (ch. ii)

The enjoyment and exultation seem to derive from what she experiences and what she goes on to imagine; the imagination of the character blends easily with the imagination of the writer. Alice's creative decisions and inventions are directed to this end as she decides how to conform, go on, begin, or stop. She adapts herself to almost incredible conditions which she not only accepts but sometimes even anticipates, as when the baby changes into a pig.

Even more important, though, is the sense of wonder, which is intellectual delight: 'and yet—and yet—it's rather curious, you know, this sort of life'. 'Curious' is plainly a term of praise. It implies intellectual interest, as in the constant references to things being queer, funny or nonsensical. Alice is appreciative of what is happening and tries to make it out, by puzzling, knowing, learning, questioning, and relating the curious events to ordinary life. The nonsense is grounded in the memory of ordinariness. The carrier will take the present to her right foot which will be found by the hearthrug near the fender and not where it is in its present displacement. She knows how the pool of tears was made and squeezes a little moral of crime and punishment out of that fantasy. She relates the story about Dinah to the usual social roles and hierarchy in which a cat who gave orders wouldn't be kept in the house. The solid bourgeois world is always just around the corner and often obtrudes awkwardly in Alice's stories, as when she says tactless things about Dinah and recognizes whiting and lobster in their dinner-table appearances.

Such recognitions are essential. Carroll constructs the story out of his own expert and inaccessible knowledge, making those mathematical and philosophical jokes over Alice's shoulder or behind her back. But he also permits her to construct the world out of her experience of art, chiefly the childhood aesthetic world of games, poetry, stories, songs and rhymes. This world of nursery culture is where the characters come from and their origin ultimately explains why she can master them. She conforms to rules, moves only as a pawn should, because she brings that tradition and knowledge from the ordinary world. She expects the Lion and the Unicorn and Tweedledum and Tweedledee to fight, and she knows Humpty Dumpty's fate. Carroll is enjoying the game of placing her in the ambiguous position of being a reader in a story where she meets fictitious characters and so knows all about them, while also toying and teasing with the idea that she may be only in the dream of one of those fictitious characters. The stories and games that make the material are frigid forms, while Alice is much more freely and passionately inventive, but she sees herself as a reader (and at one point as a potential author) while the characters are controlled and predicted by her because of her reading experience. The effect is of a comic irony which is controlled by the dreamer and this effect is clinched when the dreams end. She is both waker and author, deciding that her characters are only puppets and she will have no more to do with them, like Shakespeare at the end of *A Midsummer Night's Dream* and Bottom within it, like Thackeray at the end of *Vanity Fair* and *Pendennis*, and like Don Quixote as he faces his death. Dream is assimilated to story by being active and creatively controlled by judgement and reason, more like a day-dream than a night dream. Day-dreamer and author have in common the decision to pretend and the knowledge that it is pretence. They also share the sense of contact with the other world from which we depart and to which we return.

Alice seems to get more aesthetically conscious as she proceeds from the first book to the second. The first formal story she tells in *Through the Looking-Glass* is an arch flight of fancy which hasn't the characteristic rationality that marks the Wonderland stories, though it too is full of enjoyment and a self-conscious knowledge of fiction:

'Do you hear the snow against the window-panes, Kitty? How nice and soft it sounds! Just as if someone was kissing the window all over outside. I wonder if the snow *loves* the trees and fields, that it kisses them so gently? And then it covers them up snug, you know, with a white quilt; and perhaps it says, "Go to sleep, darlings, till the summer comes again." And when they wake up in the summer, Kitty, they dress themselves all in green, and dance about— whenever the wind blows—oh, that's very pretty!' cried Alice, dropping the ball of worsted to clap her hands. 'And I do so *wish* it was true! I'm sure the woods look sleepy in the autumn, when the leaves are getting brown.' (ch. i)

It shows the streak of whimsy in Carroll's narrative fancy and lacks the science. It also demonstrates as strongly as any of the stories in *Alice in Wonderland* the extent to which Alice longs for fiction to be true. But it is a false start and she reverts to her characteristic bent of scientific fantasy, in the first pretence that the black kitten is the Red Queen of a chess game and in the second pretence that the looking-glass is getting soft like gauze. These two day-dreams have enough intelligence and science in their fantasy for the dreamer's *fiat* to succeed. So the Looking-Glass world is created out of mirrors and chess.

Alice's pseudo-science and her genuine social realism help her to survive in the perilous dream-world, and even to participate in its dream-work. She is a Ulysses of the scientific imagination, for if one way to resist romantic seductions is to fill your ears with wax, the other way is to listen, tied to the mast. The scientist and the artist cannot bear not to listen and may even loosen the ropes that tie them. Then they have to find some means of controlling the urge to submerge and drown. Fantasy is threatening to the rational mind. For Alice there is the threat of panic, a feeling easily and naturally aroused when we lose our bearings in wonder or science. For Charlotte Brontë's characters there is the threat of overwhelming desire, from which they may not recover. The Brontë heroines remain tied to the mast, while Alice swims in the potentially destructive pool, recognizes it with typical astuteness and devises a way of getting out. This is a Carrollian anticipation of *Lord Jim*. Science and reason may help us to immerse ourselves in the dream but what Jim seems to possess is neither. His may be defined as a will to retrieve the dream after losing it in the most shattering and shameful way, as romantics do, by dithering and doddering romantically instead of acting. Jim has a rehearsal on the early occasion when he sees someone else go after the man over-board, because he is day-dreaming:

> On the lower deck in the babel of two hundred voices he would forget himself, and beforehand live in his mind the sea-life of light literature. He saw himself saving people from sinking ships, cutting away masts in a hurricane, swimming through a surf with a line; or as a lonely castaway, barefooted and half-naked, walking on uncovered reefs in search of shell-fish to stave off starvation. He confronted savages on tropical shores, quelled mutinies on the high seas, and in a small boat upon the ocean kept up the hearts of despairing men—always an example of devotion to duty, and as unflinching as a hero in a book.
> 'Something's up. Come along.'
> He leapt to his feet. The boys were streaming up the ladders. Above could be heard a great scurrying about and shouting, and when he got through the hatchway he stood still—as if confounded.
> (Lord Jim, ch. i)

Conrad's modulation from general comment about Jim's literary romanticism to the challenge of event intimates the dangers of dreaming with powerful implicitness. But Jim doesn't see them and can't even read his feelings, concluding rather that he is not angry with himself but with 'the brutal tumult of earth and sky', with nature, with the pressures of the world outside, for which he feels mistakenly readier for having seen that 'a lower achievement had served the turn'. The most damaging illusion is that of having 'enlarged his knowledge more than those who had done the work':

> ...the final effect of a staggering event was that, unnoticed and apart from the noisy crowd of boys, he exulted with fresh certitude in his avidity for adventure, and in a sense of many-sided courage.
> (ch. i)

Stein's two images for the romantic dream are well known. He uses with originality the image of the butterfly, the 'gorgeous object of his dreams', to stand for no unattainable psyche but for something realistic. The butterfly is all that survives, after friend, wife, and child have vanished, and even though it is regarded with a truthful sense of the romantic aspiration and achievement of a human work, it is also a reliable residue. The image itself invokes flight and landing, air and ground, for the butterfly has its feet on earth:

> 'This magnificent butterfly finds a little heap of dirt and sits still on it; but man he will never on his heap of mud keep still. He want to be so, and again he want to be so...' He moved his hand up, then down... 'He wants to be a saint, and he wants to be a devil—and every time he shuts his eyes he sees himself as a very fine fellow—so fine as he can never be...In a dream...' (ch. xx)

There follows the twin image of the destructive element, in which we must immerse ourselves, in which we must learn to swim and not drown. This metaphor is one of adjustment and courage and makes us understand why Marlow tells Stein that no one could be more romantic than he is and why Stein shakes his head in response. Like Stein, who insists that he has not followed all his fine dreams, Jim learns belatedly to swim, by persistence, by an act of will, by energy. His final action is romantic in its ideal of moral being but is unlike the two earlier failures in will, activity and success. There is no panic, no coming up for air, but a grappling. To swim in the destructive element is to create and to survive for a time. Jim's redemptive adventure, like Alice's Wonderland, at one moment seems like something he creates for himself. It asserts, therefore, that to be romantic and to create the dream is something like art:

> 'The story of the last events you shall find in the few pages enclosed here. You must admit that it is romantic beyond the wildest dreams of his boyhood, and yet there is to my mind a sort of profound and terrifying logic in it, as if it were our imagination alone that could set loose upon us the might of an overwhelming destiny. The imprudence of our thoughts recoils upon our heads; who toys with the sword shall perish by the sword. This astounding adventure, of which the most astounding part is that it is true, comes on as an unavoidable consequence. Something of the sort had to happen. You repeat this to yourself while you marvel that such a thing could

happen in the year of grace before last. But it has happened—and there is no disputing its logic.' (ch. xxxvi)

Jim's fate shows the possibility[3] of staying romantically ambitious, asserting an ideal character in action, finding that the dream demands resolution, energy and ability. The artist whose dream needs to be understood and developed through the arduous practice of his craft is likely to emphasize patience and cunning, likely to be ambitious in the whole domain of dream and also of nightmare. In *The Castle* Kafka's K. has to learn to adapt himself to the destructive element, imagined as more alien and more hostile than anything in *Lord Jim*. K. arrives in the village, to fall into the dream. He is a dreamer more like Alice than Jim, bringing with him the recollections of another life and the recognition that this is a threatening world, with its own new laws of time, space, and justice. Like Alice, he brings some aids with him from that other world, though his old assistants are unrecognizable when they turn up. Like Alice, he uses the artist's *fiat*, announcing that he is the land-surveyor. It seems to be his own decision. The challenge is at first refused by the people of the castle, who say they've never heard of him, but the telephone rings again, to accept the challenge and take up the game on his terms. Telephones ring differently in the village but they exist. Expectation and memory don't help much in this place where the terribly short days are more sinister than Alice's changes of size and K. the land-surveyor has to show curiosity, zeal and very great patience. His questions and explorations are backed by a willingness to immerse himself, to love, work, go to school, on the new terms. He has to use silence, exile and cunning. For Alice, Jim, and Stephen Dedalus, there are certain lessons that are painfully but productively learnt. Alice awakes, Jim dies nobly, and Stephen leaves Ireland, invoking the old artifice. For K. there is no one right stroke which will help him to survive in the castle; the mystery and intransigence of its element, in spite of or because of his resilience and energy, are renewed as long as life goes on.

Hence the claustrophobia of *The Castle*, a novel which some people find exceptionally painful to re-read. Knowing what is to come seems hard and also inappropriate, a new pain, which unlike the stops and starts of a first reading, does not seem one which K. himself has to experience. Reading the novel for a second time makes one feel more

[3] See also p. 157.

like Dostoievsky's Ivan Karamazov in his claustrophobic nightmare, oppressed by familiarity with a demonic vision. Ivan sees the devil who argues affably and indefatigably in support of his own existence until dispelled by the arrival of Aloysha. This is a threatening and repulsive nightmare. It is repulsive because Ivan is a rationalist who cannot believe in the devil talking to him in his own room. It is repulsive because he sees the devil as a sickening creation of his own imagination, very artfully put together out of his own romantic memories and inventions. It is repulsive because he thinks it may be a sick hallucination. It is repulsive because he is not absolutely sure that it may not be real, though he comes to feel he would prefer its reality to its re-flexiveness.

Jim's dreams were tales which his imagination created, tales told to Marlow, and tales which Marlow tells to his listeners. Alice's dream is the whole story and within it are a series of her fantasies, told to the creatures or to herself, responses to the story she is living, dreaming and being told. Ivan's dream is narrated as an event occurring all too steadily and stably, its only surrealistic touch being the appearance and disappearance of the devil's image. The dialogue itself is narrative rather than discursive. Not only is this an apparent dream, arranging itself sometimes as if it were real, sometimes as if it were unreal,[4] but it proceeds as talk usually does, through anecdote and rambling personal narration. The devil likes the sound of his own voice, is urbane, clever and witty and tells interesting stories, like the story of the noseless marquis and the story of the priest who seduces the penitent. Ivan's is a peculiarly unpleasant version of the artist's *fiat* since he thinks he has made the dream involuntarily. The devil is a *raconteur* who creates his identity through narrative, telling smart stories and giving the amusing account of what has been happening to him, but when he does try a little discursive reasoning Ivan can't stand its stupidity and says: 'You'd better tell me some anecdote'. But one of the most ingenious bits of his argument involves a theory of dream as art, or at least as artistic inspiration:

'Listen, in dreams and especially in nightmares, from indigestion or anything, a man sees sometimes such artistic visions, such complex and real actuality, such events, even a whole world of events, woven

[4] One feature of its unreality is its breach of convention, interfering as it does with the realism of its context, the novel as a whole.

into such a plot, with such unexpected details from the most exalted matters to the last button on a cuff, as I swear Leo Tolstoy has never invented. Yet such dreams are sometimes seen, not by writers but by the most ordinary people, officials, journalists, priests... The subject is a complete enigma. A statesman confessed to me, indeed, that all his best ideas came to him when he was asleep. Well, that's how it is now, though I am your hallucination, yet just as in a nightmare, I say original things which had not entered your head before. So I don't repeat your ideas, yet I am only your nightmare, nothing more.'

'You are lying, your aim is to convince me you exist apart and are not my nightmare, and now you are asserting you are a dream.'

(*The Brothers Karamazov*, bk. xi, ch. ix)[5]

His rambling account of his state of health and the story of his day are full of tall stories, like his tale of catching cold while hurrying through space in an evening suit to get to a soirée at the house of a lady of high rank in Petersburg:

'Spirits don't freeze, but when one's in fleshly form, well... in brief, I didn't think, and set off, and you know in those ethereal spaces, in the water that is above the firmament, there's such a frost... at least one can't call it a frost, you can fancy, 150° below zero! You know the game the village girls play—they invite the unwary to lick an axe in thirty degrees of frost, the tongue instantly freezes to it and the dupe tears the skin off, so it bleeds. But that's only in 30°...'

(ibid.)

He is an entertainer, a persuader and a liar, as one expects of the devil. Ivan is after truth and accordingly asks scientific questions, exerting himself not to believe in this delusion, 'and sink into complete insanity'. So when the devil begins to muse amusingly on what would happen to an axe at such low temperatures, Ivan doubts if an axe could exist in space and the devil readily gives his mind to the problem:

'What would become of an axe in space? *Quelle idée*! If it were to fall to any distance, it would begin, I think, flying round the earth without knowing why, like a satellite. The astronomers would calculate the rising and the setting of the axe, *Gatzuk* would put it in his calendar, that's all.' (ibid.)

[5] The translation used is that of Constance Burnett in the Everyman edition.

The devil's stories and flights of fancy are not simply charming and flashy but part of his act, manipulated to look as if they might also be manifestations of Ivan's mind representing such an act. Either he is a fiction representing fictions or a reality playing on Ivan's incredulity. His best, longest and most important story is the one about the free-thinker who went to Paradise. It is told in response to Ivan's disgusted cry: 'You are rubbish, you are my fancy!', which is followed by his despairing suggestion that he had better tell an anecdote. The free-thinker conscientiously objects to finding himself in Paradise and is punished by being made to walk a quadrillion kilometres in the dark. The story begins to work. Ivan is really curious about the man who, after refusing to walk, lay down for a thousand years: 'What did he lie on?' Then he listens while the devil explains the scale of eternity which is difficult for him to comprehend. He suddenly rejects the story when he recognizes it as his own, to which the devil replies:

'It's the new method. As soon as you disbelieve in me completely, you'll begin assuring me to my face that I am not a dream but a reality. I know you. Then I shall have attained my object, which is an honourable one. I shall sow in you only a tiny grain of faith and it will grow into an oak-tree—and such an oak-tree that, sitting on it, you will long to enter the ranks of "the hermits in the wilderness and the saintly women," for that is what you are secretly longing for. You'll dine on locusts, you'll wander into the wilderness to save your soul!'

'Then it's for the salvation of my soul you are working, is it, you scoundrel?'

'One must do a good work sometimes. How ill-humoured you are!'

'Fool! did you ever tempt those holy men who ate locusts and prayed seventeen years in the wilderness till they were overgrown with moss?'

'My dear fellow, I've done nothing else. One forgets the whole world and all the worlds, and sticks to one such saint, because he is a very precious diamond. One such soul, you know, is sometimes worth a whole constellation. We have our system of reckoning, you know. The conquest is priceless! And some of them, on my word, are not inferior to you in culture, though you won't believe it. They can contemplate such depths of belief and disbelief at the same moment that sometimes it really seems that they are within a hair's-breadth of being "turned upside down," as the actor Gorbunov says.' (ibid.)

The end of the devil's persuasion is the loss of self-belief, the impeding of action and virtue:

> ' "You are going from pride," he says. "You'll stand up and say it was I killed him, and why do you writhe with horror? You are lying! I despise your opinion, I despise your horror!" He said that about me. "And do you know you are longing for their praise— 'he is a criminal, a murderer, but what a generous soul; he wanted to save his brother, and he confessed.' " That's a lie, Aloysha!' Ivan cried suddenly, with flashing eyes. 'I don't want the low rabble to praise me, I swear I don't! That's a lie! That's why I threw the glass at him and it broke against his ugly face.'
>
> 'Brother, calm yourself, stop!' Aloysha entreated him.
>
> 'Yes, he knows how to torment one. He's cruel,' Ivan went on unheeding. 'I had an inkling from the first what he came for. "Granting that you go through pride, still you had a hope that Smerdyakov might be convicted and sent to Siberia, and Mitya would be acquitted, while you would only be punished with *moral* condemnation" ("Do you hear?" he laughed then)—"and some people will praise you." ' (ch. x)

The devil cannot stay in Aloysha's presence and it is only Aloysha who understands him, knowing him for a part of Ivan's mind, not as a type of his romantic softness but as an emissary from the virtuous dream, God trying to find a place in his heart, 'The anguish of a proud determination. An earnest conscience'. Ivan, in feeling the dangerous self-indulgence of the dream of heroic virtue, is Jim's opposite. The devil's truths, lies, jokes and legends make a dream which is indeed created by an imaginative intellect determined to scrutinize its most virtuous and idealistic stories. The fantasy of an ideal action is shaken in Ivan's missionary temptation, as he tries to improve his imaginative hypothesis in a delirium conveniently but plausibly symptomatic of strain.

No wonder Ivan is afraid of insanity. The strain of a dangerous dream, a rational self-doubt, a pride in doubt, all take their toll. Dostoievsky uses nightmare to show the perils of moral imagination in an extreme image of art and derangement. Ivan is threatened by madness because his reason inhibits immersion in the destructive element. He finds it terrifyingly risky to make the adjustment that Alice manages so easily. Cervantes, who permitted his man of genius to accept the heroic dream of love, action and tradition, also let him endure the extreme fantasies of madness. Don Quixote immerses himself in a compound dream while most other novelists have dealt with a part only. Charlotte Brontë has a dream of fulfilling love, Proust a dream of redemption through time, Joyce a dream of the freedom of the artist, Conrad a dream of heroic virtue. Don Quixote believes and lives all these visions, by going mad. Cervantes's best and daring intuition is surely the realization that only insanity could include the fullest range of fantasy. The difficulty about taking insanity as a heroic model, however, is its anarchy. If we look at some of the stories of R. D. Laing's patients in *The Politics of Experience* it looks as if schizophrenia jerrybuilds a shaky structure of passion and freedom which depends for existence on negation of control and conscious scruple. Cervantes, like Laing, sympathized with the impulse towards such freedom and wrote *Don Quixote* as a protest against hamstrung sanity. He felt the impulse to reject civilized reason and rational civilization but the rejection is mitigated. For Don Quixote is accompanied by common sense and not only in the form of Sancho Panza. His own common sense, knowledge and judgement are constantly admired by friends, relations, and strangers, not only because of their power but because these virtues live in the neighbourhood of his madness.

Cervantes endows Don Quixote with a powerful and individual mind. He has a linguistic pedantry which is amusing and shows his fastidiousness and accuracy. Sancho's malapropisms (we ought to say Mrs Malaprop's Sanchoisms) annoy him and make him interrupt Sancho's stories. On the occasion of the goat-counting story, he behaves as we would all behave and falls into the narrative trap, being unwilling to take Sancho literally. He remembers this model trap when, on a later occasion, the Ragged Knight begs him to listen without interruption, for the fascinating reason that he wants to tell the story but as fast as possible because to re-tell and especially to linger over it will bring it back too sharply:[6]

[6] Narrators are so prolific in the creation of narratives that it is impossible to isolate one kind only. In *Don Quixote* the analysis of telling and listening is rich and intricate.

'Gentlemen,' said he, 'if you intend to be informed of my mis-fortunes, you must promise me before-hand not to cut off the thread of my doleful narration with any questions, or any other interruption; for in the very instant that any of you do it, I shall leave off abruptly; and will not afterwards go on with the story.' This preamble put Don Quixote in mind of Sancho's ridiculous tale, which by his neglect in not telling the goats, was brought to an untimely conclusion. (vol. i, bk. iii, ch. x)

Don Quixote is surprisingly learned, and parades his scholarship in discussion of subjects other than chivalry, such as drama, literature, poetry, education, parents and children, government. He is capable of applying common sense even within his madness and the energy of narrative imagination is nowhere more impressively shown than when he uses it to bridge the gap between dream and reality, subjective and objective response. Because Sancho is unschooled yet perspicuous, Don Quixote tries conscientiously and sensibly to reconcile their different views, the one seeing a barber's basin, the other Mambrino's helmet:

'I fancy,' said Don Quixote, 'this enchanted helmet has fallen by some strange accident into the hands of some person, who, not knowing the value of it, for the lucre of a little money, finding it to be of pure gold, melted one half, and of the other made this head-piece, which, as thou sayest, has some resemblance of a barber's basin.' (vol. i, bk. iii, ch. viii)

He can overpower the evidence of his nose when a Dulcinea's garlic-stinking breath cannot be ignored. Having transformed himself into a don, he sees clearly the transformation he has himself undergone. The solution is a story which reverses the process—of a magician who transforms the ladies into peasant girls and dupes Sancho's senses but cannot delude Don Quixote. Ingenious and perverse, this concoction permits Don Quixote to continue in the company of Sancho's keen eyes and nostrils. When he is in the cart and Sancho asks him if he doesn't want to relieve himself, to 'do big or small waters', or 'that which no one else can do for you', he replies that he would indeed like to be let out now to relieve himself because things are 'none too clean'. Sancho presses for the reality principle: how can he be enchanted, since enchantment traditionally inhibits physical functions? Don

Quixote admits the problem but can only think that, times having changed, modern enchantments work differently.

Don Quixote not only needs to tilt at the windmills of the five senses; he has also to meet the ancient and modern argument that prefers the truths of history to the truths (or lies) of literature. After the episode in the cart the canon tries to persuade Don Quixote that the tales of chivalry belong to the past and that his intellect would be more reliably employed on works of history and scripture. Don Quixote replies that literature has a higher authenticity. His grandmother had no hesitation in appealing to it ('My boy, that lady is very like the Lady Quintanona'), and writers of romance never fail to give details which confirm the truth of what they say.

> '...setting down the father, mother, country, kindred, age, place and actions to a tittle, and day by day, of the knight and knights of whom they treat? For shame, sir,' continued he, 'forbear uttering such blasphemies; and, believe me, in this I advise you to behave yourself as becomes a man of sense, or else read them and see what satisfaction you will receive.' (vol. i, bk. iv, ch. xxiii)

He argues not only from literary tradition and authority which merge truth and legend, verity and verisimilitude. Ultimately his defence is based on delight:

> '...pray tell me, can there be anything more delightful, than to read a lively description, which, as it were, brings before your eyes the following adventure? A vast lake of boiling pitch, in which an infinite number of serpents, snakes, crocodiles, and other sorts of fierce and terrible creatures, are swimming and traversing backwards and forwards, appears to a knight-errant's sight. Then from the midst of the lake a most doleful voice is heard to say these words; "O knight, whoever thou art, who gazest on this dreadful lake, if thou wilt purchase the bliss concealed under these dismal waters, make known thy valour by casting thyself into the midst of these black burning surges; for unless thou dost so, thou art not worthy to behold the mighty wonders enclosed in the seven castles of the seven fairies, that are seated under those gloomy waves." And no sooner have the last accents of the voice reached the knight's ear, but he, without making any further reflection, or considering the danger to which he exposes himself, and even without laying aside

his ponderous armour, only recommending himself to Heaven and to his lady, plunges headlong into the middle of the burning lake; and when least he imagines it, or can guess where he shall stop, he finds himself on a sudden in the midst of verdant fields, to which the Elysian bear no comparison.' (ibid.)

The story of the story continues for some time. Don Quixote's literary criticism is that of an unusually absorbed reader who re-captures and brilliantly retells the stories that have so captivated and astonished him, 'driven away melancholy and improved the temper'. Don Quixote, like Matthew Arnold and F. R. Leavis, believes in the power of literature, a fantastic but certainly life-improving literature:

> 'This I can say for myself, that since my being a knight-errant, I am brave, courteous, bountiful, well-bred, generous, civil, bold, affable, patient, a sufferer of hardships, imprisonment and enchantments: and though I have so lately been shut up in a cage like a madman, I expect through the valour of my arm, Heaven favouring, and Fortune not opposing my designs, to be a king of some kingdom in a very few days, that so I may give proofs of my innate gratitude and liberality.' (vol. I, bk. iv, ch. xxiii)

Don Quixote's views are not only powerful in local argument but are sustained. To move from his conversation with the canon to his conversation with the gentleman in green in Volume Two is to observe the consistency of his views on literature, freedom and a liberal education. Don Quixote's power of intellect establishes him as not only 'mad nor'-nor'-west' but also as mightily sane. The artist's *fiat* in *Don Quixote* is given by Sancho but on behalf of them both, when at the beginning of Volume Two they are told that Cervantes has written their history:

> 'What,' quoth Sancho, 'does he design to do it to get a penny by it? Nay, then we are like to have a rare history indeed; we shall have him botch and whip it up, like your tailors on Easter-eve, and give us a huddle of flim-flams that will never hang together; for your hasty work can never be done as it should be. Let Mr. Moor take care how he goes to work; for, my life for his, I and my master will stock him with such a heap of matter of adventures and odd chances, that he will have enough not only to write one second part, but an hundred. The poor fellow, belike, thinks we do nothing but sleep

on a hay-mow; but let us once put foot into the stirrup, and he will see what we are about: this at least I will be bold to say, that if my master would be ruled by me, we had been in the field by this time, undoing of misdeeds and righting of wrongs, as good knights-errant use to do.' Scarce had Sancho made an end of his discourse, when Rozinante's neighing reached their ears. Don Quixote took it for a lucky omen, and resolved to take another turn within three or four days. (vol. ii, ch. v)

He is not just a passive character in fiction but a hero whose history must be written. He is also a poet who will be imitated and propitiated, whose admirers and critics try to believe him. His abilities are various, as his niece observes: '...my uncle is a poet, too! He knows every-thing. I will lay my life he might turn mason in case of necessity. If he would but undertake it, he could build a house as easy as a bird-cage' (vol. ii ch. vi). Like so many of the characters of novelists, Don Quixote is creative, in steering a way through art, idealizing reality and virtue. He is kept in touch with the real world through independence of mind and through the goodness and energy of his knight errantry. It is heroism not all wasted, though misled. He really does free the galley-slaves and his innocent amazement at their fate and punishment is a naïve but needed questioning of society, like that of the king of Brobdingnag or the Houyhnhnms. Don Quixote's folly cannot believe that society's civilized and sane mores permit or even defend injustice and cruelty. His benevolence is real, his constancy tried and true, his pity lively. Leopold Bloom, who perhaps resembles both Don Quixote and Sancho Panza more than he resembles Ulysses, shows a similar energy, pity and constancy and like Don Quixote must also be forgiven and congratulated.

Cervantes has created an anachronistic and crazed virtue, which impresses people by the company it keeps. His quixotism is infectious and changes more than Sancho. The novel makes us feel that the world is worse for its sane men, the better for the madman and the fool. Here virtue is allied with madness, as is genius, but Cervantes manages splendidly to make us feel the sanity beyond insanity of virtue and genius. When Don Quixote asks to fight the lion he is saved, as at times fools and madmen are, by chance, because the lion is not hungry. The keeper says sensibly that honour has been vindicated and shuts the cage. Don Quixote's answer is a fine stroke of sane acceptance:

'Come, shut the cage-door, honest friend, and give me a certificate under thy hand, in the amplest form thou canst devise, of what thou has seen me perform; how thou didst open the cage for the lion; how I expected his coming, and he did not come out. How, upon his not coming out then, I stayed his own time, and instead of meeting me, he turned tail and lay down. I am obliged to do no more. So, enchantments avaunt! and Heaven prosper truth, justice, and knight-errantry!' (vol. II, ch. xvii)

In the end, Don Quixote's sanity beyond insanity asserts itself unequivocally. We have seen so much of his reason, benevolence, and endurance that his perorations do not leave us feeling that he has recovered after a sickness. What is rejected has been dignified and honoured. Like Alice, Don Quixote knows he is fabulous and like her he knows the dream is over. He dies with the sense that something appropriate to life but not death, like sensuality, must go and so says that the tales 'have been only too real, to my cost. But, with Heaven's aid, my death shall turn them to my profit'. From the tales something is preserved—the goodness: 'I am Don Quixote de la Mancha no longer, but Alonso Quixano, called for my way of life *the Good*.' This is confirmed by the grief of the housekeeper, the niece and Sancho:

> ...for indeed, either as Alonso Quixano, or as Don Quixote de la Mancha, as it has been observed, the sick gentleman had always showed himself such a good-natured man, and of so agreeable a behaviour, that he was not only beloved by his family, but by every one that knew him. (vol. II, ch. lxxiv)

Death must mark the end of madness and quixotism, perhaps not so much because it reforms as because it renders sanity and insanity equal. Sancho is left at the last to recognize the inadequacy of his own common sense:

> 'Woe's me, my dear master's worship!' cried Sancho, all in tears, 'do not die this bout, but even take my counsel, and live on many years; it is the maddest trick a man can ever play in his whole life, to let his breath sneak out of his body without any more ado, and without so much as a rap over the pate, or a kick on the guts; to go out like the snuff of a farthing candle, and die merely of the mulligrubs, or the sullens. For shame, sir, do not give way to sluggishness, but get out of your doleful dumps, and rise. Is this a time to lie honing and

groaning a-bed, when we should be in the fields in our shepherd's clothing, as we had resolved? Ten to one but behind some bush, or under some hedge, we may find the Lady Madam Dulcinea, stripped of her enchanted rags, and as fine as a queen. Mayhaps you take it to heart, that you were unhorsed, and a little crupper-scratched the other day; but if that be all, lay the blame upon me, and say it was my fault, in not girting Rozinante tight enough. You know too, there is nothing more common in your errantry-books, than for the knights to be every foot jostled out of the saddle. There is nothing but ups and downs in this world, and he that is cast down to-day, may be a cock-a-hoop to-morrow.' 'Even so,' said Samson, 'honest Sancho has a right notion of the matter.' 'Soft and fair, gentleman,' replied Don Quixote, 'never look for birds of this year in the nests of the last: I was mad, but I am now in my senses; I was once Don Quixote de la Mancha but am now, as I said before, the plain Alonso Quixano...' (ibid.)

There is a last comic confirmation of the enterprise. When Don Quixote takes the last sacrament, expressing his horror of books of chivalry, 'The scrivener, who was by, protested he had never read in any books of that kind of any knight-errant who ever died in his bed so quietly and like a good Christian, as Don Quixote did.'

Don Quixote's dreams, like Lord Jim's, are formed and nourished by literature and it might look as if he had drowned in them. But his madness and its odd but faithful companion, reason, seem to permit him to move in the destructive element adroitly, kindly and actively. The Don Quixote who makes the admission in the cart is no disembodied or deranged psyche but acknowledges that we sit on a heap of dirt. In an age when we are perhaps in greater danger of denying reason and benevolence than dirt and derangement, it seems appropriate to suggest that Don Quixote is a presiding genius not only because of his capacity for extremes of fantasy but also because that capacity is subjected to the control of benevolence. The death-bed of Don Quixote reminds us that deranged exploration must have its limits and that derangement can be tolerated only if its virtue is guaranteed.

3
Memory and Memories

The descent beckons
            as the ascent beckoned
                        Memory is a kind
of accomplishment
            a sort of renewal
                        even
an initiation, since the spaces it opens are new
places
                        inhabited by hordes
                                    heretofore unrealized,
of new kinds—
            since their movements
                        are towards new objectives
(even though formerly they were abandoned)

No defeat is made up entirely of defeat—since
the world it opens is always a place
                        formerly
                                    unsuspected. A
world lost,
            a world unsuspected
                        beckons to new places
and no whiteness (lost) is so white as the memory
of whiteness
            (William Carlos Williams, *Paterson*, bk. ii, 3)

Every day has its story. Whether it has been an ordinary day or an unusual one, we tell it over, to ourselves, to our journal, to other people. The day itself is made up of narrative as we look ahead, look back and do whatever else we do besides remembering and imagining. Some characters in novels, like Proust's Marcel or Joyce's Stephen Dedalus, seem to do nothing but remember and look ahead. Proust, master of memory, even suggests that the imagination cannot work on the materials of the present. Some characters in novels, however, like Virginia Woolf's Mrs Dalloway, or Joyce's Leopold Bloom, while living alertly in memory offer more reassuring experience of responding imaginatively in the present. Time present is inextricably bound up with time past and time future, and it is the people with a capacity for the sensations and feelings of present time who bear out most simply William Carlos Williams's belief in the creative action of memory.

Mrs Dalloway's day is composed of instant responses to the people and things of the present, of the pressing plans and hopes for her party in the evening and of memories of the recent and distant past. Of all the people in fiction with good memories, she seems most at home in time. She is not bound to the past nor stupidly stuck in the present nor violently impelled towards future blisses and terrors. Her responses, her memories and her anticipations are fluid and continuously on the move, in a variegated consciousness where present, future and past co-operate, not banded in separate blocks or epochs but active in mutual stimulus. The day begins with an intention, 'she would buy the flowers herself', which is followed by her response to the outside world on her door-step, 'what a morning—fresh as if issued to children on a beach'. The images of the child and the beach move the reader easily into the past recalled for Clarissa by the open door and the breath of morning air: 'What a lark! What a plunge! For so it had always seemed to her when, with a little squeak of the hinges, which she could hear now, she had burst open the French windows and plunged at Bourton into the open air.'

The past easily and peacefully takes over, moving from the recalled sensations of freshness, calmness and silence to recalled emotions, 'solemn, feeling as she did, standing there at the open window, that something awful was about to happen'. The past is vividly present, 'with a little squeak of the hinges, which she could hear now'.

She is sufficiently aware of the act of remembering to make comparisons, 'stiller than this', and to marvel at the strange behaviour of memory, 'his eyes, his pocket-knife, his smile, his grumpiness and, when millions of things had utterly vanished—how strange it was!—a few sayings like this about cabbages'. Memory is not instantaneous or totally accurate, even the sayings about cabbages being imperfectly recalled, ' "Musing among the vegetables?"—was that it?—"I prefer men to cauliflowers"—was that it? He must have said it at breakfast one morning...'. Speculation probes sensation and feeling, memory's quotations are questioned and checked, the mind acknowledges the possibilities of being right, wrong, and blank.

While Mrs Dalloway is experiencing the summons of the past by the present, as Proust's Marcel had already done,[1] she is also achieving something which, two years after her appearance, was withheld from Marcel. She is savouring, purely and strongly, a present experience, 'this moment in June'. Virginia Woolf does not make the vivid sense of the present in any way dependent on the friction between now and then, as Proust does. She rather reverses Marcel's process so that the past is revived through the appreciation of the present freshness and excitement. Yet the texture and feeling of her novel, like Proust's, are dependent on memory. All her people are creatures of memory, despite their capacity to respond to the present. Mrs Dalloway's day ticks through the hours of morning, afternoon, evening, and night, and also strides and leaps backwards and forwards through the years. Especially backwards.

Mrs Dalloway is very much a novel of its time, presenting human vitality after the deadliness of the 1914–18 War, showing a fragile woman 'over fifty, and grown very white since her illness'. Its problems are historically determined and Mrs Dalloway's vivacity is subject to the carefully dated restrictions of a wife, a mother and a hostess. But she has no difficulty in her relationship with time. She suffers neither the hardships of recall shared by the hero of *The Prelude*, Marcel and Stephen Dedalus, nor the uncertainties about the future shared by Maggie Tulliver and Paul Morel. Mrs Dalloway accepts the intimations of mortality presented by what she sees and knows in the present, which includes death, and what she remembers of the past, which includes death. Her adjustment to the known past and present, as to the implicit future, is complete. The novel is time-haunted but its heroine moves with grace and assurance through time. It is killing her, as it kills all of us, but she never wants to kill it.

Like Lily Briscoe, the painter in *To the Lighthouse*, Virginia Woolf can use her narrative art to discern, mark and re-create meanings, connections, harmonies and unities in time. All novelists have to take time seriously, their art insisting that they must look back. Even dramatists, despite a greater commitment to the illusions of open present and unknown future, may dwell largely in the past. Mrs Dalloway presents an unusually stable attitude to the clock and calendar so evidently keeping time throughout her day, but Beckett's Krapp

---

[1] *Mrs Dalloway* was published in 1925, Proust's *A la recherche du temps perdu* between 1913–27.

lives distortedly in time past. He drinks beer (off-stage), and eats bananas (on-stage), but does nothing else in the present except play the tapes of the past and make his unfinished tape of the last year. His occupation is listening to his old, young voice, recalling the past. Even in the past, while it was present, he was engaged in retrospect and listening is a highly passive form of memory, too passive now to make conscious or unconscious selections except from what the tapes have recorded. At first he is remembering incompletely, bitterly, impotently, agedly, seemingly incapable even of the usual forms of remorseful memory, since he needs the mechanical recording machine, only remembering through its annals. Even at the end, in his assertion, 'Be again', there is nothing but memory. The play presents a discordant, unbalanced and unhappy relationship of present to past culminating in the last tape of which he has so little to record. Unlike Mrs Dalloway, he has an empty present. Like her, however, he knows that forgetting is a part of our attempts to remember. Beckett's brilliant use of the tape-recorder as up-to-the-minute *aide-mémoire* dramatizes the play of forgetfulness as it compares the recorded memory of the past with the listening memory in the present. We have an explicit comparison, a kind of memory test, in which Krapp's failures are instructive. He fails to follow his old rites of annual memory, those tapes which act as painfully perfect models of what distant memory fails to achieve, the recall of everything we once expected to remember. Mrs Dalloway compares past aspiration with present knowledge but Krapp goes even further, comparing past memorability with present oblivion. What once seemed unforgettable is forgotten, like the 'memorable equinox'. What was once known is now incomprehensible, like the word 'viduity'. Nothing is so impenetrable as the dictionary word we never use, nothing so reckless as predictions of future memories.

In *How It Is* Beckett memorably defines progress as 'ruins in prospect', and knows that nothing is as unpleasant as the recall of prospects. But for Krapp prospect ended long ago and the annual tapes look back chiefly on earlier retrospect: 'These old P.M.s are gruesome, but I often find them—(*Krapp switches off, broods, switches on*)—a help before embarking on a new … (*hesitates*) … retrospect'. Most congenial to him are the reiterated memories of love's farewell, which he quickly turns to in preference to the recorded moment of vision, perhaps because it was negative, perhaps because it would now be too cruelly rebuked by the future-present, perhaps because it was abstract or grandiose. The farewell wipes out the vision and takes over when he gives up recording his current and final tape:

> I said again I thought it was hopeless and no good going on, and she agreed, without opening her eyes. (*Pause*) I asked her to look at me and after a few moments—(*pause*)—after a few moments she did, but the eyes just slits, because of the glare. I bent over her to get them in the shadow and they opened. (*Pause. Low.*) Let me in. (*Pause*) We drifted in among the flags and stuck. The way they went down, sighing, before the stem! (*Pause*) I lay down across her with my face in her breasts and my hand on her. We lay there without moving. But under us all moved, and moved us, gently, up and down, and from side to side.

Beckett's awareness that nostalgia can be a debilitating emotion may be implicit in the repetitions of this memory, but in the absence of fresh vitality it speaks up proudly for itself, in contrast with the glimpses we get of Krapp's surviving squalid, tiring and minimal sexual life. The lyrical memory presents a nostalgia for something irreplaceable, Krapp's word 'matchless' invoking all those distance-haloed things for which we commonly feel nostalgia: youth, love, natural beauty and rhythm. But the romantic memory is the memory of a valediction, an experience which was preparing to reduce love to memory, even when it was present. Krapp insists that he wouldn't want his best years back, but the play suggests that he had and has no choice. He can exist only in memory, relies on a machine even for remembering.[2]

Krapp's Last Tape is particularly startling because it uses the dramatic present, proper to the theatre, to invoke the narrative of memory more commonly presented in the novel. On the here-and-now of the stage, memory tends to be crucial in so far as it precipitates a crisis in the present. Those plays whose present is the meeting-place of past with future—*Oedipus Rex, The Tempest, Ghosts, Rosmersholm,* or *The Master-Builder*—where the secrets or silences of the past burst into life, where telling or not telling about the past creates the dramatic tension and conflict, are strikingly narrative. But memory is such an inner and expository narrative process that *Krapp's Last Tape* flaunts the very oddity of its chosen medium as appropriate to Krapp's

---

[2] It is possible to interpret Krapp's nostalgia romantically but by underplaying the mechanics of the tape-recorder and the valedictory tenor of the memory.

paralysis and solitude. Mrs Dalloway exemplifies a sensitive balance between past and future, with genuine activity in the present. Krapp stands for the distortion or waste of a life given up to backward looks and listenings. Fictional characters may be less at ease in time than Mrs Dalloway and less fixated than Krapp but they invariably exploit active memories.

The novelist not only draws on memory for his material but may also need a good internal memory for his novel, especially if it is on the scale of *Clarissa, Tom Jones, Middlemarch, The Golden Bowl, Ulysses, A la recherche du temps perdu*[3] or *Pilgrimage*.[4] The memory with which the novelist endows his characters tends to reflect his own appreciation of memory's marvels. Fanny Price's moral life depends on a good personal and social memory and she fittingly utters the rhapsody:

> If any one faculty of our nature may be called *more* wonderful than the rest, I do think it is memory. There seems something more speakingly incomprehensible in the powers, the failures, the inequalities of memory, than in any other of our intelligences.
> (*Mansfield Park*, ch. xxii)

Fanny's sense and sensibility rely on memory as do Mrs Dalloway's vitality and harmony and even Krapp's sluggish dependence offers a wry testimony. Since the memories of characters in fiction are created out of an artist's intimate knowledge of a creative instrument, their memories often emphasize what William Carlos Williams calls initiative. Memory chooses, omits, adds, edits and collaborates with invention, exploration and disguise. All novelists superimpose invention on memory and are often especially alert to what Fanny calls its powers and failures. When George Eliot drew so lavishly on memories of early childhood in *The Mill on the Floss*, she was regretting certain losses. Her rituals mark the common diminution of innocence and freedom and of more personal sacred objects, places, epochs and people. In Jane Austen and George Eliot, memory is a base of morality.

---

[3] In this list, the only novel not centrally concerned with memory is *Tom Jones*, where the inner moral action of the hero is conducted without much reference to past behaviour though Tom's ability to forget does sometimes get stressed. But the omniscient author in the novel has a memory, and makes good use of it.

[4] Dorothy Richardson's *Pilgrimage* must be included in such a list but its moments of involuntary memory strike me as the most derivative and least interesting aspects of its analysis of feeling.

Fanny guards the family archive in the East room with love and esteem, though the treasures there have been forgotten by the other inhabitants of Mansfield Park. Maggie refuses to commit herself to a future which is not rooted in past promises and affections to which Tom and Stephen seem less sensitive. She is indulged with an end which is bound to her beginning, dying in Tom's arms in the comforting vision of recovered childhood and a new understanding. When Dickens remembers his childhood, he re-enacts bitterness, neglect and isolation. James Joyce and Marcel Proust remember parents and omit (or almost omit) brothers. The lost childhood is frequently a golden age, or a very good time indeed. The dead love is remembered reproachfully, punished and forgiven, as in Thackeray's bitter-sweet recollections in *Henry Esmond*. Sometimes the return is obsessive and undisguised, like Proust's recall of his mother's forgotten goodnight kiss. The novel plays over memories which are revised, unrevised, disguised, undisguised, painful and pleasurable. Memory, like fantasy, plays a large part in the inner action of psychological novels and the characters in novels are often efficient and self-conscious analysts of memory.

Even Robinson Crusoe is self-conscious about his recollections and records. Like all Defoe's memoir-writers, Roxana, Colonel Jack, Captain Singleton and Moll Flanders, Robinson Crusoe looks back to register a significantly misspent life. Unlike Moll and Jack, he has, as he looks back on his past self, little self-pity but plenty of remorse. *Robinson Crusoe* is a story about telling yourself stories for lack of company, and though Robinson Crusoe doesn't say that he is writing his journal out of desperate solitary need, like Pamela, Clarissa, Malloy and Malone, who tell because they must, he is aware that his journal has a function. He cannot write the story of his days until he has settled more urgent needs. Telling stories may be necessary to survival but food, drink and shelter have priority. Once those things are satisfactorily arranged and once he has made his table and chair, he starts to write a daily record which goes on as long as the pens and ink last. The materials of writing down his story are as important in Defoe as in *Pamela, Clarissa* and Golding's *Free Fall*, and he explains— wonderful detail—that ink was something he never managed to make. His journal, like his calendar of notched wood, is a means of ordering and keeping time. It is also the basis of the narrative said to be compiled by Daniel Defoe. There are some things which are told in the journal and also in the main narrative, for Robinson Crusoe, like other apparently unliterary heroes of novels, collates the different versions and takes a considerable technical interest in the timing and forming of narrative. The editor's preface praises the way the story is told, 'with Modesty, with Seriousness, and with a religious Application of Events to the Uses which wise Men always apply them', thus complimenting the moral hindsight generally found in Defoe's novels. But Robinson Crusoe is also concerned with such matters as the effects of time on a chronicle. He goes to the length of giving us three different versions of the day of his shipwreck, 30 September 1659. Once he has something to write on and sit on, he settles down to record events, but the important settling-down occurs in his thinking and feeling, as he realizes:

> But having gotten over these things in some Measure, and having settled my household Stuff and Habitation, made me a Table and a Chair, and all as handsome about me as I could, I began to keep my Journal, of which I shall here give you the Copy (tho' in it will be told all these Particulars over again) as long as it lasted, for having no more Ink I was forc'd to leave it off.

The JOURNAL

September 30, 1659. I poor miserable *Robinson Crusoe*, being shipwreck'd, during a dreadful Storm, in the offing, came on Shore on this dismal Island, which I call'd *the Island of Despair*, all the rest of the Ship's Company being drown'd, and my self almost dead.

All the rest of that Day I spent in afflicting my self at the dismal Circumstances I was brought to, *viz*. I had neither Food, House, Clothes, Weapon, or Place to fly to, and in Despair of any Relief, saw nothing but Death before me, either that I should be devour'd by wild Beasts, murther'd by Savages, or starv'd to Death for Want of Food. At the Approach of Night, I slept in a Tree for fear of wild Creatures, but slept soundly tho' it rain'd all Night. (vol. i, p. 79)[5]

This is the final, revised and authorized version, but before writing it he tells us that he found it necessary to wait for the right frame of mind:

[5] Because of the absence of chapter divisions in the novel page references are given to The Shakespeare Head Edition of *Robinson Crusoe*.

And now it was when I began to keep a Journal of every Day's Employment, for indeed at first I was in too much Hurry, and not only Hurry as to Labour, but in too much Discomposure of Mind, and my Journal would ha' been full of many dull things: For Example, I must have said thus. *Sept.* the 30th. After I got to Shore and had escap'd drowning, instead of being thankful to God for my Deliverance, having first vomited with the great Quantity of salt Water which was gotten into my Stomach, and recovering my self a little, I ran about the Shore, wringing my Hands and beating my Head and Face, exclaiming at my Misery, and crying out, I was undone, undone, till tyr'd and faint I was forc'd to lye down on the Ground to repose, but durst not sleep for fear of being devour'd.

(vol. i, p. 78)

The authorized extract shows the ordering and generalizing powers working on the records of memory; they erase much of the circumstantial physical and emotional detail, and display his concern for moral summary. The specimen of what he might have said is scarcely full of dull things. It also differs from the first version given earlier in the main course of the narrative, which has no visible status, since Robinson Crusoe does not discuss its place or form. This version is very much longer and more detailed than either of the others, taking about a page and a half to tell what the shorter versions tell, but with certain differences of fact, such as the account of his startling pleasure at being saved, which he describes, analyses and evaluates. It has more particularity of movement, thoughts, food, and drink though some of the immediacy of the unwritten 'specimen' is lacking:

I was now landed, and safe on Shore, and began to look up and thank God that my Life was sav'd in a Case wherein there was some Minutes before scarce any room to hope...I walk'd about on the Shore, lifting up my Hands, and my whole Being, as I may say, wrapt up in the Contemplation of my Deliverance, making a Thousand Gestures and Motions which I cannot describe, reflecting upon all my Comrades that were drown'd, and that there should not be one Soul sav'd but my self...

After I had solac'd my Mind with the comfortable Part of my Condition, I began to look round me to see what kind of Place I was in, and what was next to be done, and I soon found my Comforts abate, and that in a word I had a dreadful Deliverance: For I was wet, had no Clothes to shift me, nor any thing either to eat or drink to comfort me, neither did I see any Prospect before me, but that of perishing with Hunger, or being devour'd by wild Beasts . . . I had nothing about me but a Knife, a Tobacco-pipe, and a little Tobacco in a Box; this was all my Provision, and this threw me into terrible Agonies of Mind, that for a while I run about like a Mad-man . . . I walk'd about a Furlong from the Shore, to see if I could find any fresh Water to drink, which I did, to my great Joy; and having drank and put a little Tobacco in my Mouth to prevent Hunger, I went to the Tree, and getting up into it, endeavour'd to place myself so, as that if I should sleep I might not fall; and having cut me a short Stick, like a Truncheon, for my Defence, I took up my Lodging, and having been excessively fatigu'd, I fell fast asleep and slept comfortably as, I believe, few could have done in my Condition, and found my self the most refresh'd with it, that I think I ever was on such an Occasion. (vol. i, p. 53)

Robinson Crusoe's journal is a deliberated and reflective form of record, making full use of moral summary. Defoe seems to be interested in showing the small changes and shifts of memory, especially the generalizations of reflective memory and the loss of particulars, the growth of judgement, and the shortage of time and materials. Before starting to write the journal, Defoe draws up a balance sheet, setting the good against the evil and explaining the purpose of this part of his narrative:

...I drew up the State of my Affairs in Writing, not so much to leave them to any that were to come after me, for I was like to have but few Heirs, as to deliver my Thoughts from daily poring upon them, and afflicting my Mind; and as my Reason now began to master my Despondency, I began to comfort my self as well as I could, and to set the good against the Evil, that I might have something to distinguish my Case from worse... (vol. i, p. 74)

Once again there is an act of comparison between two versions of narrative: 'I am divided from Mankind, a Solitaire'; but, 'I am not starv'd and perishing on a barren Place'. This testimony is a survey of the present and acts as a necessary preliminary to the retrospects of the journal, which begins with a recall of the past year when he has been too busy to write. It is gradually brought up to date. It often merges with the narrative and Robinson Crusoe sometimes has to pull himself up in the middle of lengthy reflection to remind himself that he must return to his journal. This is no highly complex analysis of memory but Defoe is plainly aware that the act of narrative recall is variable. He knows that its emotional causes and effects are worth pondering and he sees that memory depends on present emotion, that writing the story of an experience can be a solace, and an elucidation. Robinson Crusoe's insights are not so very far from those of Edouard Passavant in Gide's *The Counterfeiters*. Edouard has more people to talk to than Defoe's 'solitaire', but he says that he doesn't feel that experience is clearly imprinted on the mind until it is narrated in his journal: 'I cannot feel that anything that happens to me has any real existence until I see it reflected here'. Edouard's simple image for his journal, 'the pocket-mirror', would not do for Defoe's three versions of the shipwreck.

Dickens usually seems to assume that we can control the choices and speeds of memory. He attaches considerable importance to his own possession of a good memory, seeing it as a novelist's gift, and links it with powers of observation. His novels calmly set out to say everything about past, present and future, as explicitly as possible. The memory within the novel, David Copperfield's, Esther's or Pip's, must be capable of remembering everything. David's powers of observation and Esther's 'noticing way' are certainly relevant to the convention of total recall but it does not get discussed in the novels, being taken for granted. Defoe was interested in the variations of memory induced by different emotional states but Dickens seems to feel that memories are fixed in their tones or tonalities.

Proust's Marcel has his galleries, Krapp his tapes, David Copperfield his retrospects. 'I Observe', the second chapter of *David Copperfield*, is not presented as one of the four chapters called 'Retrospects' but resembles them in having a distinct tonality of feeling and a rapid pace. Dickens, at the very beginning of his hero's life, wants to stress observation. David is remembering a time before he had begun to remember. But the chapter is linked with the later retrospects by its present tense, which stands for past-present. It is most formally and analytically concerned with memory, beginning with David's very early memories of learning to walk between his mother and Peggotty and his memory of detached, sensuous images of sight and touch. As he recalls the nutmeg-grater roughness of Peggotty's finger, held out to support him in his enterprise, he observes:

This may be fancy, though I think the memory of most of us can go farther back into such times than many of us suppose; just as I believe the power of observation in numbers of very young children to be quite wonderful for its closeness and accuracy. Indeed, I think that most grown men who are remarkable in this respect, may with greater propriety be said not to have lost the faculty, than to have acquired it; the rather, as I generally observe such men to retain a certain freshness, and gentleness, and capacity of being pleased, which are also an inheritance they have preserved from their childhood.

I might have a misgiving that I am 'meandering' in stopping to say this, but that it brings me to remark that I build these conclusions, in part upon my own experience of myself; and if it should appear from anything I may set down in this narrative that I was a child of close observation, or that as a man I have a strong memory of my childhood, I undoubtedly lay claim to both of these characteristics. (*David Copperfield*, ch. ii)

The apology for meandering is most unlike Proust, but the meandering itself is an anticipation of Marcel's wayward form of narrative. It represents the shifting tenses and perspectives of memory. There is vividness and nostalgic longing in the present tense, 'I see', 'I could draw distinctly'. Its historic immediacy allows for such local effects as the uncomfortably memorable presence of Murdstone, or the happy picture of his mother's image, which shows a natural preference for the newly-widowed Mrs Copperfield rather than Mrs Murdstone. 'I Observe' also marks the beginning of the pattern of appropriately seasonal imagery which runs throughout the novel, as well as in the retrospective passages:

Now I am in the garden at the back, beyond the yard where the empty pigeon-house and dog-kennel are—a very preserve of butterflies, as I remember it, with a high fence, and a gate and padlock; where the fruit clusters on the trees, riper and richer than fruit has ever been since, in any other garden, and where my mother gathers some in a basket, while I stand by, bolting furtive gooseberries, and trying to look unmoved. A great wind rises, and the summer is gone in a moment. We are playing in the winter twilight, dancing about in the parlour. When my mother is out of breath and rests herself in an elbow-chair, I watch her winding her bright curls round her fingers, and straightening her waist, and nobody knows better than I do that she likes to look so well, and is proud of being so pretty. (ch. ii)

The 'great wind' and the shift of season point the beginning of maturer observation; his indulgent recognition of his mother's delight in her looks leads on to the appearance of Murdstone, with the brilliantly observed upsurge of unselfconscious, intuitive questioning about second marriages.

Dickens invokes the sad irrevocability of the past by the natural images but also by a change of pace. A speeding-up of time is especially apparent in 'I Observe' and in the four 'Retrospects' (Chapters viii, xliii, liii and lxiv), where it also conveniently gathers together the periods and epochs he wants to summarize but not to record in detail. Memory in Dickens lends itself to a generalization of experience. This generalization is variously appropriate to the comically accelerated episodes of calf-love, the swooning dreaminess of the marriage to Dora, the blurred solemnities of her death-bed and the formality of the happy ending. In certain episodes, Dickens is using the generalizations and knowingness of memory to deflate past experiences, to suggest that they were mistakes, or not to be taken too seriously. This emotional divorce of past and present is most marked in the memories of calf-love and the marriage to Dora. Comedy disowns the past, though it is sweetened by a certain solicitude towards his absurd early affections. But throughout *David Copperfield* Dickens combines a solemn nostalgia for that early reliance on Agnes, which forms the moral basis of David's conversion with a comic or satiric deflation of the romantic past. Such contrivances and distortions of memory are often necessary for survival and renewal and seem to have worked efficiently for David, perhaps for his author. The image of the past self as distinct from the present self, which occurs in the second 'Retrospect' marking the end of school, is not presented with the strong emotional significance which colours similar images of the older, younger self in Proust or Joyce; it simply marks the astonishment we may feel at earlier images, especially at times of rapid growth: 'That little fellow seems to be no part of me; I remember him as something left behind upon the road of life—as something I have passed, rather than have actually been—and almost think of him as someone else' (ch. xviii).

The image of a separate self may have some significance in a novel which depends so much on the act of disowning the past. Dickens uses memory to create a comic, mock-romantic feeling for experiences his hero regrets and such tones contrast markedly with the strong and loving nostalgia for the very early days of childhood and the complacent sense of completeness in the final 'Retrospect'. The third 'Retrospect' does not entirely discredit Dora's ghost but recalls her in a decorous and even tender act of memory. The past is not totally devalued but its more youthful ignorance and stupidity are recorded with comic ruefulness, a convenient tone for a novel about conversion and maturity.

Thackeray is also concerned with maturity but treats the past more decently than Dickens. An implicit distaste for the easy treacheries of memory prevents him from treating Pendennis's passion for 'the Fotheringay' as Dickens treats David's schoolboy attachments. Thackeray manages to keep faith with the genuine feelings of the past, misplaced though their raptures may have been. *Pendennis* is not a first-person narrative of memory but retrospective tones are present in the author's voice. Comic and serious tones are tolerantly blended in the recollections of saner age smiling at sillier youth and of worldly wisdom envying sincerity and innocence: 'Love had roused him—and said, "Awake, Pendennis, I am here". That charming fever—that delicious longing—and fire, and uncertainty; he hugged them to him— he would not have lost them for all the world' (*Pendennis*, ch. v). Thackeray knows precisely how deluded Pen is by his Dulcinea but feels a certain paternal nostalgia and envy for the delicious fever and fire which are now lost and not altogether unregretted. It is the absence of regret for the passions of young manhood that gives a ruthlessness to Dickens's comic memories of love.

Thackeray's greatest novel of memory is not *Pendennis* but *Henry Esmond*, perhaps the only mid-nineteenth-century novel to concern itself with the forms as well as the content of memory. In *Henry Esmond* Thackeray presents a complex attitude to time and to the memory of past passions. The form of his novel is that of a personal memoir, written by Henry Esmond in his old age for his descendants. In it he looks back with a calm melancholy on the loves and ambitions of his youth. He is also looking back at England from America, so that place as well as time is peculiarly hallowed for him and redolent of the past, as it is to be for Henry James's Strether and Proust's Marcel. The editor of the memoir is Esmond's daughter Rachel, who writes a tendentious preface after her father's death in which we see the first appearance of Esmond's dominant passion for Beatrix Castlewood. Rachel, her half-sister, jealous both of Beatrix and of her mother, tells how the aging Beatrix, grown fat and ugly, was defended faithfully by Esmond. Through her devoted account of her parents' happy marriage, Rachel lets us glimpse that love-in-memory which is one of the chief interests of the novel.

In *Henry Esmond* there are three layers of time, that of the supposed publication, that of the time of writing and that of the early memories. Thackeray liked to build the novels in which he domesticated the Muse of History through linked generations of memory, a series stretching back from the early nineteenth century which he could remember himself, to the age of Queen Anne. *Esmond* begins by stretching back to the times remembered by the adults in Esmond's early life and his memory is a part of the bloodstream of memory which flows through successive periods of time. But Esmond's memory is at the centre of the novel. Like David Copperfield, he keeps reminding us of the act of memory and the act of penning his memoirs. Like David, he is a professional writer and he is also dwelling on what is the hardest thing to recapture, the past life of feeling. Unlike Dickens, Thackeray is concerned with past passions and also with the present's passionate act of memory. Esmond's recollected moments are usually experiences of intense joy, desire or surprise, often fixed by a visual detail, but sometimes they are generalized memories of a whole period of time: 'He will remember to his life's end the delights of those days. He was taken to see a play by Monsieur Blaise...'. Sometimes even the early memories are incisively engraved:

> To the very last hour of his life, Esmond remembered the lady as she then spoke and looked, the rings on her fair hands, the very scent of her robe, the beam of her eyes lighting up with surprise and kindness, her lips blooming in a smile, the sun making a golden halo round her hair. (bk. i, ch. i)

> Harry Esmond recollected to the end of his life that figure with the brocade dress and the white night-rail, and the gold-clocked red stockings, and white red-heeled shoes, sitting up in the bed, and stepping down from it. (ibid.)

> He remembers, and must to his dying day, the thoughts and tears of that long night, the hours tolling through it. (ibid.)

The images display a concern for the tonality of recollection, as with the simile for the memory of the dead, 'holiday music from within a prison wall' (bk. i, ch. ix). Isolated patches are retained by visual memory. Unlike David Copperfield, Esmond makes no claim to have an exceptionally good memory but refrains from arranging all early memories in a sequence of the kind we get in the second chapter of *David Copperfield*. He jots them down piecemeal, sometimes remarking on the blanks, like much of his life at Ealing. Esmond remembers images of 'a different country; and a town with tall white houses; and a ship', but such snippets are from very early memory and the convention soon shifts to the familiar Victorian form of total recall, gaps being accounted for not by normal fits, starts and chills but by the uneventful nature of what is passed over.

In the story of Esmond's love for Rachel and Beatrix Castlewood, mother and daughter, the use of visual association becomes more sustained and elaborate, sometimes more arbitrary, to fix the particularity of intense moments:

> There was in the court a peculiar silence somehow; and the scene remained long in Esmond's memory;—the sky bright overhead; the buttresses of the building and the sundial casting shadow over the gilt *memento mori* inscribed underneath; the two dogs, a black greyhound and a spaniel nearly white, the one with his face up to the sun, and the other snuffing amongst the grass and stones, and my Lord leaning over the fountain, which was bubbling audibly. 'Tis strange how that scene, and the sound of that fountain, remained fixed on the memory of a man who has beheld a hundred sights of splendour, and danger too, of which he has kept no account. (bk. i, ch. xiv)

The scene stays in Esmond's memory because of its emotional charge of jealousy and premonition, Rachel watching her husband and Lord Mohun, then Castlewood watching Mohun's departure, his face livid, cursing and kicking his dogs. What fixes the scene is the static assembly of innocent and random objects that surround the sundial's *memento mori*, avoiding melodramatic emphasis and thinning out symbolism into a realistic record of a moment when accidents are charged with dominant feeling. This kind of accidental visual detail is something George Eliot later uses in Dorothea's recall of the red drapery of St Peter's, which stayed with her 'like a disease of the memory' in certain moments of 'dull forlornness', and of Featherstone's funeral, watched reluctantly from Lowick's high window, and attached forever to some 'sensitive points in memory'. Thackeray and George Eliot make much of the imprinting of visual and aural particulars through emotional association.

When Henry Esmond writes about his past, the act of remembering Beatrix revives the vivid particulars of a dead feeling. He tells us, near the end of the novel, that when he finds her with the Pretender and recognizes her wanton ambition his love of ten years is killed in an instant. With it comes the crash of all the enterprises in which he has engaged for her sake, as a Quixote tilting at the windmills of literary fame, military adventure and political revolution. *Henry Esmond* is a novel of disillusionment and the losses are not only sexual, the shallowness and corruption of all he has undertaken for love being eventually recognized and rejected. Esmond leaves England with his eyes open not only to Beatrix but to the shams and vanities of the great world and the great men of his age. In order to show the process of disillusion, it is necessary to start with the elations of faith; and since Thackeray is writing about a writer and using his self-awareness in an analytic fashion the connection between illusion and disillusion is scrupulously made. Thackeray is faced with a problem rather like that of Dickens in *David Copperfield* but instead of sacrificing the quality of his first love he takes risks with the second. He is reticent about his love for Rachel. His passion for Beatrix is fully evoked and, with the additional link never made by Dickens, blind to the action of depreciating memory, Thackeray makes him recognize that the resurrecting act of memory denies the so-called finality of love's death. Perhaps because of carelessness, perhaps because of a not uncommon mixture of revenge and nostalgia, Esmond brings back the past by writing about the past. The emotion of memory is not recollected feeling but the emotion of that recollection. The revival of old love creates a forceful, even surprised, celebration of it, its strength admitted after its death-sentence is written. In *Pendennis*, we see Thackeray joining the rueful and amused tones of emotional recovery with those of hankering. In *Henry Esmond*, we find such a strength in the resurrection that the competition between the two loves remains, as it never does in *David Copperfield*, where Dora's pathetic ghost is never a threat, but made to know its own ghostly place. Love grows, says Proust, like a book in the writing. Thackeray shows that the memories of love can sprout in a disconcerting second growth. Memory, like the poetic composition of which it forms a part, takes fire from its own motion.

Rachel's early description of her mother's love for Esmond as 'so passionate and exclusive as to prevent her, I think, from loving any other person except with an inferior regard', draws attention to the unexclusive nature of Esmond's passion. When he feels his love fall down 'dead on the spot' his memory hardens, 'he wondered that he could ever have loved her'. But the hardness, like the earlier passion, is also changed by time and he comes to say:

> Years after this passion hath been dead and buried, along with a thousand other worldly cares and ambitions, he who felt it can recall it out of its grave, and admire, almost as fondly as he did in his youth, that lovely queenly creature. I invoke that beautiful spirit from the shades and love her still; or rather I should say such a past is always present to a man; such a passion once felt forms a part of his whole being, and cannot be separated from it...
>
> (bk. iii, ch. vi)

This is no momentary admission but a considered insight into the act of memory. Like Marcel, Esmond recognizes that the past sleeps, to be woken by the voluntary and involuntary work of memory: 'a thousand beautiful memories of our youth, beautiful and sad, but as real and vivid in our minds as that fair and always-remembered scene our eyes beheld once more. We forget nothing. The memory sleeps, but wakens again...'(bk. iii, ch. vii). The remembered scene is the Hall, the clustering lights, shadows, sundial and fountain of which have aroused the sleeping associations. Thackeray recognizes that the past does not have to wait until it is accidentally awakened but may be deliberately invoked, as Esmond invokes his 'beautiful spirit from the shades'. It is this sense of the voluntary but unpredictable memory of a past in competition with the present that makes the memorial enterprise of this novel so defiant and ambiguous. Esmond dismisses the 'unworthy' love along with other corruptions of mind and spirit and rejoices in his Indian summer, his America and his autumnal love. But the novel uncovers a melancholy wish to unsettle such security and perversely but constantly looks back to what he cannot entirely wish away, since it remains part of him.

The novel presents a way of remembering, voluntary in some of its decisions, involuntary in others, making a knowing return to the past whose force may be alarmingly or elatingly stronger than we thought we remembered. What Esmond engages in is a familiar enterprise, showing Thackeray's recognition of the twin needs of memory, the need to kill the past and the need to preserve it. Both can appear as acts of fidelity to other people, as well as to ourselves. In *Vanity Fair*, Thackeray had damned a clinging or sentimental memory. Amelia turns her back on the genuine calls of the present in an idolatry of a dead past which was false even when it was alive. She waits slightly too long before she stops worshipping George Osborne's picture and his memory. Esmond has wisely and naturally moved on to another grand passion, so in his case it is necessary to acknowledge the vitality of the past. Thackeray reflects on the dangers and powers of memory, its constancy and its sentimentality.

George Eliot is chiefly interested in the moral implications of memory. She takes care to make her characters conform to rituals and traditions and Maggie Tulliver's decision not to break with her personal and social past is put most forcibly to the test. George Eliot's treatment of the childhood scenes in *The Mill on the Floss* lays a careful groundwork of feelings. Tom and Maggie are created in and by their environment. Like many other George Eliot characters, even Fred and Rosamond Vincy in *Middlemarch*, they are creatures of a Midland landscape. As in Thackeray, the emphasis is not simply on being true to one's background but to one's associations with the sacred objects and natural scenes which have entered into us, made us what we are, taught us how to love. To deny associations is most painfully to risk alienation, unreality and a thinning of the personal life. Hetty Sorrel in *Adam Bede* and Gwendolen Harleth in *Daniel Deronda* are rootless, their associations weak, and their efforts at memory accordingly very painful, especially when they are forced to look back and make sense out of the past.

For Maggie, the roots are deep, the retrospect inevitable. Her favourite mode is that of memory and all her attempts to live in the future are essentially attempts to stay in the past. Even her religious conversion which helps her to live without the opiates of personal and poetic fantasy affords the opiate of duty and humility and so allows her to live as a good child. Philip insists that she is dangerously denying a part of herself which will take its revenge; even after she comes to feel the force of his argument she still lives in the past, for her feeling for

Philip is founded in the fairy-tale memory of two children. It is scarcely surprising that Maggie tells Stephen that she can't be rent away from her past, 'can't set out on a fresh life, and forget that'. But George Eliot defends the vulnerable childhood attachments, not simply because they are a part of ourselves, but because, as Wordsworth had recognized, they are the beginning of our education in love:

> Life did change for Tom and Maggie; and yet they were not wrong in believing that the thoughts and loves of these first years would always make part of their lives. We could never have loved the earth so well if we had had no childhood in it,—if it were not the earth where the same flowers come up again every spring that we used to gather with our tiny fingers as we sat lisping to ourselves on the grass—the same hips and haws on the autumn hedgerows—the same redbreasts that we used to call 'God's birds,' because they did no harm to the precious crops. What novelty is worth that sweet monotony where everything is known, and *loved* because it is known?
>
> The wood I walk in on this mild May day, with the young yellow-brown foliage of the oaks between me and the blue sky, the white star-flowers and the blue-eyed speedwell and the ground ivy at my feet—what grove of tropic palms, what strange ferns or splendid broad-petalled blossoms, could ever thrill such deep and delicate fibres within me as this home scene? These familiar flowers, these well-remembered bird-notes, this sky, with its fitful brightness, these furrowed and grassy fields, each with a sort of personality given to it by the capricious hedgerows—such things as these are the mother-tongue of our imagination, the language that is laden with all the subtle inextricable associations the fleeting hours of our childhood left behind them. Our delight in the sunshine on the deep-bladed grass to-day, might be no more than the faint perception of wearied souls, if it were not for the sunshine and the grass in the far-off years which still live in us, and transform our perception into love. (*The Mill on the Floss*, bk. i, ch. v)

There are objections to George Eliot's transference of the argument from love of nature to love of people and her definition of the 'mother-tongue of imagination' involves a metonymy which is more fully argued and explained in Wordsworth's 'Tintern Abbey' and *The Prelude*, which helped to form her own mother-tongue. The feelings of time-rooted characters like Maggie are related also to the powers of ritual which, in a crisis, determine the behaviour of Aunt Glegg and Mr Tulliver, who both act according to the imprinted lessons of the past. Mr Tulliver's act of memory is by no means facile, because his traditions and rituals are not as simple as George Eliot's natural imagery suggests. In book iii, chapter viii, we see him responding to the recorded memory of the family Bible, a memory of births, deaths and marriages. Mrs Tulliver remembers the marriage vow, varies it and puts it to the test: 'I never thought it 'ud be for so worse as this'. Tulliver is moved by the memory of his marriage, of its stability and its changes. In the next chapter we see these memories reinforced by others:

> But the strongest influence of all was the love of the old premises where he had run about when he was a boy, just as Tom had done after him. The Tullivers had lived on this spot for generations, and he had sat listening on a low stool on winter evenings while his father talked of the old half-timbered mill that had been there before the last great floods which damaged it so that his grandfather pulled it down and built the new one. It was when he got able to walk about and look at all the old objects, that he felt the strain of this clinging affection for the old home as part of his life, part of himself. He couldn't bear to think of himself living on any other spot than this, where he knew the sound of every gate and door, and felt that the shape and colour of every roof and weather-stain and broken hillock was good, because his growing senses had been fed on them. Our instructed vagrancy, which has hardly time to linger by the hedgerows, but runs away early to the tropics, and is at home with palms and banyans,—which is nourished on books of travel, and stretches the theatre of its imagination to the Zambesi,—can hardly get a dim notion of what an old-fashioned man like Tulliver felt for this spot, where all his memories centred, and where life seemed like a familiar smooth-handled tool that the fingers clutch with loving ease. And just now he was living in that freshened memory of the far-off time which comes to us in the passive hours of recovery from sickness. (bk. iii, ch. ix)

But then George Eliot shows another, older, pagan tradition arousing his memory and his action:

It was still possible, even in that later time of anti-Catholic preaching, for people to hold many pagan ideas, and believe themselves good church-people notwithstanding; so we need hardly feel any surprise at the fact that Mr Tulliver, though a regular church-goer, recorded his vindictiveness on the fly-leaf of his Bible. (bk. iv, ch. i)

The memory of the Christian past is qualified, even in the family Bible, as a commitment to another ritual, in response to another social and religious memory.

Daniel Deronda, too, is impelled by a need for memory so strong that George Eliot supports it with a suggestion of a race-memory. Mordecai's fantasy is created by a racial history and Daniel feels the need to succumb to it, though also to preserve an identity created not only by the mystical race-memory of the Jews but by the Christian roots which he has put down. In George Eliot's last novel of memory, the very form is an experiment in retrospect made in order to reveal Daniel's strong foundations and Gwendolen's insecurity. Daniel Deronda strikes a balance between a total fidelity to the past and too energetic a liberation. Hence his desire to commit himself to a nationalism with a difference, to a combination of community and separateness. It is ironic that George Eliot's qualification of Jewish nationalism should now create a very wry memory.

Wordsworth presides explicitly over *Adam Bede* and *Silas Marner*. His traces can be found in most of George Eliot's work but she is concerned with the powers of ritual as a communal memory which instructs and strengthens, whereas Wordsworth is more inclined to create his own rites of memory. Even when George Eliot shows people acting very individually, like Dorothea and Mrs Bulstrode, she makes them maintain continuity and morale by ritual behaviour. Wordsworth is fully aware of ritual behaviour but his is almost always original and inventive, even when traditionally or naturally inspired. He marks what George Eliot calls epochs; he calls them spots of time. His memorials remain absolutely stable and prepare for future stability when they first occur. His story of memory in *The Prelude* anticipates Proust's discovery of vocation, which is made afresh each time it is contemplated. The fresh beginning, in love or art, must be grounded in memory. Wordsworth knows that we may buy the sense of personal unity too dearly and admits that he may be falsifying the past, back-reading meanings into memory and planting 'snowdrops in the winter snows'. He takes the risk because he has not experienced the debilitating pressure of familiar associations but has suffered badly from the sense of discontinuity in time and disassociation of feeling and reason. Restoration was brought about by using his sister Dorothy as another memory, through whose presence he could relive his past, as well as by those sacramental moments, guardians of time, which preserved the valuable past, 'for future restoration'. *The Prelude* explicitly discusses and substantiates the needs and powers of the memory, demonstrated locally in the spots of time.

Wordsworth and George Eliot show a value placed on tradition and plead for a personal memory to act as a microcosm of that social memory felt to be of particular value at times of rapid social change. In Jane Austen and Thackeray also, memory is a type of fidelity to other people and to our past selves. But memory can plead romantically and dangerously, appealing to the nostalgia felt by experience for innocence, by disillusion for illusion, by scepticism for belief. The solicitations of romantic memory are plainly though subtly present in Henry James's *The Ambassadors*, a novel where involuntary memory is of decisive importance.

Like *Henry Esmond* and *The Mill on the Floss*, *The Ambassadors* is concerned with a sense of the past and a sense of the future. Maggie Tulliver's moral conflict led to a fight to the death between past and future. Strether's story is of a man whose fantasy is strongly and thoroughly grounded in memory, taking the form of a projection into the past and the future, the story of Chad's enlightened and enlightening passion for Madame de Vionnet. Sometimes Strether sees Chad as his own self, as he might have been; sometimes as a 'fair young man', the son he might have now if his son had lived. Strether's failure as a husband, a father and a man of letters is compounded in his involuntary memory of a visit to Paris in his youth. When he comes to Paris as Mrs Newsome's ambassador, on the diplomatic mission to Chad, he has already been unsettled by Chester, London and the ambiguous tutelage of Maria Gostrey. In Paris, the ambassador from Woollett, Massachusetts, meets his old self, who is not only a ghost of the past but evokes that other ghost Henry James delighted to imagine, the self he might have become. The scene of Strether's encounter with the past is Paris and its action is complex. Light, form, air, space, architecture, painting and books join to remind him that he has forgotten to remember. What finally disturbs the sleeping memory is something visual, something bright, something unchanged, something whose surface is a delicate but lucid symbol of its value. It is a lemon-covered, lemon-coloured book, that peculiarly French object. On his earlier visit Strether had bought some books, intending to have them bound, intending to read them, intending to embark on the life of the mind. The lemon paper bindings, so fresh, so clean, so delicate, did not wear well. Strether is also to blame for never having taken the books to the binder but there may also lurk a faint suggestion in their fragile and soiled covers of an ominous might-have-been, like the sinister presence of Paris, the great Babylon, whose lights twinkle ambiguously and deceptively. But the involuntary memory strikes a startled joy: 'something that made him hover and wonder and laugh and sigh, made him advance and retreat, feeling half ashamed of his impulse to plunge and more than half afraid of his impulse to wait' (*The Ambassadors*, bk. ii, pt. ii).

Strether is almost more Proustian than Proust's Marcel. Marcel's recognition of Albertine is an image he has to develop as a photograph in his private darkness, but Proust's involuntary springs of memory are immediately accompanied by the sense of joy, which heralds the sense of familiarity and identification. Henry James joins Proust's involuntary memory with an experience of even more gradual development. His awakening memory is somewhat generalized but eventually lights on the lemon-coloured volumes. Strether's sense of retrospect is looked at retrospectively on the day after it has begun to work. It first appears as an admonition and even the admonition is only indirectly related to the core of feeling which is making itself slowly felt. Henry James does as well as his brother William[6] in giving the sense of the slow, indistinct stirring which sets about its business in ways so obscure that we have no language to describe them:

> More than once, during the time, he had regarded himself as admonished; but the admonition, this morning, was formidably sharp. It took as it hadn't done yet the form of a question—the question of what he was doing with such an extraordinary sense of escape. (bk. ii, pt. ii)

A lengthy analysis covers both his admission of fatigue and a sense that he was almost finished but 'had just detected in his cup the dregs of

---

[6] William James, *Principles of Psychology* (London, 1918), ch. xvi.

youth'. The tentative image of 'just' detecting 'dregs' is typical of the whole dense and delicate account. Strether is stimulated by the feeling of difference, of realizing that he would like 'a single boon—the common unattainable art of taking things as they came'. After the feelings in the present, comes the remembered past. It is rapidly but not simply summarized, with mildness and controlled remorse. Its key image is the sad group in the distance, 'the pale figure of his real youth, which held against its breast the two presences paler than itself—the young wife he had early lost and the young son he had stupidly sacrificed'. It is against this pallor that the image of the present comes to fresh life, as one of various impressions, but the only one to be sensuously particularized:

> The process of yesterday had really been the process of feeling the general stirred life of connexions long since individually dropped. Strether had become acquainted even on this ground with short gusts of speculation—sudden flights of fancy in Louvre galleries, hungry gazes through clear plates behind which lemon-coloured volumes were as fresh as fruit on the tree. (bk. ii, pt. ii)

The colour is tasted like a tang, and satisfies that hungry gaze, stinging with brightness and sharpness. It is picked out, like Marcel's uneven paving-stones, and the *madeleine*, and ringing spoon, but without the freedom and randomness of attachment. Both the surface of the image and its contents are appropriate to his youth and its intentions: 'the vow taken in the course of that pilgrimage that, newly-married, with the War just over, and helplessly young in spite of it, he had recklessly made with the creature who was so much younger still' (bk. ii, pt. ii). It had been a plan for 'a relation planned with the higher culture', but one expected to bear 'a good harvest'. The promise had been sealed with the lemon-coloured volumes, 'he had gone back in the sixties with lemon-coloured volumes in general on the brain as with a dozen—selected for his wife too—in his trunk'. The old books provide a contrast as well as a link, 'somewhere at home, the dozen—stale and soiled and never sent to the binder'. He uses the words 'sharp initiation' for what they had represented and then introduces a new contrast with volumes of another colour:

> ...he glared at the lemon-coloured covers in confession of the subconsciousness that, all the same, in the great desert of the years,

he must have had of them. The green covers at home comprised, by the law of their purpose, no tribute to letters; it was of a mere rich kernel of economics, politics, ethics that, glazed and, as Mrs Newsome maintained rather against *his* view, pre-eminently pleasant to touch, they formed the specious shell. (bk. ii, pt. ii)

The glossy covers of Mrs Newsome's review show up badly, a 'specious shell', against the natural roughness both of the book and the imagined fruit, and a green unripeness beside the Parisian yellow. Strether is drawn back to an unacted past inspiration, an initiation neglected, a fruit untasted. Its freshness appeals now to his middle-age as to his youth and the image he uses for the process of awakened memory is very close to Proust: 'Buried for ten long years in dark corners at any rate these few germs had sprouted again under forty-eight hours of Paris'.

In *The Beast in the Jungle* and *The Jolly Corner*, the past returns with violence, to assert something sadly, or something happily, missed. *The Ambassadors* can stand with *Henry Esmond* as the only novel before *A la recherche du temps perdu* to assert a similar quest, in terms of similar psychological subtlety. But James's lost past is not the same as Proust's and for Strether a complete return is not possible. The lemon-coloured volumes offer him a chance he cannot seize. We see his attempts to seize it, in his advice to little Bilham to 'live' and in his own vicarious and fantastic attempts to love again through the deceptive and uncongenial passions of Chad. Strether is saluted by memory in middle-age and his aridity becomes avidity. But he is not so changed that he can have life over again. Memory can remind him but not return him to the past.

The moment when he comes to see this also invokes the past. Literature spoke in the lemon-coloured volumes and on the second occasion it is the turn of painting. Strether has to give up the role of ambassador in order to listen to his own inner embassies, one from the past and one from the future. He uses the story of the future in an attempt to return to the past but by trying to leap over the present. Later, as he looks at the river, he imposes his dream of unused vitality on to Chad's insufficiently passionate, insufficiently loving and insufficiently creative experience.

It is because of his memories of Paris that he tells Chad's love story as he does. Past shapes future. As he approaches the real thing which moves slowly out of the vagueness into specificity, he is living through his past, making up a story with a different ending. Jane Austen's *Emma* is curiously and damagingly not interested in the past; her fantasies are tested by intelligence, seldom by memory; but Strether's fantasies recreate the past from its sterilities. The life he has lived has not been good enough and the lovers in the present seem to proffer compensation for his losses.

What Strether explicitly remembers, before he re-writes his story, recognizes the lie in the affair and sees the other side of the romantic idyll, is a fantasy and a fancy in the past. It is another sad blend of memory and anticipation, like the lemon-coloured books, because what he is so moved by in the past is again imaginary, not actual. He remembers the mild adventure of intention in Tremont Street when he nearly bought the Lambinet:

> Romance could weave itself, for Strether's sense, out of elements mild enough; and even after what he had, as he felt, lately 'been through', he could thrill a little at the chance of seeing something somewhere that would remind him of a certain small Lambinet that had charmed him, long years before, at a Boston dealer's and that he had quite absurdly never forgotten. It had been offered, he remembered, at a price he had been instructed to believe the lowest ever named for a Lambinet, a price he had never felt so poor as on having to recognise, all the same, as beyond a dream of possibility. He had dreamed—had turned and twisted possibilities for an hour: it had been the only adventure of his life in connexion with the purchase of a work of art. The adventure, it will be perceived, was modest; but the memory, beyond all reason and by some accident of association, was sweet. The little Lambinet abode with him as the picture he *would* have bought—the particular production that had made him for the moment overstep the modesty of nature. He was quite aware that if he were to see it again he should perhaps have a drop or a shock, and he never found himself wishing that the wheel of time would turn it up again, just as he had seen it in the maroon-coloured, sky-lighted inner shrine of Tremont Street. It would be a different thing, however, to see the remembered mixture resolved back into its elements—to assist at the restoration to nature of the whole far-away hour: the dusty day in Boston, the background of the Fitchburg depot, of the maroon-coloured sanctum, the special-

green vision, the ridiculous price, the poplars, the willows, the rushes, the river, the sunny silvery sky, the shady woody horizon.
(bk. xi, pt. iii)

The books are unbound. The picture is unbought. Strether is a curious mixture of romantic dreamer and realist, knowing enough about himself and time not to expect complete restoration, not wishing for the past to turn up in its old form, not believing that the years can come again to the same point. What he wants is a possible thing, the impressions that had made him dream of buying the picture. The picture itself had been nearly within his means. His fantasy, like his memory, works on feasibilities. His dreams of the past and of the future are those especially sad things, the near-misses.

He was enthralled by the picture's realism and there is a sense in which it can come back, in bits and pieces, in blurred delicious impressions:

His theory of his excursion was that he could alight anywhere—not nearer Paris than an hour's run—on catching a suggestion of the particular note required. It made its sign, the suggestion— weather, air, light, colour and his mood all favouring—at the end of some eighty minutes; the train pulled up just at the right spot, and he found himself getting out as securely as if to keep an appointment. It will be felt of him that he could amuse himself, at his age, with very small things if it be again noted that his appointment was only with a superseded Boston fashion. He hadn't gone far without the quick confidence that it would be quite sufficiently kept. The oblong gilt frame disposed its enclosing lines; the poplars and willows, the reeds and river—a river of which he didn't know, and didn't want to know, the name—fell into a composition, full of felicity, within them; the sky was silver and turquoise and varnish; the village on the left was white and the church on the right was grey; it was all there, in short—it was what he wanted: it was Tremont Street, it was France, it was Lambinet. (bk. xi, pt. iii)

Strether's low-key expectations are perfectly done. Even the fashion is superseded, the excursion is undertaken casually, the station chosen at random, the pleasures are the inexpensive, innocent and available pleasures of sight and speech. James's looming irony that the 'whole episode' is going to remind him of Maupassant insists on the difference between his innocent fantasy and the picture that changes so disturbingly when he steps inside the frame. His true memory of the past has nourished and enlightened Strether. It has also been dangerous, making him wildly over-estimate the claims of culture and sexual passion, particularly when appealing in conjunction. He can never go back to being the name on the glossy green cover. He cannot live vicariously through Chad, who is avid for a successful career in advertising, obliquely praising and patronizing his mistress as he prepares to move. He cannot linger with the ghost of his old self, buying the lemon-coloured volumes and nearly buying the Lambinet. Art, passion, and even memory are all suspect, though their benefits are real enough to make it impossible for him to return to Woollett unchanged. The honourable course is to stear clear of living too strongly in past or future, to claim nothing for himself. *The Ambassadors* shows as clearly and more subtly than *The Jolly Corner* that the imagination needs to hear but also to suspect the calls of memory and its fantasy. Strether was in danger of the perils that destroyed Lot's wife and Orpheus, as well as those that threatened Odysseus.

Proust's Marcel finds a way of getting back. Undeterred by discouraging myths of the backward glance and the return journey, he makes the long and difficult return to his childhood paradise seem arduous and brave. Like Alice, Lord Jim, and Don Quixote, artists in the fantasy of the future, he uses the artist's *fiat* to justify and elevate the processes of memory. The past is the only hope, alert as he is to the treacheries of the dream, particularly of that dream of love which keeps so many people active in the present and the future. Proust could accept no guarantees from love, for him an elusive, irrational fantasy which was so far from being a reliable means of knowledge that it could fix on anything at all, however worthless. Marcel's loves, like Swann's, or Saint-Loup's, are destroyed by time, which shows their flimsiness, their arbitrariness, their cheating and their transience. Art, on the other hand, stands all the tests of time. Best of all, it can guarantee that safe-conduct to the past which Proust needed with particular urgency. He was disinclined to tell the story of the present, perhaps because he had no faith in adult loves, most at home in the beds of childhood, longing for his mother's kiss, in a lost paradise offering pains and pleasures.[7] What we can all observe is the importance of the congenial forms of memory.

Proust is, of course, not exclusively devoted to memory. He offers

[7] See G. D. Painter, *Marcel Proust; a biography* (2 vols. London, 1959, 1965).

copious narratives of gossip, scandal, curious or jealous investigation, exhibitionism, solicitation, dream and fantasy, but subordinates these other forms of life-narrative to his favourite mode of memory. Perhaps only Wordsworth equalled him as a specialist in retrospect. *The Prelude* presides silently over *A la recherche du temps perdu*, as over so many memoirs. Wordsworth's creations and re-creations of what Coleridge called 'the streamy train of association', lingering relic of the rejected Hartley, join with his more Kantian affirmations of the harmony and autonomy of poetic imagination to anticipate Proust's achievements. *The Prelude* and *A la recherche du temps perdu* both have the function of demonstrating and analysing the power of art and the artist; they are about themselves. They are concerned with the artist's memory, with the making of his vocation, and with their own exemplariness. They discuss their creators' perils, doubts, and ultimate assurance. *The Prelude* seemed to Wordsworth and Coleridge to be a prelude to a philosophical epic poem of broader human concern but Wordsworth went on writing prologemena to such a poem, instead of the poem itself. His achievement is therefore similar to Proust's less preliminary sense of achievement. Both masters of memory defend art in general, their own arts in particular, but above all, the imaginative use of retrospect, the poem and the novel of memory.[8]

Wordsworth went on procrastinating. Proust's novel shows how the procrastinator turned his attention from tomorrow to today, aided by the brilliant reassurance of yesterday. Memory taught him how to tell his story, giving him method, form, subject and faith. His claims for art are general, established and widened in the portraits of Vinteuil, the musician, Elstir, the painter, Bergotte, the writer, and Berma, the actress, but most fully explicated in the form of his own narrative fiction. Proust illuminates the nature of his novel, the nature of his genre and the nature of memory, and does it all as a novelist, critic and psychologist. With various necessary powers, he presents his view of time as a subject of universal and professional concern. Clocks tick, calendars turn, seasons glide, eras and epochs merge into each

[8] One of the resemblances between these two masterpieces of memory is their compromise between truthful memory and deceit. In *The Prelude* Wordsworth left out the story of his attachment to Annette Vallon, but told it in the story of 'Vaudracour and Julia'. Proust left out the story of his homosexuality, but told it in the histories of Charlus, Saint-Loup, Albertine, and a large number of other characters. In each case, memory seems to have insisted that the whole story got told somehow, however obliquely.

other. Time passes quickly and slowly, with wit, purpose and meaning. Proust shows the social memory at work in the dining-rooms, drawing-rooms and bedrooms of his society, chronicling the movements and shifts of classes, groups, sub-classes, factions, and families, of social, political and professional successes, failures, rivalries, and allegiances. Madame Verdurin and Odette marry into the Guermantes family, Rachel draws the crowds while Berma dies. His aging acquaintances startle Marcel as masqueraders wearing the powdered hair and masks of age. He shows the personal memory at work in all the activities of love and *désamour*, of waking and sleeping, of getting to know people, rightly and wrongly, of reading, listening to music, going to the theatre, looking at pictures, thinking about writing and writing. He shows us the internal memory of the novel itself, suspending its discoveries until its end, but using them at its beginning, showing the erratic course of time but keeping faith with biographical sequence, creating essential and accidental symbols.

These three aspects of memory, being aspects and not distinct kinds, work together. Proust, in telling the tale of his childhood, allows Swann to appear on its fringe, then moves him in to occupy its centre, to illuminate Marcel's life through his experiences of society, art, love and memory. The best narrators in fiction have always had an imperative reason for narrating. Marcel is disposed to impart his joyful discovery of unity and meaning to others. Conrad's Marlow, who desperately makes the most of what shreds of nobility this sublunary life can yield, Defoe's saddler, Charlotte Brontë's Jane Eyre, and the Ancient Mariner, are all avid to explain and instruct. Marcel tells his story because he loves to remember the whole of his life in great detail, as do Henry Esmond, David Copperfield and Maggie Tulliver. He needs to tell of the sicknesses and jealousies, to relive them or to exorcise them like Richardson's heroines or Beckett's heroes. Even the place of the telling is important. Marcel tells the curious story of his restless journeys and adventures in the great world, like Beckett's travellers, Captain Singleton or Robinson Crusoe. He tells the private and introverted story from the cave of his bed, as do Beckett's bed-ridden and pot-bound paralytics.

The novel starts in privacy and quiet, in a meditation on sleeping and waking. The tone is casual and easy, as if we are turning simply to one of many possible subjects, or stopping casually to reflect on some one interesting aspect of a rambling discourse. This is a very cunning beginning. Proust wants Marcel in the adult world, where his memories begin, but needs to get him back to childhood, where the novel's memory will begin. The return to Combray has an imperative interest for the novelist but he disguises urgency in the interests of plotting the wayward course of memory and of analysing its nature. Proust weaves story and analysis together. So we begin with some account of memory. We have to wait for fifty pages or so before we come to the key incident of the *madeleine*, which is Marcel's first encounter with involuntary memory. Proust has in fact put it earlier in Marcel's life than it came in his own; he transplants experiences as Wordsworth did, though Wordsworth apologizes for the inadvertent shifts in time in *The Prelude*. The analogy of the invalid transplants experience too and most indirectly and subtly, comparing our loss of memory on waking with the disorientation of the invalid waking in a strange hotel and mistaking the last lights of midnight for dawn. As we might expect in an 'Overture', the themes of time, childhood, memory, isolation and malady are all introduced. The simile of the invalid is expanded into an anecdote which introduces the first mention of solitude and darkness, for 'he must lie all night in agony with no one to bring him any help'. Next comes the example of waking from a dream. It is a nightmare based on a memory of childhood terror, though Marcel tells us that the originating event has been forgotten during sleep. It is, however, remembered so clearly on waking that he has to bury his head in the pillow. Then follows the illustration of waking from a sexual dream which may be traced on waking to an actual woman, to be pursued in memory until that memory 'would dissolve or vanish'. There is a dense impression of time, place, dreams, awakenings and memories, experiences common enough to attach the reader to their generalization, but permitting individual instances to emerge in sharp particularity. Information about Marcel seeps through, in his images, his examples, and his analysis. The analysis seems discursive but is actually dramatic. His images and examples are biographical too. The philosophy of memory goes hand in hand with its operations. Memory is content and form.

The individual examples embedded or blurred in generalization, picked from different ages and stages, lead to an image of waking as an automatic reading-off of our position in time, on 'the chain of the hours, the sequence of the years, the order of the heavenly host'. The most impressive anecdote of disorientation brilliantly joins detail with generality. This kind of ruminative narrative makes the analysis of memory morbid and yet entirely representative:

> I had only the most rudimentary sense of existence, such as may lurk and flicker in the depths of an animal's consciousness; I was more destitute of human qualities than the cave-dweller; but then the memory, not yet of the place in which I was, but of various other places where I had lived, and might now very possibly be, would come like a rope let down from heaven to draw me up out of the abyss of not-being, from which I could never have escaped by myself: in a flash I would traverse and surmount centuries of civilisation, and out of a half-visualised succession of oil-lamps, followed by shirts with turned-down collars, would put together by degrees the component parts of my ego. (*Swann's Way*, vol. i, pt. i, 'Overture')[9]

It is a sickened, exaggerated version of many of our wakenings. The early pages of the first volume, *Swann's Way* (*Du côté de chez Swann*), are full of such analyses of routine but indefinable states, when the awareness of self and surroundings sits loosely on the mind, and compared with Proust's most versions of the stream of consciousness in fiction seem over-plotted, too committed to the particularities of event to render the freedom and drift of rumination. Proust needs particularities too but uses his pondering as a theatre for many dramas of memory. In *Eyeless in Gaza*, Huxley attempts something like Proust's combination of a free erratic flow of time with a slow revelation of meaning. Huxley's scrambling of chronology, brilliantly though it disorders and orders, retards and advances, is totally committed to his plot. Proust's discourse is at times minimally narrative, yet one cannot imagine a better medium for the development of narratives of memory. His narrator is a man musing on his habits, merging specific cases in generalization without losing vividness. The psychologist joins the novelist.

Soon the actions of memory become wholly specific. He moves from one fixed memory of his childhood in Combray, limited in space and time, to a suddenly expanded recall. In the last volume, *Time Regained* (*Le Temps retrouvé*), we realize, looking back, that this

---

[9] All references are to C. K. Scott-Moncrieff's translation, *Remembrance of Things Past*. I have retained the original title, *A la recherche du temps perdu*, because of its precise significance.

revolution of memory made the novel possible, though it is only one of several such revolutions, whose full significance Marcel does not grasp until the time recounted in *Time Regained*.

The 'Overture' is also about itself. It relates the clearing and preparing of the mind for narrative action and sounds the themes of longing, solitude and delighted imagination. Wordsworth's imagination was 'impaired and restored'. Proust's was darkened but took a series of extraordinary steps backward. We move from vagueness to definition in the first step of the image Marcel uses for his revived memories of Combray: 'a sort of luminous panel, sharply defined against a vague and shadowy background, like the panels which a Bengal fire or some electric sign will illuminate and dissect from the front of a building the other parts of which remain plunged in darkness' (vol. i, pt. i, 'Overture'). This image of vague memory seems to become part of what is being vaguely remembered, connected by the other image of architectural shape and the contrast of light and dark. The luminous panel becomes part of the pyramid of the house, which has its base in the hall and slopes up the stairway to the pointed ceiling of his bedroom. This image is sufficient to represent his fixed memory of the light, the guest, the bedroom and its glass door through which his mother came to him:

> ...in a word, seen always at the same evening hour, isolated from all its possible surroundings, detached and solitary against its shadowy background, the bare minimum of scenery necessary (like the setting one sees printed at the head of an old play, for its performance in the provinces) to the drama of my undressing, as though all Combray had consisted of but two floors joined by a slender staircase, and as though there had been no time there but seven o'clock at night. I must own that I could have assured any questioner that Combray did include other scenes and did exist at other hours than these. But since the facts which I should then have recalled would have been prompted only by an exercise of the will, by my intellectual memory, and since the pictures which that kind of memory shows of the past preserve nothing of the past itself, I should never have had any wish to ponder over this residue of Combray. To me it was in reality all dead.
>
> Permanently dead? Very possibly. (vol. i, pt. i, 'Overture')

There follows the image of the imprisoned spirit of the past which introduces the episode of the *madeleine*. The innocent event, the exquisite and mysterious happiness, and the identification of the experience are described in a long, slow drama of effort, failure and success. Nothing could provide a greater psychological contrast to the ruminations of the early pages than this breath-held account of Marcel's sense of the past as a something unknown, rising up within him very slowly, sometimes sinking back, letting its resistance be felt and sounding 'the echoes of great spaces traversed'. Proust makes it plain that something astonishing is happening in the mind. Marcel even tries to control and guide the rise of memory but he also manages to give the impression of depths and space scarcely to be contained within the human psyche. There is the attempt at identifying the experience: 'Undoubtedly what is thus palpitating in the depths of my being must be the image, the visual memory which, being linked to that taste, has tried to follow it into my conscious mind' (ibid.).

Then we are there, 'Suddenly the memory returns'. Proust identifies the association of the past, 'the contemporary, the inseparable paramour', with the crumb of *madeleine* his aunt Léonie used to dip in her real or lime-flower tea. He postpones the full explanation of 'why this memory made me so happy' because he had himself to wait for a long time before he knew why. But its fruits are real, ripe and fresh. Memory takes in light, enlarges the panel which was all he could see, moves out of the house, creates streets, buildings, rooms, garden, pavilion, 'like the scenery of a theatre', is mobile, finds itself in the square, the streets, the country roads. The whole day, 'from morning to night', becomes available and with the outside world, 'all weathers'. The restoration of memory allows the curtain to rise on *Swann's Way*. It makes its surprising but graceful movement from Marcel to the family guest who detained his mother on that memorable night and from the inner meditation on memory to something clearly and precisely seen as a first instance of memory's new gains. Figure and ground change position and we leave Marcel's emergent memory for the story it tells:

And just as the Japanese amuse themselves by filling a porcelain bowl with water and steeping in it little crumbs of paper which until then are without character or form, but, the moment they become wet, stretch themselves and bend, take on colour and distinctive shape, become flowers or houses or people, permanent and recognisable, so in that moment all the flowers in our garden and in M. Swann's park, and the water-lilies on the Vivonne and the good folk of the village and their little dwellings and the parish church and the whole of Combray and of its surroundings, taking their proper shapes and growing solid, sprang into being, town and gardens alike, from my cup of tea. (ibid.)

Proust's symbols are of two kinds. There is the symbol proper, like the luminous screen, the Japanese flower, or the theatre, which is accessible and rational in vehicle and tenor; and there is the private symbol, of the *madeleine*, the hawthorn bush, the smell in the mind, the bending to the boots, the uneven paving-stones, the rough linen napkin, the pipes, the ringing spoon, the book, and Vinteuil's little phrase. Perhaps most resonant of all the private symbols is the group of three trees which never yield the secret of their past. Wordsworth was rather good at surrounding the symbols of his spots of time, the louring cliff or the girl struggling against the wind, with a random and arbitrary fringe, though they are images of solitude and strong feeling in a natural scene. Even though they have a sensuous glow, Strether's involuntary memories of the books are highly schematic symbols, but Marcel's arbitrary objects advance far beyond the rationally evocative lemon-coloured volumes to evoke what is more or less than rational and what must hide from the reason.

It might be said that all the greatly exciting moments in *A la recherche du temps perdu* are such moments of memory. There are great descriptions of still-life but these usually turn out to be aided by artistic memory, influenced by Marcel's brilliant recollections of Elstir which make the world of things, lights, shadows and forms look like a painting. Visual impressions evoke a memory which has evoked them, in a fashion not private and mysterious but rational and lucid. (Elstir's painting stands for impressionist painting in a painterly equivalent of Proust's fiction, since it depends on impression not intelligence.) Marcel's response to art and music respond to his own test, depend on and nourish the memory, link time and place, or transcend them. His strong moments of feeling are also displaced in time. He responds to Albertine after the first impression can be developed in the dark. He grieves for his grandmother a year after her death, the realization of great loss released involuntarily by the action of bending down to fasten his boots, which she had formerly done for him in the same place. This is one of the involuntary memories, incidentally, which is neither arbitrary nor irrational in content, since the action recollected is a typical one of love, service and abasement. Marcel's memory is the medium for his record and his primary experience of the feelings.

Time Regained completes the long narrative of memory and memories by going beyond the 'mnemonic resurrection'. The first eleven volumes retrieved and revived time and place in epoch after epoch. It was plain that the book was being written but it was also plain that it was written about a man who had not yet written it. The final gathering of mnemonic release, the desperate increase in the efforts of soliciting memory, the plaintive summoning of resources and reinforcements, appear at first to elicit a recognition that the past was not only remembered piecemeal but wholly remembered. It also acquaints Marcel with the principle of structure implicit in the series of private symbols which released the individual memories, as promised in Marcel's early warning in the 'Overture' that he did not understand the feeling of joy which accompanied the experience of the *madeleine* until long afterwards.

What is revealed, of course, is more than this, much more than the unity and harmony of a life revealed by memory and memories. Memory is recognized and transcended. The narrative is identified as the narrative of affective life, the novel of self-communion, an answer to the false claims made for the novel by ideology and realism, those distortions of art which offer surfaces in place of depths, sketches instead of impressions, outlines without passions. The miracles of memory are not the only instances of imagination but are accessible models of imaginative penetration. Certainly Marcel works away from them towards harder cases of what he calls the compelling image:

> And yet I reminded myself after a moment and after having thought over those resurrections of memory, that in another way, obscure impressions had sometimes, as far back as Combray and on the Guermantes' side, demanded my thought, in the same way as those mnemonic resurrections, yet they did not contain an earlier experience but a new truth, a precious image which I was trying to discover by efforts of the kind one makes to remember something, as though our loveliest ideas were like musical airs which might come to us without our having ever heard them and which we force

ourselves to listen to and write down. I reminded myself with satisfaction (because it proved that I was the same then and that it represented a fundamental quality of my nature) and also with sadness in the thought that since then I had made no progress, that, as far back as at Combray, I was attempting to concentrate my mind on a compelling image, a cloud, a triangle, a belfry, a flower, a pebble, believing that there was perhaps something else under those symbols I ought to try to discover, a thought which these objects were expressing in the manner of hieroglyphic characters which one might imagine only represented material objects.

(Time Regained, ch. iii)

'They did not contain an earlier experience but a new truth.' He substantiates this new truth's advance on memory by distinguishing

> memories like the sound of the spoon and the taste of the *madeleine* or of those verities expressed in forms the meaning of which I sought in my brain, where, belfries, wild herbs, what not, they composed a complex illuminated scroll, their first characteristic was that I was not free to choose them, that they had been given to me as they were.

Only in a thorough experience and appreciation of memory can we discover that memory alone is insufficient. Marcel insists on this thoroughness as a receptive intuition and an intellectual strenuousness. He describes intuition as the literary equivalent of experiment in which the work of intelligence succeeds, rather than precedes, the work. The part played by the intelligence is strenuous and it is forced to decipher what is unclear, to make an effort to extract the full individual experience 'from the darkness within ourselves and which is unknown to others'. Intuition is primary but it is no good on its own. The argument itself demonstrates this labour but because Marcel is a novelist he gives a narrative example of the extracted and recomposed experience:

> An oblique ray from the setting sun brings instantly back to me a time of which I had never thought again, when, in my childhood, my Aunt Léonie had a fever which Dr Percepied had feared was typhoid and they had made me stop for a week in the little room Eulalie had in the church square, where there was only a matting on the floor and a dimity curtain at the window humming in the

sunlight to which I was unaccustomed. And when I think how the memory of that little room of an old servant suddenly added to my past life an extension so different from its other side and so delightful, I remember, as a contrast, the nullity of impressions left on my mind by the most sumptuous parties in the most princely mansions.

(*Time Regained*, ch. iii)

Marcel is using his intelligence after the intuitive event. It is not accidental that this case of the narrative imagination should follow an attack on what he sees as attempts of propaganda and realism to use art 'to assert the triumph of Justice, to recreate the moral unity of the nation'. The moral and social argument succeed the image. The image itself is composed of two memories related by contrast. One is a memory of a memory, 'when I think how the memory of that little room...added to my past life', and it evokes another, distinct, and time-separated memory, 'I remember, as a contrast, the nullity'. It is an instance of the imagination's mode of assembly, its superiority over time and space, its subordination of intelligence to intuition, its use of memory and its intuitive agility. The imagination is more than memory, impossible without memory.

Marcel's story is composed of memories of feeling. The pleasant time in Eulalie's room is fully recollected down to the last detail of the only distressing thing he suffered there: the noise of trains, arousing a moderate fear, qualified by knowing 'that this roaring proceeded from regulated machines'. One feeling is set against another feeling and strong feeling itself against 'the nullity of impressions'. A second example follows, not plucked from the past by the ruminating mind but actively improvised in the present, worked out 'just now'. As Marcel looks at the Guermantes' first editions, he is surprised by a violent feeling which he first identifies as inharmonious. He is inattentively opening a George Sand novel and, realizing that the emotion is released by the past when his mother read the book to him on the memorable night in Combray, he sees that in fact there is harmony. The book he was looking at in the present with a bibliophile's eye refused to respond to his present self, summoning instead the past self, 'the child I once was whom the book had revived in me, for recognizing only the child in me, the book had at once summoned him, wanting only to be seen with his eyes, only to be loved with his heart, and only to talk to him'. The friction set up between the bibliophily of the

Prince de Guermantes and what Marcel calls his own psychic bibliophily is another case of the evaluation made by the moral intelligence,
after memory has been added to memory to produce a new form and
new impressions. In a brilliant shifting of the bibliographical image
which makes his point poetically as he argues it discursively, Marcel
surmises that if he were to be a bibliophile he would be interested in the
history of ownership, 'that beauty of a book which is in a sense
historical, would not have been lost upon me'. But he concludes that
he would find it most congenial to extract such beauty from his own
history. This is just what he is doing. George Sand's *François le
Champi* is the key example in the book, in the fictional autobiography
of Marcel and the biography of Proust, taking him back to 'the first
abdication from which I was able to date the decline of my health and
my will', on the night when his mother had not kissed him goodnight
but had subsequently healed his distress by reading him this book all
through the night. Marcel needs no psychoanalysis to elicit the past
and its significance. Memory advances to imagination both in the
anecdote and in the discursive rumination. He considers the surface of
experience as a carrier of meaning, memory he understands as feeling
and sensation: 'The taste of our morning coffee brings us that vague
hope of a fine day'. Once more he insists on the superficial and false
claims of realism:

> An hour is not merely an hour, it is a vase filled with perfumes, with
> sounds, with projects, with climates. What we call reality is a
> relation between those sensations and those memories which
> simultaneously encircle us—a relation which a cinematographic
> vision destroys because its form separates it from the truth to which
> it pretends to limit itself—that unique relation which the writer
> must discover in order that he may link two different states of being
> together for ever in a phrase. In describing objects one can make
> those which figure in a particular place succeed each other in-
> definitely; the truth will only begin to emerge from the moment that
> the writer takes two different objects, posits their relationship, the
> analogue in the world of art to the only relationship of causal law in
> the world of science, and encloses it within the circle of fine style.
> (*Time Regained*, ch. iii)

The arts of memory were only preparations, taught by nature 'on
the track of art' when she 'often only permitted me to realize the beauty

of an object long afterwards in another, mid-day at Combray only through the sound of its bells, mornings at Doncières only through the groans of our heating apparatus'. He attacks the literature which wants only the description of things, listing what he calls waste experience, in phrases like 'bad weather' and 'lighted restaurant'. Salvaged experience is conveyed in the difficult rendering of 'what takes place in us at the moment a circumstance or an event makes a certain impression'. In this effort of salvage memory is essential; to render particularity we must interpret what lies within each one of us, in past and present.

Proust gives examples of the attempt to get at the truths of feeling. They are examples of common human effort, like the attempt to straighten out the 'oblique inner utterance' which has deviated from the original impression in any experience of feeling. What is demonstrated is no purely artistic endeavour but the candour, courage and intelligence demanded by all attempts at understanding the affective life. The dishonesty of love, for instance, 'where that same straightening-out becomes painful', is related to the falsities of art, but in such a way that no division is made between the artist and the non-artist. In love, as in art, we should labour to make out what we felt, 'to bring back what was really and truly felt from where it had strayed'.

Proust goes on to give one of the most valuable accounts ever uttered of the idleness of much response to literature. It is made memorable by his image of the relationship between the recipient and the art: 'all impression is twofold, half-sheathed in the object, prolonged in ourselves by another half which we alone can know'. We tend to concentrate on the easier exterior half, thus avoiding the laborious probing of our own affective experience. And what tempts the reader tempts the writer also. He may find it easy to refuse the effort of memory and imagination and reproduce what has 'accumulated little by little in the memory, the chain of all the obscure impressions where nothing of what we actually experienced remains'. Art's honourable purpose is the attempt to recapture 'our true life ... revealed and illumined, the only life which is really lived and which in one sense lives at every moment in all men as well as in the artist'. What art needs is 'sentimental courage', the courage to develop those negatives of past experience, 'abrogating our most cherished illusion, ceasing to believe in the objectivity of our own elaborations', and, of course, using the power of intelligence which is also necessary to 'distinguish, and with how much difficulty, the shape of that which we have felt'. As well as memory and intelligence, the imagination at work on shaping what it has felt, may use the emotional experience of the present, 'a new tenderness, a new suffering comes which enables us to finish it and fill it out'. The novel is founded on attempts to put memories together in order to understand the true life of feeling and in order to do so may incorporate new experience, joining the present to the past. Memory is not enough.

Proust appears to claim a distinction between the imagination of the artist and the imagination of the man who is not an artist, like Swann. Marcel observes, for instance, that Swann failed to understand the joy he felt at the reverberations of Vinteuil's little phrase because, not being an artist, he could only mistakenly account for it as associated with the delights of love. Although all Proust's efforts move towards the growing discovery of Marcel's 'vocation', *A la recherche du temps perdu* is not exempt from Lawrence's warning that we must trust the tale, not the teller. Because Marcel postpones for so long the identification of mnemonic resurrection with inspiration, his 'ignorance' frees him to keep intact the processes of imaginative memory, sentimental courage and intellectual labour which he shares with men who are not artists. His moments of memory, his revival of feeling and sensation, his yoking of memories which correct, rebuke and judge each other, form an analysis which moves against the grain of his conclusion, that such activity is the exclusive sphere of the artist. The analysis and its anecdotes are larger than the aesthetic conclusion, offering a description of memory as the basis of the moral life. In *Ulysses* the imaginations of Stephen Dedalus, Leopold and Molly Bloom are all fully appreciated, whereas Swann's inadequacies demonstrate the superiority of Marcel's artistic imagination. But Proust is more like Joyce than he might have liked.

Proust's renovations of experience depend on his destructions. His ability to record the shape of what was really felt in such particularity and over such tracts of time and space is matched only by what we have to take on trust, his self-styled capacity for obliteration. Samuel Beckett observes that 'Proust had a bad memory. . . . The man with a good memory does not remember anything because he does not forget anything' (*Proust*). Beckett's Krapp should be a figure in a nightmare to Marcel, a case of purely voluntary and therefore of supersaturated, dead memory, though he does come to discard most of what he taped. The narrators in Beckett's novels, like Marcel, know that silence and darkness are needed for memory. They are self-dubbed paralytics and travellers, resembling Marcel, Don Quixote and Alice. They know that imagination needs silence and privacy. They also know that it needs to cover vast expanses of new ground. Like the Descartes of *Whoroscope* they are all horoscopic, watching the hour. Stuck in their bins, jars, beds, or void, wandering through terrains, marsh, woods and mud, cosy and restless as Marcel, they refuse to take his responsibility for time. They are desperately uncertain of the status and reliability of memory or imagination. Sometimes they remind us of Marcel's insights into memory. Didi in *Waiting for Godot* observes that 'habit is a great deadener'. The narrator in 'The Expelled' agrees with Marcel that memory must not become a routine of mind but ruminates on the ways of killing that past which Marcel needed to keep green, by losses:

> Memories are killing. So you must not think of certain things, of those that are dear to you, or rather you must think of them, for if you don't there is the danger of finding them, in your mind, little by little. That is to say, you must think of them for a while, a good while, every day several times a day, until they sink forever in the mud. That's an order.

Proust sees the falsity of the surfaces and willed choices of memory but his memory-founded imagination, in art or out of art, depends on some belief in the past. He distrusts love, friendship, intelligence and ideology but pins his faith to memory. However hard we have to work to remember properly, it is assumed that there is such a thing as remembering properly. In Beckett there is a conspicuous absence of this faith and its absence is at least as understandable as its presence in Proust. Beckett challenges the availability of truth in telling the stories of the past or the future to ourselves or to each other, and in remembering the stories we have been told.

Beckett's people might appeal to Marcel, however, because their distrust of memory is a recognition of the difficulty of the affective recall. Beckett never likes to claim much for our knowledge of feeling and with the passage of time the difficulties are horribly multiplied. Memory is up against all the confusing pressures of shifting circumstance and identity. Even though Proust saw the personal history as composed of different selves, he seems to have had no doubt that imaginative labour can get us back to each successive *moi*. It is precisely this process of recovery that Beckett doubts. What seems to be memory may be invention or retrospective fantasy. Proust looks trusting beside Beckett. In Beckett we can't always tell what is memory and what is not:

> I got up and set off. I forget how old I can have been. In what had just happened to me there was nothing in the least memorable. It was neither the cradle nor the grave of anything whatever. Or rather it resembled so many other cradles, so many other graves, that I'm lost. But I don't believe I exaggerate when I say that I was in the prime of life, what I believe is called the full possession of one's faculties. Ah yes, them I possessed all right. I crossed the street and turned back towards the house that had just ejected me, I who never turned back when leaving. How beautiful it was! There were geraniums in the windows. I have brooded over geraniums for years. Geraniums are artful customers, but in the end I was able to do what I liked with them. I have always greatly admired the door of this house, up on top of its little flight of steps.
>
> (*No's Knife*, 'The Expelled')

> In the street I was lost. I had not set foot in this part of the city for a long time and it seemed greatly changed. Whole buildings had disappeared, the palings had changed position and on all sides I saw, in great letters, the names of tradesmen I had never seen before and would have been at a loss to pronounce. There were streets where I remembered none, some I did remember had vanished and others had completely changed their names. The general impression was the same as before. It is true I did not know the city very well. Perhaps it was quite a different one. I did not know where I was supposed to be going. I had the great good fortune, more than once, not to be run over. My appearance still made people laugh, with that hearty jovial laugh so good for the health. By keeping the red part of the sky as much as possible on my right hand I came at last to the river. Here all seemed at first sight more or less as I had left it. But if I had looked more closely I would doubtless have discovered many changes. And indeed I subsequently did so. But the general appearance of the river, flowing between its quays and under its bridges, had not changed. Yes, the river still gave the impression it was flowing in the wrong direction. That's all a pack of lies I feel. My bench was still there. (*No's Knife*, 'The End')

Objects get by more easily than people. Nostalgia is permitted if suitably comic, trivial, or incongruous. Beckett's bicycles show a distressing tendency to be Cartesian but at least one is loved for itself alone:

> Dear bicycle, I shall not call you bike, you were green, like so many of your generation. I don't know why. It is a pleasure to meet it again. To describe it at length would be a pleasure. It had a little red horn instead of the bell fashionable in your days. To blow this horn was for me a real pleasure, almost a vice. I will go further and declare that if I were obliged to record, in a roll of honour, those activities which in the course of my interminable existence have given me only a mild pain in the balls, the blowing of a rubber horn—toot!—would figure among the first. And when I had to part from my bicycle I took off the horn and kept it about me. I believe I have it still, somewhere, and if I blow it no more it is because it has gone dumb. Even motor-cars have no horns nowadays, as I understand the thing, or rarely. When I see one, through the lowered window of a stationary car, I often stop and blow it. This should all be re-written in the pluperfect. What a rest to speak of bicycles and horns. (*Molloy*, pt. i)

But the memory of his bike comes in handy to show the difficulty of more personal nostalgia, especially his memory of his mother and his mother's memory, both decidedly uncertain: 'She who brought me into the world, through the hole in her arse if my memory serves me correct'. He and his mother share ancient, dim memories, 'like a couple of old cronies, sexless, unrelated, with the same memories...'. The old cronies' memories are scarcely sentimental. His mother is always asking him if he remembers but calls him by his father's name: 'Dan, you remember the day I saved the swallow. Dan, you remember the day you buried the ring', and Molloy flatly and matter-of-factly puts memory in its place: 'I remembered, I remembered, I mean I knew more or less what she was talking about, and if I hadn't always taken part personally in the scenes she evoked, it was just as if I had'. At the beginning of his story he says without making or expecting a fuss, 'perhaps I'm inventing a little, perhaps embellishing, but on the whole that's the way it was'. Likewise, at the beginning of the twelfth of the *Texts for Nothing* he writes: 'It's a winter's night, where I was, where I'm going, remembered, imagined, no matter...'.

Memory is sharply imagined in those works where its status is doubtful or unstable, its presence minimal. In *How It Is*, the speaker says that memories have not been given to him, instead he has images of the life in the light. These images are eventually discredited along with everything else except the mud but they act like lyrical glimpses of memory. Evoked by someone's memory or imagination, dictated by someone's caprice or knowledge, there appear the crocus, the girl, his mother, and marriage, well-lit and circumstantial images, Proust-like in their involuntary and spasmodic emergences, but guaranteeing nothing. In *Ping* everything is reduced to an enclosed visual shape, colour and size, and memory is minimally present in a short murmur, seemingly because language implies memory. In the spareness and tautness of *Lessness*, the images are not discussed. The blue seems to hover between memory and fantasy and performs like a product of memory since it is what the reader at least might expect to be remembered in the whiteness and greyness. In the attempts to do without story in *Texts for Nothing*, to present the minimum of life through the reduction of narrative, the past is barely present but it is sometimes seen as a struggle for possession, as if someone else is receiving the narrator's dreams and memory, or as if it is forcibly inserted 'into him still living'. Sometimes it is presented as chosen with a brutal or brutalized arbitrariness, as in *From an Abandoned Work*. And if *Krapp's Last Tape* is the great drama of reminiscence run wild, statically taking over life, *Eh Joe* presents the memories' violent aggressions in that form of memory known as remorse.

Proust's reliance on memory forces and helps the reader to remember, so it seems only right that *Waiting for Godot* should make us feel, in the theatre of all places, what it is like to find memory useless. After Proust, there had to be a Beckett.

4
Abuses of Narrative

The well-skill'd workman this mild image drew
For perjur'd Sinon, whose enchanting story
The credulous old Priam after slew;
Whose words like wildfire burnt the shining glory
Of rich-built Ilion...
               (Shakespeare, *The Rape of Lucrece*, 1520–4)

For what soeuer good by any sayd,
Or doen she heard, she would streightwayes inuent,
How to depraue, or slaunderously vpbrayd,
Or to misconstrue of a mans intent,
And turne to ill the thing, that well was ment.
Therefore she vsed often to resort,
To common haunts, and companies frequent,
To hearke what any one did good report,
To blot the same with blame, or wrest in wicked sort.

And if that any ill she heard of any,
She would it eeke, and make much worse by telling,
And take great ioy to publish it to many,
That euery matter worse was for her melling.
Her name was hight *Detraction*...
        (Spenser, *The Faerie Queene*, bk. v, canto xii, v. 34–5)

To make out the truth about the past or to check an ideal of the future demands what Proust calls sentimental courage. His distinction between the power of the artist and the shallowness of the non-artist should not obscure his valuable formulation of imaginative passion and knowledge. For Proust, the errors of imagination were the products of sluggishness or incompetence and he nowhere considers *imaginative* perversions or defects, profound and impassioned misuses of his powers of composition and recomposition. If the good dream and the resonant memory are offspring of the narrative imagination, so also are lies, slanders, gossip, aggressive confidences, persuasive temptations, secrets, deceits and cold reserve. Stupid and superficial illustrations from life or literature come to mind at once, but the most interesting examples, and doubtless the most dangerous, are intelligent and profound. It may, of course, be unwise to draw conclusions in this instance from the narrative perversions imagined by great artists, since they endow them with their own power. But it is for this very reason that literature can valuably shake our credulity by evidence that imagination is not invariably benign.

Great narrative artists are drawn to abuses of narrative. Homer is interested in lies and boasts, Virgil in lies and rumour, Shakespeare in slander, Milton in temptations, George Eliot and D. H. Lawrence in gossip. Thomas Hardy is the rare narrative artist who does not imagine such perversions, with the occasional exception of a comic abuse like the narrative withdrawal practised by the story-telling parson in *A Pair of Blue Eyes*, who begins stories but won't finish them because they are improper. The interest in perverted forms is made up of various strands, including the interest of the craftsman in his genre. The proper study of the novelist is narrative, in all its forms.

The analysis of narrative distortion in great narrative works, novels, plays and epic poems is imaginative, analytic, and consequently instructive. There may or may not be explicit analysis of narrative error, like Lawrence's comparison of the novel with gossip or Proust's attacks on naturalism but there is always an implicit analysis and judgement. Analysis emerges from the very composition of narrative, which contains narratives within itself and compares them with each other. An instance of slander or solicitation is almost always demonstrated in a context of cause and effect, plot and character.[1] The nature of the communication is laid bare, lies and gossip related to the liar and the gossips, and to their victims. The bad narrative is criticized, is necessarily exaggerated or schematic and self-analysing. It is also implicitly evaluated by its neighbourhood to true story-telling.

Lie is set beside truth, aggressive confidence beside wise reserve, gossip beside sympathetic understanding. Most important, the lies and slander and gossip are masterpieces, products of imagination imagining imagination. They are the most complete and dangerous abuses, not interesting errors of blindness, stupidity or generalization but distortions of passion and intelligence. They are usually not failures in communication, like Proust's literary examples of failure, but all too

---

[1] There are, of course, exceptions like Wycherley's *The Country Wife*, Thackeray's *Barry Lyndon*, and Thomas Mann's *Felix Krull*, where the normal value is assumed, not illustrated.

successful manipulations of the human spirit, knowing, thorough, well-formed and eloquent. Virgil and Shakespeare know a lie when they hear one and their liars are Sinon, Falstaff, Iago and Edmund. Milton never stopped investigating forms of illicit persuasion and his tempters are Satan and Comus. There are, of course, times when our attention is drawn to incompetence. Gabriel sets a trap for Satan's pride, when he asks him why he has come to Paradise and scorns the first reason given as an admission of cowardice, not leadership. Satan hastily changes his story, eliciting Gabriel's retort that 'to say and unsay…argues a liar traced'. In *Samson Agonistes*, Dalila changes her story several times. Thackeray shows Becky Sharp's successes as a liar but also her failures, her lack of control over plausibility, her overreaching. But even though many of the perverted story-tellers do ultimately fail, their actual art is not by any means to blame, and the effectiveness of Sinon, Iago, or even Satan is scarcely in doubt.

Narrative is of crucial importance in the epic, drama and the novel, not only as a means of establishing history and character but as an important aspect of action. A story frequently shapes and precipitates the turning points of the action. The *Aeneid* contains a powerful lie and a powerful rumour. The lie was crucial. Troy fell not because of the wooden horse but because of Sinon's persuasive story. The horse was essential but by itself a mere object; filled with armed men but inert until moved by the powers of narrative. The technical imagination of Ulysses needed the story-teller to complete the military exercise and make his machine work. Sinon's lie is so effective that the Trojans do not just agree to take the horse into the city but jump at the chance, are terrified in case they can't get it in and tear down their walls. Sinon, like Mosca, Tom Sawyer, the Man Who Sold the Eiffel Tower[2] (twice), and all good con-men and salesmen, knows that willingness is not enough; you must gull the victims into a passionate desire for the dangerous or worthless thing on offer. Virgil's story is self-analysing, evaluated by its context.

Sinon's is a story within a story, a lie within a memory within an epic. It is a part of that all too effective story which Aeneas tells at Dido's request, in anguished memory and understanding, all through the night. Sinon's story is also set in conflict with two other stories: the prophecy of Cassandra and the earlier interpretation of Laocoon,

---

[2] J. F. Johnson, *The Man Who Sold the Eiffel Tower* (London, 1962).

who nearly breaks a hole in the horse and speculates accurately about its probable contents. His story is brief, spontaneous, artless, sensible, ineffective and interrupted by the arrival of Sinon. He gives Sinon the perfect cue and the Trojans the hint they cannot take, by warning them against the Greeks bearing gifts. The warning comes to apply to Sinon, offering the gift of good advice, which purports to be a solemn act of gratitude and revenge. Brilliant con-man that he is, he makes them a present in order to get what he wants from them. His story is perfectly designed for the anxious, suspicious, decent audience, taking them aback by a show of anxiety, innocence and hopelessness and encouraging them to encourage him to tell, 'who he was/What he could say for himself'. It gives him the form and excuse of answering a question, not taking the initiative. Like Iago, he needs pressing, and like Iago, he flaunts his honesty, says he is going to tell the whole truth, not having been shaped by Fortune as a liar. He tells his story with a show of unwillingness, breaking off in the middle of an interesting sentence to ask, 'What's the point, I ask you, going on with this sorry tale?' His technique is one of apologetic and distressed self-deprecation, playing on pity, burying and suspending the point of the story, ending with an impressive ritual declaration that it is no sin for him to disclose the secrets of the Greeks, in revenge and gratitude.

His lie is big enough to move the horse. He persuades the Trojans that it has been made so big because it must on no account be taken into the city to become a guardian and defeat the Greeks. Had it been damaged it would have been 'quite disastrous (may the omen sooner recoil/On its own prophet!)'. The lie is awesome, as it needs to be. It works, and Troy falls. Aeneas remembers and tells his story as a gulled listener, a loser, and a man regretting great losses. As he tells, Dido listens, also to prepare for later regrets.

Virgil shows the same interest in narrative contrasts in the famous appearance of *Fama* or Rumour in Book IV. The story of Dido and Aeneas, so fatally blown up by Rumour, is told first quietly and reticently in a few lines which do not intrude on the consummation in the cave but briefly salute it with delight, solemnity and foreboding:

Now Dido and the prince Aeneas found themselves
In the same cave. Primordial Earth and presiding Juno
Gave the signal. The firmament flickered with fire, a witness
Of wedding. Somewhere above, the Nymphs cried out in pleasure.

That day was doom's first birthday and that first day was the cause of
Evils: (iv. 165–70)³

The terse account barely looks at the lovers, turning away towards
another story of their consummation. Only the line and a half of bare
factual report, 'Now Dido and the prince Aeneas found themselves/In
the same cave', narrates the happening. If Dido cried out in pleasure,
we hear her only through the amplification of the Nymphs. Reserve
and brevity are immediately followed by the galloping and exuberant
garrulousness of *Fama*, that vile Rumour whose gossip swells into
many lives, and Virgil inflates her story by combining with it his own
analysis of the nature and power of her energy. She is 'Loud-speaker
of truth, hoarder of mischievous falsehood', announcing 'fact and
fiction indiscriminately'. Persistence, glee and effectiveness are all
analysed and then shown as effective in the precipitation of Aeneas's
departure and Dido's death. When the story reaches Iarbas, he tells
it to Jove in inflamed resentment, driven out of his mind 'by that bitter
blast of Rumour' and doing his best to poison Jove's mind too.

Virgil is instructive about the gravity and the sinister workings of
gossip, scandal, and rumour. We see how *Fama* grows and smears,
combining truth and falsehood, reducing Aeneas to a philanderer with
oily hair and an effeminate following. Virgil knows that rumour doesn't
grow simply of its own accord but is stimulated by personal malice
and jealousy. Iarbas is susceptible because he is a jealous suitor; both
his listening and his telling are prompted by personal interest. Jove
too is scarcely disinterested, intent on the founding of Rome. Aeneas is
wasting his time instead of getting on with the destiny of nations and
Jove is especially sensitive to Iarbas's story because he is afraid that
Aeneas is dallying too long. Gossip is powerful. The contrast with the
quiet privacy of that line and a half's record is striking, as we see *Fama*
'thriving on movement, gathering strength as it goes', beginning as
small and cowardly and relentlessly awake, imaged by multiple
tongues and multiple eyes. Each feather has a sleepless eye, tongue
and ear. She terrorizes cities, never sleeping, driven by anger, the last
child of earth borne in destructive rage 'as a winged angel of ruin'.
Fama is closely attentive, untiringly energetic and cunning in her
choice of listeners. Her story-telling is as effective as Sinon's.

³ *The Eclogues, Georgics and Aeneid of Virgil*, translated by C. Day Lewis
(London, 1966).

Narrative within narration is crucial in *Othello*. The story which marks the first step in Iago's seduction of Othello's mind is the story of Cassio's dream. It is a lie about a dream, a double unreality. It is carefully plausible in its circumstantial detail: Iago is spending the night with Cassio but is kept awake by raging toothache, Cassio is 'loose-souled' enough to talk in his sleep. It is offered in disingenuous self-deprecation, as only a dream, so that its significance shall be interpreted by Othello, who observes that the dream shows a 'foregone conclusion' in Cassio's mind. It is violently aggressive in its sexual particularity, to feed and rouse jealousy:

> I lay with Cassio lately,
> And being troubled with a raging tooth,
> I could not sleep.
> There are a kind of men so loose of soul,
> That in their sleeps will mutter their affairs:
> One of this kind is Cassio.
> In sleep I heard him say 'Sweet Desdemona,
> Let us be wary, let us hide our loves';
> And then, sir, would he gripe and wring my hand,
> Cry 'O sweet creature!' and then kiss me hard,
> As if he plucked up kisses by the roots,
> That grew upon my lips; then laid his leg
> Over my thigh, and sighed, and kissed, and then
> Cried 'Cursèd fate that gave thee to the Moor!'
>
> (III. iii. 415–28)

It is brazenly offered instead of the ocular evidence which Othello's sanity says he must have, so vivid in every respect that Othello forgets that it is not ocular evidence. It is a lie brilliantly designed by the liar, whose imaginative relish is shown in the urgency and physical vehemence of every detail.

It is a perversion of the true stories in *Othello*, which it opposes. Like the narratives in the *Aeneid*, they are spontaneous, sincere and accurate. There is the story of Othello's life which he tells to Brabantio and Desdemona; his 'round unvarnished tale' which he tells about the wooing and marriage to Brabantio and the Duke; Desdemona's story of the maid called Barbara; Emilia's story of Iago's villainy; and the final story which Othello tells to declare his integrity and create the opportunity for suicide. They are all crucial narratives, each one acting as a hinge of action: the falling in love, the marriage, Desdemona's acceptance of fatality, the discovery and the death are precipitated or marked by a story. The malevolent stories of Iago work in the same way, as lies pitting their strength against truths, but there is no opposition without some affinity, so particularity, passion and intelligence are found in truths and lies, destruction and love, antipathy and sympathy. The truthful stories are artless, the false ones carefully designed, but since Shakespeare's contrivance is behind them all, even art and artlessness own an affinity. Othello's story of his story-telling makes plainest the resemblance between his powers and Iago's, but even Desdemona's most distracted story, a bare outline, takes its place in the pattern. In telling someone else's story, like Fontane's Effi Briest, she speaks her own while keeping its secret:

> My mother had a maid called Barbara.
> She was in love; and he she loved proved mad
> And did forsake her. She had a song of 'willow'—
> An old thing 'twas, but it expressed her fortune,
>
> (IV. iii. 26–9)

The mode of art most thoroughly used and analysed within plays is, of course, drama. Role-playing, illusion, impersonation, deceit, performance, acting, scenes and stage are frequent metaphors and themes in Shakespeare, Marlowe, Ibsen, Brecht, Sartre and Beckett. Since narrative is a part of drama (as drama is a part of fiction), it has an important part to play in Shakespeare's theatre. In literature as in life, it is impossible to separate story from performance,[4] and the interest in truthful and lying stories is obviously one with considerable histrionic implications. Shakespeare's characters perform the stories they tell. Prospero tells Miranda a perfectly timed and spellbinding story, with effective majesty and sentiment. Falstaff's lies are magnificently huge, carelessly self-aggrandizing, drawing attention to Hal's politic secrecy and reserve. Goneril and Regan tell Lear the story of their love, Cordelia says nothing. Edmund tells each victim the story he is most likely to believe, with those liar's skills he shares with Sinon and Iago, but tells

---

[4] This is also true of novels where the narrator must have an imperative reason for telling his story, like Pamela, Clarissa, Robinson Crusoe, the Man of the Hill in *Tom Jones*, Molloy, Stephen Dedalus in the last pages of *A Portrait of the Artist as a Young Man* or Marcel. But in drama the narrative is more of a total performance.

the truth to the audience. The soliloquy of the deceiver creates a peculiar confidential freedom and intimacy, an aspect of narrative which can have no equivalent in ordinary life, since it depends on a movement in and out of convention. The nearest thing to it would be the confidence we make to the stranger in the train but that scarcely matches the intimate candour of such story-tellers as Edmund or Richard III, whose narrative medium in public is totally dishonest and deceptive. Lear's dream of joyful love, privacy, and communion in prison 'We two will sing alone like birds i' the cage', is a story about story-telling. Lear and Cordelia will tell each other the stories of the remote world, of 'who's in, who's out'. It is made of the same materials as Edmund's deceitful stories or Edgar's bitter ones but redeemed by loving conversation, perhaps by seclusion. The lies, contrivances and slanders that appear in every play are criticized by the standards of truth, warmth, and relationship in story-telling, whether the stories meet in collision or not.

The Winter's Tale offers a variant on Shakespeare's favourite subject of slander. Leontes's jealous slander of Hermoine and Polixenes is totally irrational, uncontrolled and unpersuasive. His sick fantasy is effective because of its power over his own mind and his executive authority. Leontes completes the range of Shakespeare's investigations of slander, which is not always rationally contrived but often patho-logical. Iago is driven by cold passion, constructing his story carefully and skilfully, to play on the passions of one man. Leontes's narrative, like his language, is tortured and uncontrolled. His rhetoric is Shakespeare's, unmediated by the character's 'control'. His hesitations, interruptions and digressions, unlike those of Sinon and Iago, are fits and starts of his mind. It is the pressure of his feeling that seizes a brutal language as he attacks Camillo with confidences which are aggressive, gross, and self-mutilating:

> Ha' not you seen, Camillo?
> (But that's past doubt: you have, or your eye-glass
> Is thicker than a cuckold's horn) or heard?
> (For to a vision so apparent rumour
> Cannot be mute) or thought? (for cogitation
> Resides not in the man that does not think)
> My wife is slippery?   (I. ii. 267–73)

This grossness and aggressiveness contrast perfectly with the sweetness and friendliness of the story elicited from Polixenes by Hermione:

> We were as twinn'd lambs, that did frisk i' th' sun,
> And bleat the one at th' other: what we chang'd
> Was innocence for innocence: we knew not
> The doctrine of ill-doing, nor dream'd
> That any did. Had we pursu'd that life,
> And our weak spirits n'er been higher rear'd
> With stronger blood, we should have answer'd heaven
> Boldly, 'not guilty', the imposition clear'd,
> Hereditary ours.   (I. ii. 67–75)

It is the story good lovers love to hear, the story of the beloved's childhood. It is a story of innocence but it is form as well as content that completes the contrast. Polixenes's story is simple, free, relaxed and full of goodwill; Leontes's is tortured, tense and hostile. Leontes is talking to himself, even when he tells his story to Camillo, whereas Polixenes's story is part of a trusting conversation, so amicable and happy that it is drawn into Leontes's fantasy, which has the magnetism of imagination unimpeded by reason. Leontes seizes on any materials to make up his story and makes his obsession explicit in a general condemnation of faith and love.

Coleridge used Shakespeare's portrayal of madness (and Wordsworth's) because they were studies in mania, models of imaginative dissolution, diffusion and dissipation of experiences, though without the subordination to judgement. Leontes, like Lear, sees one story and one story only. In *King Lear* Shakespeare's own story all but confirms Lear's obsession, but *The Winter's Tale* takes care to distinguish aberration from truth. Even so, the false story and the true story have a long way to go before they meet to make an end.

The awareness of narrative is there in the title, to which, as Coleridge says, the play is exquisitely responsive. *The Winter's Tale* tells a fabulous tale of seasonal rhythm and reconciliation, of a wintry sadness, chill and barrenness. The winter's tale within the play is promised and begun by Mamillius, who is not allowed to finish either his story or his childhood. Leontes murders innocent story-telling just as Macbeth murders sleep, but his own winter's tale is permitted its spring.

The principle of narrative contrast between the good and the bad story is fundamental in Shakespeare. Enobarbus tells the full story of

Antony's meeting with Cleopatra and his appreciative, detached version contrasts with the curter and grosser versions, like Philo's:

> ...you shall see in him
> The triple pillar of the world transform'd
> Into a strumpet's fool....   (I. i. 11–13)

Hamlet's solitary and secret speculations about the ghost's crucial story is filled with memories, dreams, fantasies, alternatives, plans and intentions. They contrast violently with the stories other people make up in their attempts to pluck out the heart of his mystery in this play where all narratives are, rightly, suspected. Shakespeare is as good at reticence as he is at eloquence and if Cordelia's unspoken truth is matched by her sisters' flattering lies, Edgar's mad inventions by Edmund's persuasive stories, story-telling is ultimately exonerated and glorified in Lear's dream of prison.

In *Paradise Lost, Paradise Regained, Samson Agonistes* and *Comus*, Milton's is the story of the temptation, successful once and three times unsuccessful. The temptation is always the same in its attempt to subvert integrity and mind by a stong, unbalanced and unworthy appeal to imagination through pleasure and power. *Paradise Lost* shows most elaborately the pattern of contrast which is there in all four poems. Within the explicit epic attempt to justify Providence, the good story is the story of creation and redemption, narrated in many local forms, as well as through the poem as a whole. Michael and Raphael are the angelic and professional story-tellers, instructed by God to tell the retrospective story of the fall of the angels and the prophetic story of the redemption. They are powerful and thoughtful narrators. Raphael is much occupied with the problem of symbolic representation, needing urgently to tell his human listeners a story which cannot be conveyed wholly in terms of their world and experience, 'for how shall I relate/To human sense th' invisible exploits/Of warring Spirits?' His doubts touch on more than the problem of inaccessible or ineffable conceptions, for he is also aware of the danger of the enterprise, even though God (admittedly in very general terms) has told him what to do. He also shows an impassioned scrupulousness in his reluctance to relive the anguish through the telling of the painful and regrettable story, and, like Aeneas, finds it hard to recount 'without remorse/The ruin of so many...'. Adam and Eve are told the story as an urgently needed illustration of free will and as a warning against disobedience, and hear it 'attentive', and 'fill'd with admiration and deep muse'. They are amazed by hearing what was unimaginable, 'hate in Heav'n', and Adam responds with insistent and relevant questions about the origin of heaven and earth, which Raphael answers 'within bounds'. Like Faust, Adam needs to know the story of creation, but unlike Faust, he is satisfied with the edited narrative, not yet having eaten the forbidden fruit.

The good story not only plays a large part in Milton's analysis of narrative but demonstrates the response to story. Intellectual curiosity is roused but the moral warning is not taken. The narrative part of Raphael's history done, Eve leaves Adam and the divine Historian to 'studious thoughts abstruse', intending later on to ask her husband, her preferred 'Relater', for his version, which will be relieved by 'grateful digressions' and 'conjugal Caresses'. The angelic narration, while using stories for instruction, makes no concessions to the listeners.

Adam and Eve are also story-tellers, Adam being invited by Raphael to give his version of his own creation, which Raphael missed by being on duty outside Hell. Adam tells his extraordinary and beautiful memory of the awakening in Paradise:

> As new wak't from soundest sleep
> Soft on the flourie herb I found me laid
> In Balmie Sweat, which with his Beames the Sun
> Soon dri'd, and on the reaking moisture fed.
> Strait toward Heav'n my wondring Eyes I turnd,
> And gaz'd a while the ample Skie, till rais'd
> By quick instinctive motion up I sprung,
> As thitherward endevoring, and upright
> Stood on my feet; about me round I saw
> Hill, Dale, and shadie Woods, and sunnie Plaines,
> And liquid Lapse of murmuring Streams; by these,
> Creatures that livd, and mov'd, and walkd, or flew,
> Birds on the branches warbling; all things smil'd,
> With fragrance and with joy my heart oreflowd.
> My self I then perus'd, and Limb by Limb
> Surveyd, and somtimes went, and somtimes ran
> With supple joints, as lively vigour led:
> But who I was, or where, or from what cause,
> Knew not;   (viii. 253–71)

The details of his wonder, motion and delight at once establish man's energy, vigorous in a vigorous world, happy in a happy one. He does not simply enjoy creation passively but takes an imaginative initiative in desiring and asking for a companion. He pleases God by showing his 'image, not imparted to the brute', perhaps the more ingratiatingly because he asks for someone to talk to. That social converse, which he misses almost as soon as he becomes conscious, largely takes the familiar domestic form of story-telling. Before and after the Fall, Adam and Eve's talk is more narrative than discursive, even though its trend and purpose are philosophical.

After the noble story of Creation comes the slanderous story of destruction. The story of Creation is one of the most imaginative narratives in Milton but it fails to influence Adam and Eve. Satan's story offers successful opposition which subverts where Raphael's history failed to strengthen. Satan might almost have read Eve's thoughts about liking digressions and caresses for he begins with a salute of inordinate flattery. Eve is no easy prey, rebuking his grossly obsequious explanation that the fruit of the Tree of Knowledge has made him appreciate her with the sharp rejoinder that the value of the tree must therefore be overrated. But Satan approaches subtly and his earlier flattery has more guile than is immediately apparent, to Eve or to us. He tells her he has eaten the fruit of a tree, but not of The Tree. Although Milton's misogyny devised Satan's flattery, the 'proem' that he 'tunes' being largely a commiseration with Eve for having only one man to appreciate her, and although this 'glozing' is said to make its way into Eve's heart, she seems less impressed by his repeated 'Empress' than by hearing an animal speak. But the long-term purpose of the imperial epithets shows itself when Eve gets to the tree and says that they might have spared the journey. The serpent has moved serpentinely, laying on flattery so thickly that Eve rejects his 'overpraising' but at the same time more subtly laying the foundation for his own plausible innocence and surprise when he asks, guilefully:

> 'Indeed? hath God then said that of the fruit
> Of all these garden trees ye shall not eat,
> Yet lords declar'd of all in Earth or Air?'   (ix. 656–8)

The story is acted in the telling. When Eve answers this question, he is silent, 'new part puts on', and 'Fluctuats disturbd, yet comely'. Milton invokes the analogy of the Greek or Roman orator whose mute gesture and act won his audience before he said a word. After the powerful muteness, there follows the impassioned invocation, 'O Sacred, Wise, and Wisdom-giving Plant', and the address to Eve, 'Queen of this Universe'. The arguments are various. The tree gives knowledge, not death, as proved by the newly-gifted serpent. What beast has, man should surely have. God will be pleased with courage and if He is not will not punish for so small a fault. If He did, He would not be just, and therefore would not be God and should not be feared or obeyed. The ethical and political reasoning moves fast, the appeals to reason, courage, justice, knowledge and power unite. Then the argument degenerates into an appeal to sentiment. Perhaps the whole idea of the forbidden fruit was to keep them low and ignorant. To eat is to be 'as Gods', and once more there is the plausible appeal of the tempter's accomplishments. The speciousness which Eve cannot possibly see lies in the argument *ad hominem*, since she cannot know that the serpent is not a real serpent promoted to human power. Eve's response, sharpened by noontime hunger, shows what has impressed her in his acquisitions of elocution and reason, and in his survival:

> hee hath eat'n, and lives,
> And knows, and speaks, and reasons, and discernes,
> Irrational till then.   (ix. 764–6)

Satan's arguments are not only imaginatively grounded on a fair insight into Eve and her response but also appeal to her imagination. And his last argument is the denial of the story of Creation:

> And what are Gods that Man may not become
> As they, participating God-like food?
> The Gods are first, and that advantage use
> On our belief, that all from them proceeds;
> I question it, for this fair Earth I see,
> Warmd by the Sun, producing every kind,
> Them nothing: (ix. 716–22)

Neither Adam nor Eve make any response to this denial but it significantly completes the analysis of Satan's perverted imagination. Eve's longings for freedom after she eats the fruit make her play with the idea of not tempting Adam but preserving a secret equality and are only dismissed when she thinks of the possibility of dying and leaving him free to take another wife. This temptation certainly bears the mark of Satan's flattery, though her quick survey of advantages testifies to the effectiveness of the fruit. But there are aspects of Satan which are only visible to the reader, for Milton does not show the extent and depth of imaginative denial simply in the temptation of Eve. Satan's slander of Creation makes this plain and it is a tribute to the good story which Raphael tells to quench Adam's 'drouth' that Satan's subversion should be so shattering. If the story of Creation had been less impressive, Satan's denial would seem to be an ideological footnote, but its attack relies on our acquaintance with Raphael's praise:

> Thus God the Heav'n created, thus the Earth,
> Matter unformd and void: Darkness profound
> Coverd th' Abyss: but on the watrie calme
> His brooding wings the Spirit of God outspred,
> And vital vertue infus'd, and vital warmth
> Throughout the fluid Mass, but downward purg'd
> The black tartareous cold infernal dregs
> Adverse to life: then founded, then conglob'd
> Like things to like, the rest to several place
> Disparted, and between spun out the Air,
> And Earth self-ballanc't on her Center hung.
>
> (vii. 232–42)

Satan's story comes to be answered by Michael's final narrative, accompanied by those visions of the future which heavily depress Adam until they stretch to include the Covenant and the Redemption. Raphael remembers, Michael prophecies, and Satan's slander is placed between their paeans. Eve finds Satan, then God, in dreams. Keats took Adam's dream for his type of imagination, which dreams and wakes to find that the dream is truth, and in Milton's story of creative energies the denial of imagination needed to be profound and passionate.

The most Miltonic of novelists is Richardson, analyst of defeated temptation. In *Clarissa*, story is pitted against story, but the conflict is not only ideological as in *Paradise Lost* and *Paradise Regained*, it is also psychological, as in *Comus*. Clarissa is subjected to persuasions, deceptions and lies. The novel's force depends on the unequal conflict of a malevolence and virtue which are both highly articulate, as also on the exchange of stories by the four main characters. Clarissa and

Lovelace correspond and argue and she has eventually to put on his duplicity, surviving through those examples of the virtuous lie which have appealed to the imagination of such different novelists as Mrs Gaskell and Henry James. The initial contrast is created by Lovelace's dishonest narrative as it is set against the sincere stories of Clarissa. This is the contrast between deception and candour. If the story of Creation was the utmost that angelic narrative could do in the way of adoration, justification and teaching, Clarissa's intelligent virtue surely does the utmost in arguing and explaining its own nature. As she relates, explains and analyses her narrative in the open and self-critical letters to Anna Howe, Lovelace writes his story to Belford, explaining past and future plots. The contrast is certainly not a simple one. If Clarissa is open, so in a sense is Lovelace, who tells Belford the whole story of his deception. Two most intimate narratives are woven together, the rational confidence and equal exchange between Clarissa and Anna, and the gradually disintegrating correspondence which begins as the complicity of rakes exchanging sexual boasts and becomes an argument between Lovelace's unstable bravado and Belford's reformed conscience. Lovelace's cock-pride finds a pornographic outlet in a fantasy combined with boast. His letters convey something of the outrageous complicity of Laclos's *Les Liaisons dangereuses*, where seduction enjoys a narrative dimension in confidence and conspiracy. The combination of sexual gloating, boast, advice, fantasy and confidences is especially repulsive when placed beside the ignorant stories of the innocent victims. In Laclos, innocence is pathetic, but in Richardson it is tough and well-armed. In Laclos, no one triumphs, but Richardson allows Clarissa's stronger mind to defeat Lovelace.

There is a moral and an intellectual clash between Clarissa's confidences to Anna and Lovelace's to Belford. Clarissa's shining chastity is lofty, monumental and earnest, but Anna's spirit and humour complements it to create a perfect balance of telling and listening. The uncertain boasts of Lovelace are balanced by the invisible revenges of Clarissa, who also tells all. Both Clarissa and Lovelace try to get at the other's plans and secrets, both work out their feelings and their actions by telling the story of the past and the present. Clarissa is not always right but she is impressively rational in her scrupulous attempts to respond to the probing and teasing of Anna, who takes her up on such words as 'a conditional kind of liking' and forces her to think out their implication. Their correspondence presents a candid human relationship, unreserved, trusting and mutually dependent. The friends' congeniality of mind and contrast of temper create that ideal which Lovelace denies, destroys and misses. Clarissa's independent candour is even more impressive than the mutual openness. After the rape, she becomes less dependent on the correspondence, more solitary, and more heaven-centred. One of Richardson's best insights makes Lovelace conventional, so that he is surprised and shocked by Clarissa's unabashed insistence on telling the whole story. Her clarity moves into the ascendant, while he deteriorates as he has been afraid she will after the drugs and the rape.

The epistolary medium of narrative becomes involved in the action. When Lovelace intercepts and forges letters in another type of false narrative, it is a serious attack on free and trusting communication, an appropriately literary rape. One of the worst consequences of the rape itself is the disturbance in the clarity of Clarissa's narrative. It becomes incoherent:

> O what dreadful, dreadful things have I to tell you! But yet I cannot tell you neither. But say, are you really ill, as a vile, vile creature informs me you are?
>
> But he never yet told me truth, and I hope has not in this: and yet, if it were not true, surely I should have heard from you before now! But what have I to do to upbraid? You may well be tired of me! And if you are, I can forgive you; for I am tired of myself: and all my own relations were tired of me long before you were.
>
> How good you have always been to me, mine own dear Anna Howe! But how I ramble!
>
> I sat down to say a great deal—my heart was full—I did not know what to say first—and thought, and grief, and confusion, and (O my poor head!) I cannot tell what—and thought, and grief, and confusion, came crowding so thick upon me; *one* would be first, *another* would be first, *all would* be first; so I can write nothing at all. (vol. iii. letter xxxiii)[5]

A little later coherence is regained but narration takes the form of dark allegories, like the story of the lady and the bear or tiger cub, pathetic in its content and in its uncharacteristically enigmatic form. Clarissa is forced to be clandestine but what she tells Anna has been the full story. Clarity is restored, however, and she defies the idea of shame, having

[5] All references are to the four-volume Everyman edition.

nothing to be ashamed of, so that the truthful story comes into its own, to accuse mealy-mouthed lechery.

Richardson's characters are sufficiently introverted to praise the epistolary medium that creates them, thereby naturalizing and publicizing it. Clarissa, Lovelace and Belford all insist on the value of recording and preserving events. After the rape Lovelace thinks ahead to melancholy future readings of Clarissa's distracted fragments and Belford longs to enjoy his literary executor's privilege of reading her correspondence, 'so *much more* lively and affecting...her mind tortured by the pangs of uncertainty (the events then hidden in the womb of fate), *than* the dry narrative, unanimate style of a person relating difficulties and dangers surmounted'. Clarissa herself appreciates the point of her author's immediacy, the 'writing of and in the midst of *present* distresses', aware, like Thackeray's Esmond penning his memoirs, of the value of imprinting and enlarging experience. Among the advantages of writing Clarissa includes mental relief and passing the time, having 'no other employment or diversion'. She also sees the need to write, even without anyone to read, in the double purpose of opening and expanding 'the ductile mind', and fixing good intentions:

> ...every one will find that many a good thought evaporates in thinking; many a good resolution goes off, driven out of memory perhaps by some other not so good. But when I set down what I *will* do, or what I *have* done, on this or that occasion, the resolution or action is before me either to be adhered to, withdrawn, or amended; and I have entered into *compact* with myself, as I may say; having given it under my own hand to *improve*, rather than to go *backward*, as I live longer.
>
> I would willingly therefore write to *you* if I *might*; the rather as it would be more inspiriting to have some end in view in what I write, some friend to please, besides merely seeking to gratify my passion for scribbling. (vol. iii, letter xxxvi)

Lovelace also needs his 'scribbling vein' to keep him from distraction after Clarissa's escape and like her writes that he 'must write'. For him, to write is to escape from lies into boasts. The boast can be an interesting revelation of imagination, involving some spirit and power of ingrown appreciation, but Lovelace's boasts are ludicrous failures of mind. They show his instability, for he knows and admits that the resolution he works up in writing—another instance of the effect of literary narrative —may not be maintained when he is face to face with Clarissa. His stories to Belford work up intention, 'O my charmer, look to it!...*Art thou not in my* POWER?' and are unintelligently self-flattering, 'Nor, if thou lovest me, think that the female affectation of denying thy love will avail thee *now*, with a heart so proud and so jealous as mine', which is almost anticipating Mr Collins. His narrative is often incoherent as he swings from one intention to another, 'But how I ramble! This it is to be in such a situation, that I know not what to resolve upon'. His pride is even pleased by the rambling of his narrative: 'Regardless, nevertheless, I shall be in all I write, of connection, accuracy, or of anything but of my own imperial will and pleasure'.

This contrast between the good and bad narrative is the opposition of a fair and strenuous reasoning to a coarse and slack irrationality. Clarissa painstakingly works out her survival and the meanings of her experience, Lovelace wavers from blind confidence to blind floundering. Her analysis makes room for the acknowledgement of error and doubt. Even as he deteriorates he shows flashes of spirit and inventiveness, but they are spasmodic compared with hers. They both show fertility of imagination: Clarissa expands mind and feeling by repetition and reflection, Lovelace works up intentions in isolation from the tests and trials that exist in the world of flesh, not in his world of paper. Richardson's own paper world convinces us of the value and short-comings of writing down our stories, making sense of past and future while attending most urgently to the present. Clarissa has to learn to remember as scrupulously as Marcel but Lovelace cannot afford to remember much.[6] The lies of Sinon, Iago and Satan maintain a certain solemnity and seriousness but Lovelace's grossly displaced sense of comedy creates and reflects his limitations. He is like a man carrying a distorting mirror whose image he has come to accept. The structures of Lovelace's story use but pervert the imagination's inventiveness and growth, and the friction between his lies and boasts and Clarissa's truths and scruples creates the total imaginative structure which analyses and judges narrative imagination.

Although scandal and rumour play their part in Chaucer, Shakespeare and Fielding, they do not seem to become generally important for a

---

[6] He prefers his sentimental story of the woman who wronged him and so begins his misogynous rake's progress. His is not an imaginative memory but a mere self-excusing fable, outlined for convenience.

whole genre of narrative until the nineteenth- and twentieth-century novel. In *After Many a Summer*, Aldous Huxley's Mr Propter complains about the mindless descriptiveness of literature and longs for its interminable anecdotes to create a theory of anecdote. Like Sinon's lie or Lovelace's boast, the gossip which plays so full a part in the Victorian novel is more than an imitation of narrative form and genuinely implies a theory of gossip. It is no merely literary theory but an account of the limitations, powers and shapes of this most common form of narrative. The novelist's curiosity and speculation resemble, sometimes emerge from, the curiosity and speculation of the gossip. Henry James's case is significant in its refusal to go on gossiping. Once an anecdote addressed his imagination, he needed to be alone in his private darkness to develop the idea. Gossip can go too far to inspire imagination. It is not only an inspiration but, like the lie and the temptation, it is a narrative theme very useful to plot and action. Gossip is crucial in so many stories of a close but segmented society, making destinies, relationships and reputations by its knowingness and its ignorance. It is useful in the expansive novels of Thackeray, George Eliot and Trollope by helping to shift and show different psychological points of view and a many-faced morality. Implicit in the imaginative presentation of gossip is some sense of its motives and effects, its trivialities, shallowness and spite. George Eliot uses the web and connective tissue of gossip, frail but strong enough to stop and snare people. In a small society of a village or provincial town, life is lived very privately and very publicly. In *Adam Bede*, rituals of funeral liturgy, harvest festival and the young squire's coming of age join gentry and tenants. Within the rigid class structure are associations of some warmth and affection, like the friendship of Adam and Arthur, or the Reverend Irwine's affection for his parishioners. But even when they seem to get close to each other's lives across the divisions of class and occupation which sympathy seems to pass, there are impassable barriers. The rector loves his parish but gets his facts wrong, taking the most superficial hearsay rather than genuine information. The lady of the manor scarcely knows her tenants. What looks like an 'organic' connection, is ignorance. Gossip displaces knowledge.

In St Ogg's and its environs, private life cannot be kept private, as in the city. Aunt Pullet and Bob Jakin let fall their idle remarks about Philip Wakem's frequent appearances in the Red Deeps and Maggie's secret is out. In *The Mill on the Floss*, as in *Adam Bede*, gossip is powerful and dangerous, even when apparently trivial. Tulliver asks Riley's advice about a school for his son and without either malice or thought Riley finds it pleasanter to say something than nothing, to give bad advice rather than say that he doesn't know, and Tom's education is blundered into. The whole novel makes subtle use of the visibility of the private life. When you plan the education of your son, lose your lawsuit, make a will, fail in business, or stay too long on the river with a man you decide not to marry, you are visible and vulnerable. George Eliot recognizes the so-called harmlessness of much idle gossip, and Aunt Pullet's damaging, casual talk is typical of her vague rambling flow of conversation, her superficial, well-meaning sympathies which shed tears for every piece of bad news of illness and death. There is something understandable in Aunt Glegg's fiercely familial refusal to weep for those she doesn't know and her consistency is shown at the end of the novel, when she stands grimly and condescendingly by Maggie and refuses to accept the rumours of St Ogg's. George Eliot shows at every turn of her action the difference between the complex, disturbing, inner facts of Maggie's life and the simplicities and externalities of the town's talk. She sometimes dramatizes the voice of collective opinion. *Middlemarch* ends with the contrast between what the novelist knows and the reader has come to expect, with the sheer erroneousness of Middlemarch views and verdicts. Gossip can be well-intentioned in the novels of George Eliot but on the whole it prefers not to think the best of anyone. Middlemarch makes Lydgate's marriage, determines his allegiances in local politics, weaves its stories about Rosamond and Ladislaw, jolts Dorothea into protest and action, rejects and discovers Bulstrode, acts at times like a blundering god and at others like a shallow reporter. Its voice is heard in the Finale:

In Middlemarch admiration was...reserved: most persons there were inclined to believe that the merit of Fred's authorship was due to his wife, since they had never expected Fred Vincy to write on turnips and mangelwurzel.

But when Mary wrote a little book for her boys, called 'Stories of Great Men, taken from Plutarch,' and had it printed and published by Gripp & Co., Middlemarch, every one in the town was willing to give the credit of this work to Fred, observing that he had been to the University, 'where the ancients were studied,' and might have been a clergyman if he had chosen.

In this way it was made clear that Middlemarch had never been deceived, and that there was no need to praise anybody for writing a book, since it was always done by somebody else.

Collective opinion is created by the whispers and surmises of gossip which grow and speculate, asking questions and providing answers with energy and abandon. Gossip is an occupation, has its kindly side and its accidental good results, but it is inspired at best by idleness, at worst by social or sexual jealousy. Unlike the question-and-answer of thorough imagination, gossip propagates itself through the superficial view, wags its heads and tongues with more malice than benevolence. D. H. Lawrence's portrait of nineteenth-century communities in the early and middle sections of *The Rainbow*, lacks dense social detail, his village society is outlined in skeletal and imagistic fashion. It is as if his only historical novel left out what he could not imagine, the way people talked about each other at another time. As soon as he comes into his own time in *Women in Love, The Lost Girl* and *Lady Chatterley's Lover*, he is most concerned to define and dramatize in some detail the shallowness and jealousy of gossip. He uses its irresponsible sketchiness, its pious terms and tones, and its erratic stabs at analysis in his definition of the novelist's imagination. For the most part he sees gossip not as a type of parody of imagination but as unimaginative. However, he creates in Mrs Bolton a gossip of power and magnitude, who enthralls Clifford Chatterley and even holds Connie. Lawrence knows perfectly well that it is hard not to be interested in gossip but he also knows what is wrong with too avid a listening:

> Connie was fascinated, listening to her. But afterwards always a little ashamed. She ought not to listen with this queer rabid curiosity. After all, one may hear the most private affairs of other people, but only in a spirit of respect for the struggling, battered thing which any human soul is, and in a spirit of fine, discriminative sympathy. For even satire is a form of sympathy. It is the way our sympathy flows and recoils that really determines our lives. And here lies the vast importance of the novel, properly handled. It can inform and lead into new places the flow of our sympathetic consciousness, and it can lead our sympathy away in recoil from things gone dead. Therefore, the novel, properly handled, can reveal the most secret places of life: for it is in the *passional* secret places of life, above all,

that the tide of sensitive awareness needs to ebb and flow, cleansing and freshening.

But the novel, like gossip, can also excite spurious sympathies and recoils, mechanical and deadening to the psyche. The novel can glorify the most corrupt feelings, so long as they are *conventionally* 'pure'. Then the novel, like gossip, becomes at last vicious, and, like gossip, all the more vicious because it is always ostensibly on the side of the angels. Mrs Bolton's gossip was always on the side of the angels. (*Lady Chatterley's Lover*, ch. ix)

Like George Eliot, Lawrence is particularly concerned with the contrast between the most private affairs of people, their struggles, sufferings and their spirit, and the crude, jealous, outside view. His lovers are most literally exposed, in body and language, more intimately than in any previous English novel. The title, *Lady Chatterley's Lover*, can be pronounced in two very different ways, the one jeeringly and pruriently dwelling on the *Lady* and the *Lover*, the other appreciating the meaning of every word and all their implications of class and love in the spirit of fine, discriminative sympathy. Lawrence created his chief gossip, Mrs Bolton, who leads her deprived life after her husband's death, and except for one genuinely open conversation with Connie, is regarded as a monster living on curiosity, easy virtuous judgements, and energetically salacious talk.[7] Her imaginative judgements may be crude but the energy is undeniable. She is paired well with Sir Clifford, a listener who is impotent, analytic and intensely curious. His affective life also finished, he too needs to live like a fish, to use his image[8] for her, by breathing in the air of other people's lives. A great deal of vituperation goes into this portrait, which scarcely shows a fine, discriminative sympathy for Clifford's very battered human spirit. The victim of gossip (as Lawrence himself was on several occasions) falls easily into shrill recrimination. It is not astonishing that Lawrence's novel about gossip, partly provoked by his dispiriting return to England in 1923 which recalled so many old hostilities, should be simplified and coarsened by his own failures of imagination.

He shows that gossip can disturb and corrupt even those people who know the story to be grossly distorted and aggressive. Connie is

[7] See above pp. 15–16.
[8] One of Lawrence's self-revealing insights is his perception of Clifford in his glass-house stoning Mrs Bolton.

shattered by gossip about sexual intimacies which she, like his wife, has enjoyed with Mellors. When Clifford writes about what he has heard from Mrs Bolton and refers to Mellors with a superficial sympathy as a dog with a can tied to his tail, Connie is put in the unpleasant situation of seeing someone she loves attacked from an external and malevolent viewpoint and having to be silent. As the intimate details of Mellors's marriage-bed are violently made public, she cannot immediately feel love and sympathy but responds with revulsion, fatigue, fear, anger and even a nostalgia for respectability.

Lady Chatterley's Lover lapses into the crudity of fable, unfortunately for Lawrence's decisive claims for the penetration of imaginative sympathy. He registers the crude response often provoked by the stimulus of gossip in Connie's correction of Mrs Bolton. Mrs Bolton judges someone's marriage too slickly, 'And he was such a *bad* fellow, and she was such a *nice* woman', but Connie's instant response is scarcely convincing. It is also glib and superior: 'Whereas, Connie could see even from Mrs Bolton's gossip, the woman had been merely a mealy-mouthed sort, and the man angrily honest'. Unlike George Eliot, who must also have suffered from gossip, but kept her head and her temper as she anatomized the blatant beast, Lawrence lets his own angry honesty get in the way of that fine discriminative sympathy. Not only does he humourlessly narrow the range of gossip to exclude its haphazard justices, mildness and harmlessness, but he is himself driven into the crude and harsh judgements of imaginative failure.

Aldous Huxley gets much closer to the psychology of creative gossip in the salacious conversation of two people whose sophisticated self-indulgence is remote from the pathetic pillow-talk of Chatterley and Mrs Bolton. In *Eyeless in Gaza* his rational hero, Anthony Beavis, slowly learns to put reason in its place, as part of love. He comes to discover and value the affective response to people, instead of the largely appetitive relation which is permitted and regulated by detached rationality. On one occasion in his youth, when his detachment has still room to grow, he hits on the idea of feeding his mistress's flagging interest with the story of his best friend's neurotic chastity. Huxley's dramatic analysis of the language, feelings and motives of this treacherous act of gossip shows a grasp of the temptations of narrative imagination. Anthony boasts, showing off his superiority, wit and sexual snobbishness, as he regales Mary Amberley with the amusing exposure of Brian Foxe's battered spirit.

Anthony arrives in Mary's drawing-room announcing that he has a story for her, and she hopes it is a coarse one. He feels the situation is extraordinary and heady, the mere fact of sexual talk still being new to him. One unpleasant detail is his sudden thought of diverting Mary at the very moment when Joan is confiding in him, 'at last releasing in speech a flood of distressing feelings too long debarred from expression'. He starts in imagination to betray the confidence before it is even finished, showing the first essential characteristic of gossip, its detached and predatory amusement and lack of sympathy, 'Tragic—but also grotesque, absurd. It occurred to him that Mary would find the story particularly ludicrous' (ch. xxvii). He tends to collect divertingly rude stories for her, including extracts from De Lancre's *Tableau de L'Inconstance des Mauvais Anges* and an anecdote about a urinating goat. Brian and Joan become characters in 'Another one for Mary'. Anthony is a writer, no run-of-the-mill teller of dirty stories, and he plans the telling of the story: 'he was ambitious about his story, wanted to make it a good one, at once amusing and psychologically profound; a smoking-room story that should also be a library story, a laboratory story'. He wants admiration as well as laughs. Like Sir Clifford Chatterley, he exhibits what Joyce calls the vivisecting spirit of modern fiction, telling the story patronizingly and wittily, by 'the right of the enlightened and scientific vivisector, to anatomize and examine'. He is amusing: '...poor old Brian! That maniacal pre-occupation of his with chastity! Chastity—the most unnatural of all the sexual perversions, he added parenthetically, out of Remy de Gourmont.' Mary's appreciation spurs him on, as she compares Brian's mother to St Monica, provoking him to add, 'St Monica by Ary Scheffer', inaccurately, 'But the end of his story-telling, which was to provoke Mary's laughter and admiration, was sufficient justification for any means whatever'. The jokes fly, ranging from the 'uterine reactions' of Mrs Foxe, Joan, and Brian, to the early Christians. Mary's superior contempt pulls him up momentarily to realize 'for the first time since he had begun this story, that Brian was his friend, that Joan had been genuinely unhappy', and he embarks on a revision, 'retro-spectively and in imagination'. 'Inside his head', he becomes eloquent on the subject of his devotion to Brian, realizing that his anecdote is an inexcusable betrayal, a piece of malice 'without apology or qualifying explanation'. He becomes rather less pleased with his own acuteness, feeling 'these betrayed confidences, the indispensable facts without

which the acuteness could not have been exercised'. He is confused,
tries to stammer out amends and sympathy, but the structure of superior
malice is self-perpetuating and turns his genuine feelings of perplexity
into justifications, 'Perplexed, he was justified in betraying Joan's
confidences; he had told the story (he now began to assure himself)
solely for the sake of asking Mary's advice—the advice of an experienced woman of the world'.

Mary is bored, and over the weeks that follow she encourages the
malicious betrayals of what becomes a serial story, exposing it and him,
to make a fool of him in front of another admirer, 'obstinately determined to be only "civilized" '. He recognizes that he is committed to
the story he has told in the style of a 'vivisecting comedian'. The story
not only takes on a life and death of its own, forcing upon him the
role of unenthusiastic but effective seducer, as Mary makes the amusing
bet that he won't console Joan for Brian's chastity, but the narrative
betrayal also becomes the sexual betrayal which drives Brian to
suicide. Huxley's betrayals often take a narrative form, like Helen's
public revelation of her husband's impotence, or Anthony's reluctance
to tell Brian the story of what really happened.

The structure of this narrative perversion is a collaboration, an
abuse of entertainment and wit, and yet an instance of the strength of
art. Anthony tells the story with detachment and the role of heartless
and amused narrator is wished on him outside the story-telling, though
the breach of confidence for amorous titillation is a major betrayal.
Anthony is aware of his own abuses and the autonomy and power of
his art of anecdote is brought out as he passively feels its powerful
existence outside himself. The novel ends with Anthony resisting a last
temptation to betray and before he arrives at that final certainty he
has the experience of many betrayals, unerringly located by Huxley as
failures in imagination. If one were to pick out the good story to
balance the treacherous anecdote, it might be the straightforward,
brief autobiography which Miller tells when they meet, filled with
essential details of occupation, marriage and his wife's death, followed
by Miller's asking for the story of Anthony's life in return and
questioning him with the utmost interest and goodwill about his
occupation, his marital status and the state of his health. Anthony
wonders 'whether it would be agreeable if everybody were to talk
to one in this sort of way. A bit tiring, perhaps, to have to treat
all the people you met as human beings, every one of them with a right

to know all about you' (ch. xlix). Miller's stories and requests for Anthony's *curriculum vitae* may seem sanctimoniously interrogative but they represent the extreme of decent matter-of-fact curiosity after the betrayals of story by story.

Huxley is a brilliant dissector of gossip, his own tendency to vivisection alerting him to the heartlessness and cleverness of clever gossip. Dylan Thomas's *Under Milk Wood* and Iris Murdoch's *An Accidental Man* follow him in a stylization of public talk. Iris Murdoch provides a mid-twentieth-century, urban version of the kind of collective voice that George Eliot caught so well in *The Mill on the Floss* and *Middlemarch*. Her touch is light and appropriately hard. She presents the outer shell of human relations which covers with its brittle case the feelings we see in the private discourse of private lives. Throughout the novel there is a choric refrain of party gossip, a game most of us play:

'Charlotte Ledgard is living with a weight-lifter.'
'I can't quite see Char reposing on a hairy bosom.'
'My dear, it's a female weight-lifter.'
'What a charming idea with the cushions.'
'Isn't it a charming idea.'
'Patrick is going to read history at Balliol.'
'George and Geoffrey are discussing the crisis.'
'Isn't Austin gorgeous.'
'He nestles in the bosom of the Tisbourne family.'
'He always was a friendly little viper.'
'Gracie adores him.'
'Mavis is furious.'
'Oliver and Andrew have borrowed Richard's yacht.'
'Richard is charging them the earth.'
'Isn't Ann looking happy.'
'How long for though.'
'Andrew is spending his sabbatical term studying Oliver.'
'Matthew is making another million in New York.'
'Mollie Arbuthnot has paella for breakfast every day.'
'Ralph is going to read history at Balliol.'
'There's Dr Seldon.'
'He looks as if he's got something.'
'Doctors are so infectious.'

'People ought not to invite doctors.'
'I hear that chap's in prison.'
'What chap?'
'That American chap.'
'What was his name? Lucas Leferrier or something.'
'Where is he in prison?'
'In America.'
'Oh, in America.'
'Wasn't he the chap that used to dangle after Gracie?'
'Sssh. Hello, Gracie, what a lovely party.'

(An Accidental Man, pp. 374–5)

This chorus shows divertingly and devastatingly the schematic nature of gossip. Her own selection scarcely simplifies the simplicities of party talk and might almost have been made by a tape-recorder. Almost, but not quite. Individual idiosyncracies are reduced to a common style. The talk sounds desultory but has a regular rhythm. The nice things are always said to the face and the things said behind the back are never nice. Sometimes they start to be, or try to be, but are soon deflected by the impulse to belittle or undermine. Scurrilousness is sometimes disguised as tolerance but only to ensure that gossip is safely licensed. It is patronizing, entertaining and agile, illustrating Huxley's point about the demoralizing effects of play and wit. Its impulses are sometimes the motiveless malignities of party talk, stimulated by drink, and company. Sometimes they are motivated by jealousy—of money, success, being grand and getting away with it. The device of quick shift from face-talk to behind-back-talk illustrates the falsities with amusing economy. The flow of talk is rapid but cautious and has to pull up as the groups change and victims turn into listeners, with the warning signal 'Ssh' which transforms spite into sweetness. The schematic form in the novel seems excellently approximated to the schematic narrations of life.

The communal act of imagination is analysed. Gossip invents and elaborates its inventions, passion deepens, inspiration rises, the wheels take fire from their own motion. One of the best instances of communally inspired narrative occurs in Constance Holme's novel, *The Trumpet in the Dust*, where village gossip is seen at its finest and most fluent in two decent and hard-working women. They have a standard dialogue about a destructive woman, almost a witch, who has undermined her son's life, and whose own special line in narrative abuse effects a subtle but potent discouragement and depression of the spirit. Mrs Clapham and Mrs Tanner combine in their narrative performance:

> The Saga of Poor Stephen who had fallen in the War began all over again, with precisely the same zest as if sung for the first time. It was a sort of duet into which they fell quite naturally whenever they happened to meet, and however often it was repeated it never palled. Conversation is almost the only form of artistic expression open to most of the poor, and on this subject at least these two had reached a high level. The Saga of Poor Stephen was, indeed, their star performance. Knowing it like their prayers, they played up to each other with mechanical ease, yet found always some shade of inflection which might possibly be bettered, some sentence intro- duced or eliminated which shed new light upon the whole. And always, as soon as they had parted, their minds set to work again upon the scene they had just played, half consciously rehearsing it for its next public appearance, and seeking some fresh touch which should cause it to live anew. (pt. ii, ch. i)

The narrative stresses pity rather than blame. Constance Holme is aware that virtuous people enjoy denigration. This example supple- ments the analyses of Lawrence and Huxley with its awareness that creative denigration is not necessarily a game played fast and super- ficially in smart parties or in pornographic conversation but is an aspect of the rituals of conversation between intimates. She actually calls her conversation a form of art and like Iris Murdoch and Huxley, she is interested in the structures of gossip, in its arias, duets and choruses, its rehearsals, repetitions and renewals, its power to work itself up, to improve, with a creativity of form and feeling and an accompanying delight, which makes very plain its kinship with art. This form of familiar gossip relies on continuity, it has been played before and will be played again.

When Christopher Isherwood was planning *Lions and Shadows* he thought of making its form loose and rambling, 'like gossip', but when we look closely at the forms of gossip they seem to have strict principles and patterns. There is certainly an element of open-endedness, allowing for improvisation, but as in other forms which allow for an impromptu element, like jazz, or *commedia dell'Arte*, there is a basic impulse which shapes collective enterprise. Gossip is moved by a basic desire, un-governed or ungovernable, to see life as interestingly but as securely as possible. Gossip and slander are apparently at different extremes of a moral spectrum but both are equally undeterred by the checks of reason and respect. Gossip, like slander, can be lazy or energetic but is also anarchic in spirit, flattering in judgement, fertile in fancy, making objects out of its human materials. Imagination moves in the opposite direction, to animate and plumb what looks rigid and fixed. Ultimately, slander and gossip are self-defeating because to look closely and profoundly at the world outside ourselves is the only creative work worth doing, reaching beyond self to discover other selves, not moving in circles to return to self. Satan is a fallen angel, seditiously revealing the perversions of what was imagination. He begins by recognizing the beauty of human love in Paradise and envy-ing it. In order to destroy it, he has to stop thinking about it and deny it. Marlowe's Mephistopheles plays fair and tells Faustus the limitations of hell's knowledge and the precise nature of its losses but has to leave behind such profundities for the frivolous games of damnation which will pass the time for Faustus. The more familiar forms of perverted imagination don't go so far, but circle curiously over the surfaces, like dragonflies over scum.

In Edna Lyell's *The Autobiography of a Slander*, one of the few Victorian anticipations of the stylized gossip-games of Aldous Huxley and Iris Murdoch, a distinction is drawn between cruel scandal and the kind of gossip which is curiously interested in other people but is 'in the main kindly'. It is almost impossible to find instances in novels of this communal kindliness. The game of whispers seems impelled towards malignancy by its very imperfect communication. Gossip is a form of joint egging-on, whose moments of kindliness gloss over, license, or prop up unworthier speculations. Where the novel presents benign table-talk, it tends not to be concerned with people's private lives. Or it may touch on them so superficially as to say nothing and encourage nothing, as in one of the anecdotes of Mrs Gaskell's Mrs Forrester in *Cranford*, who tells a good but brief story of the marriage of Mr ffoulkes, who married Mrs ffarringdon, 'all for the sake of her two little ffs'. But this is a static anecdote with no pretensions and not an evolving narrative. Slander and spiteful gossip are bad children of imagi-nation and grow, reproduce and multiply themselves, like more benign forms of narrative. Therein lies their ambitiousness, and their danger.

5
Good Stories, Good Listeners

There can be no literary equivalent to truth. If, in writing,
truth is the quality of what is said, told, this is not a literary
achievement: it is a simple human achievement.
(Laura (Riding) Jackson, *The Telling*[1])

Cranford is maligned in *Lady Chatterley's Lover*, where Lawrence
describes Mrs Bolton's gossip as 'Mrs Gaskell and George Eliot and
Miss Mitford all rolled into one'. When Rumour sets to work in
Cranford, creating the panic about burglars or Mr Peter's possible
marriage, it is to illustrate credulity but not malevolence. Miss Matty
is not the only model of an innocence, unselfishness and sense of
justice which does not feel impelled to speculate wildly about other
people's lives. The inhabitants of Cranford have the common experiences of love, loss and loneliness but the novel is about stoical
pride and reticence, and its stories get told sparingly, piecemeal,
obliquely. What does get told may seem petty but the telling of the
unimportant details of life is important to us all and little anecdotes
play a part in the harmony and communion of Cranford that is far
from trivial.

Mary Smith, the good-tempered narrator, explains the trivialities of
conversation in Cranford: 'As we did not read much, and as all the ladies
were pretty well suited with servants, there was a dearth of subjects for
conversation'. Little anecdotes tend to get much talked over, like the
story of Captain Brown's 'taking a poor old woman's dinner out of her
hands one very slippery Sunday'. The Cranford ladies are almost
critical of this breach of good manners, but even their criticism is
benevolent and 'in a kindly pity for him' they decide that the act
showed great goodness of heart and resolve 'that he should be com-
forted on his next appearance amongst us'. Cards and light suppers are
more prominent than conversation in the Amazonian parties of
Cranford but there is some talk. Mrs Forrester tells one of her stories

[1] Athlone Press, 1972.

on the occasion of Mrs Jamieson's evening party for her sister-in-law, Lady Glenmire, a policy of social exclusiveness having proved too tedious. Cranford society, though forgiving, has been wounded, and the politely overdressed ladies are curious but wary. Doubts about subjects for appropriate conversation end in the happy discovery that Lady Glenmire is not interested in court gossip but is one of themselves, and the harmony is aided and confirmed by one of the small stories that go a long way in Cranford, Mrs Forrester's story of the lace collar, the cat and the emetic. The story is a set-piece, known to her intimates, but new to her hostess and the guest of honour, and the occasion for telling arises smoothly and naturally when Lady Glenmire admires Mrs Forrester's old lace collar. The story is therefore politely addressed to 'Your Ladyship', because she has started the recollection, and has a few special turns of address, like the touch of domestic complicity in 'your ladyship knows that such lace must never be starched or ironed', the transformation of her little charity-girl into 'my maid' and the pleasant archness of 'your ladyship must excuse me' when she reaches the climax with the emetic and the top-boot. The story is rounded off with a friendly flourish: 'But now your ladyship would never guess that it had been in pussy's inside.'

It is the very smallest of small-talk, absorbing to ladies, and such domesticated ladies, dealing with the trivialities of dress, housekeeping, and pets. It is a tale of amusingly inventive solutions, its neat style matching its subject of practical housewifery and its familiarity and formality courteous and companionable. Condescension would be out of place. Mrs Gaskell's story of the story shows how anecdote enlivens and lubricates, how a tactful and personal pleasantness of address need involve no exhibitionism or egoism but a modest sense of occasion. There has been offence and the thoroughly inoffensive story is healing. There has been snobbishness, and the good guest's story demonstrates the kinship of the women after everyone has been put at their ease by Lady Glenmire:

> After tea we thawed down into common-life subjects. We were thankful to Lady Glenmire for having proposed some more bread and butter, and this mutual want made us better acquainted with her than we should ever have been with talking about the Court, though Miss Pole did say she had hoped to know how the dear Queen was from some one who had seen her. (ch. viii)

Even the tall story is entirely benevolent in Cranford. The book ends with another rift in the old sociability and there is something like uneasy gossip in Miss Pole's conjecture that there may be something 'in the matrimonial line' between Mr Peter and Mrs Jamieson, since Mrs Jamieson has asked for a footstool to be put to the warmest seat at the George on the occasion of Mr Peter's address. The usual pattern is lightly sketched, including the old maid's jealousy, the magnifying of slight evidence and the spoiling of feeling, especially for Mary, who was 'angry and irritated and exaggerated every little incident which could add to...irritation'. Conjecture is banished and peace restored when Mary hears what Mr Peter is talking about so animatedly to Mrs Jamieson. He is 'up to his old tricks' and giving the lady the strong narrative stimulant which she required 'to excite her to come out of her apathy':

> Mr Peter wound up his account by saying that, of course, at that altitude there were none of the animals to be found that existed in the lower regions; the game—everything was different. Firing one day at some flying creature, he was very much dismayed when it fell, to find that he had shot a cherubim! (ch. xvi)

Mr Peter turns out to have learnt the appropriate use for his tall stories, which originally exiled him from Cranford, and is pulling Mrs Jamieson's leg in order to bribe her, stop her rancour and allow 'everybody to be friends'. Though presented very mutedly, Mr Peter should be put with Odysseus, Jingle, and Huckleberry Finn as a teller of tall tales. He too comes to discover a proper time, place, and use for lying.

Mrs Gaskell is interested in the lies we tell for love and even more interested in the place of narrative in social communion. Lawrence joins her name with George Eliot's in his list of gossips but George Eliot is also one of the very few novelists to show benign public conversation. In *Silas Marner* she is anatomizing exile and community. The social ritual of story-telling is prominent in the Rainbow Inn, where a purely masculine assembly tells and listens to familiar stories and histories. The story-telling here, as in *Cranford*, passes the time and makes human connections. George Eliot presents the conversation in a relaxed and expansive way. She takes her time, partly to dramatize with extreme precision the rhythm of the slow-burning evening talk and partly to distract the reader's attention from Silas Marner, whose hand is lifting the latch of the kitchen bar at the end of Chapter Five, but who suspends his entry, like Uncle Toby and Walter Shandy coming downstairs, until the beginning of Chapter Seven. The initial desultory conversation rises gradually into Mr Macey's reminiscences of the Lammeter family with the two anecdotal set-pieces, the story of the marriage ceremony where the questions were mixed up and the bride was asked, 'Wilt thou have this man to be thy lawful wedded wife?' and the groom, 'Wilt thou have this woman to thy lawful wedded husband?', and the comic ghost story of Cliff's holiday. Entertainment at the Rainbow is largely narrative and Mr Macey, chief performer and parish clerk, receives the congratulatory prompting which brings him 'up to the point of narration'. He needs to be given cues by a grateful landlord, and his story-telling and the listening is a ritual, having occurred before and falling into expected rhythms. Mr Macey always gives 'his narrative in instalments, expecting to be questioned according to precedent'.

Mrs Gaskell's Mrs Forrester and George Eliot's Mr Macey are good story-tellers and good company. They have a marked individual style and are conscious of performance, Macey in his grand, assertive and professional way, Mrs Forrester with modesty, attentiveness, humour and finish. Such style and stylishness are especially marked when we compare these individual narratives with the styleless, seamless garment of gossip in St Ogg's and Middlemarch, woven by many tongues at the expense of imagination and sympathy for the individual case. Mrs Forrester and Mr Macey are both narrators who make important contributions in the company of their neighbours by benignly and imaginatively recording the annals of the parish, whether these are trivial, tragic, harrowing or amusing. They elicit an animated interest and sympathy and rely on an existing community of interest. Mrs Forrester expects her listeners to know about lace, to stoop to humble and intimate physiological detail, to be interested in the history of an object and an animal, and to smile at triumphant strategy and happy ending. Mr Macey expects his listeners to ask, to praise and to be amazed, not in spite of familiarity but because of it, 'according to precedent'. He makes allowances for 'the impotence of his hearers' imagination' which he pities and hopes to educate: 'Every one of Mr Macey's audience had heard this story many times, but it was listened to as if it had been a favourite tune, and at certain points the puffing of the pipes was momentarily suspended, that the listeners might give their whole minds to the expected words'. Ritual and repetition is emphasized, as in Constance Holme's *The Trumpet in the Dust*. Mrs Forrester's narrative style is clear and unfussed, her faintly apologetic tone the product of rhetorical confidence, not embarrassment. Mr Macey is proud of his skill, his knowledge and his strong responses to experience. He is not only the parish story-teller but is telling his own story too: the story of his two occupations, of parish-clerk, which accounted for his feeling of responsibility and fear when the ritual questions of the marriage ceremony were crossed, and of tailor, which gave him a special interest in the story of Cliff's Holiday, since Cliff was a 'Lunnon tailor, some folks said, as had gone mad wi' cheating', who wanted his frightened son to take up riding, 'to ride the tailor out o' the lad'. His strong personal and appreciative response softens his pride in performance; his role as local historian is appropriate to his age and to his conservative longing for the past. He looks back nostalgically at things which are dying out, is proud of his family's musical prowess and insists on his role as historian, 'ther's no voices like what there used to be, and there's nobody remembers what we remember, if it isn't the old crows'. His story-telling has a value and a function and although he is dealing with more profound and passion-ate matters than Mrs Forrester's cats and collars his role should illumine hers, not overshadow it. Both story-tellers inherit their author's narrative artistry. Their stories are very much part of a ritual activity, working through response and chorus. Both narrators are fluent and vivid narrative artists who keep an eye on the subject, on the listeners, and on the occasion. They are sincerely involved and engrossed in their stories but self-consciously practised in that manipulation of effect which belongs to all oratory and is essential to the art of narrative improvisation. They are sympathetic and benign, like their listeners.

Silas Marner doesn't need to be a master of narrative like Mr Macey for his story brings news of urgent immediate experience. His story-telling is visibly less skilful than the accomplished comic narrative of the old parish clerk, which first holds Silas's entry in the background and then allows it to burst excitingly into the scene at the beginning of Chapter Seven. The scene in the Rainbow is not just cleverly con-trived entertainment and distraction but a self-analysing drama of the community from which Silas has been excluded. The drama consists of telling and listening to stories which are a part of the history of the parish. Mr Macey's anxiety about the mixed-up ceremony and his tart but sympathetic judgement of Cliff are testimonies to a benign and inviting public life. Silas needs its warmth and welcome as he comes in to tell his story, having told no one anything for twenty years.

The story is new, its teller shy and barely articulate, and both the teller and his story are mysterious. Silas's story-telling takes a first step towards that social restoration which is the subject of the novel, and the society into which he steps is that of the communal story, those annals of the parish to which he will belong. The Rainbow decides that Silas is not a ghost and takes him into the company, which has been impressively and solidly established through the story-telling, making him free of its ease and its humanity. A company of gossips or loose-talkers would not have provided the right fellowship, but here Silas can sit in the centre of the circle and in the rays of the fire. But he sits apart from them, because this telling marks a transition. The scene of his story-telling has been most thoroughly imagined.

The interest of the listeners is not sentimentalized. They are curious because of Silas's alarming entry and because he accuses Jem Rodney of the theft. He is instructed by the landlord to sit down, dry himself and prove that he is in his right mind by speaking out 'sensible' and 'straight forrard'. This narration is badly needed to ease the tension of the speaker and the listeners. Silas's story is interrupted by feverish questions, not rituals of rhetoric, and the telling and the listening mark an initiation for the isolated weaver whose old community cast him out long ago:

> Silas now told his story, under frequent questioning as the mysterious character of the robbery became evident.
>
> This strangely novel situation of opening his trouble to his Raveloe neighbours, of sitting in the warmth of a hearth not his own, and feeling the presence of faces and voices which were his nearest promise of help, had doubtless its influence on Marner, in spite of his passionate preoccupation with his loss. Our consciousness rarely registers the beginning of a growth within us any more than without us: there have been many circulations of the sap before we detect the smallest sign of the bud.
>
> The slight suspicion with which his hearers at first listened to him, gradually melted away before the convincing simplicity of his distress: it was impossible for the neighbours to doubt that Marner was telling the truth...(*Silas Marner*, ch. vii)

The act of telling is an admission of need. The act of listening meets that need.

The story of the robbery brings Silas closer to his neighbours but there is no instantaneous transformation. George Eliot later observes wryly that the presents of Silas's neighbours were more comforting than their words which tended, as words often do, to adulterate goodwill, 'in spite of ourselves, before it can pass our lips'. Dolly Winthrop gets closer than anyone else but at first what she says seems to Silas 'like a report of unknown objects, which his imagination could not fashion'. The crucial change comes when he adopts Eppie and is eventually able to tell Dolly the story of his life, though the narrative is 'a slow and difficult process'. The telling and listening of neighbourliness whose 'words of interest were always ready for him' marks his social restoration but the conversation of love is stronger than the rituals of neighbourliness.

Novelists like to remember and imagine the stories parents tell their children when telling and listening is easy. Silas Marner's talk to Eppie mostly takes place after she grows up. He does not tell her fairy-tales but the puzzling story of his 'past, and how and why he had lived a lonely man until she had been sent to him'. He needs to tell the story of the past because it remains a mystery for him and though telling it to Dolly has helped to adjust his sense of injustice and revive his sense of the 'good i' the world', he tells it again with a deeper affection to Eppie, as we do tell over and over again to the people we love. He also has to tell her the story of her own past, in so far as he knows it:

> For it would have been impossible for him to hide from Eppie that she was not his own child: even if the most delicate reticence on the point could have been expected from Raveloe gossips in her presence, her own questions about her mother could not have been parried, as she grew up, without that complete shrouding of the past which would have made a painful barrier between their minds.
>
> (ch. xvi)

Eppie asks for one story but never thinks of asking for another. She never thinks about her father:

> ...had she not a father very close to her, who loved her better than any real fathers in the village seemed to love their daughters? On

the contrary, who her mother was, and how she came to die in that forlornness, were questions that often pressed on Eppie's mind.

(ch. xvi)

So she asks 'again and again' for the story of how Silas had found her mother against the furze bush, led there by her own footsteps. The ritual and memorial of this story leads them to take the furze bush into the garden and plant against it snowdrops and crocuses which 'won't die out'.

Silas Marner is a novel about hiding and finding, secrets, discovery and mystery. The coming to light of Dunsey's skeleton completes Silas's unfinished story of the stolen gold. Godfrey takes the discovery as a sign that secrets will out and fills in the gaps in the other mystery by completing the story of Eppie. But the oldest secret in the novel is never revealed. The story of the injustice done to Silas in Lantern Yard remains 'dark', and the image lingers after the frustrated journey to the past when Silas admits that since he has Eppie, he has 'light enough to trusten by'. Silas's story is told finally by his neighbours, most appropriately in the yard of the Rainbow Inn where the wedding-guests assemble before Eppie's wedding and have leisure 'to talk over Silas Marner's strange history'. He has become part of the history of Raveloe and of all the stories that make up his story the most significant are those that create and confirm the companionship of neighbourliness, friendship and parental love. Silas's story is told with a properly regulated sentiment and given place and definition through social rituals of narrative and history. Just as Virgil's and Milton's lies, rumours or slanders are set against full and truthful narratives, so George Eliot's good story-telling is imagined in company with a parallel failure of communication. Godfrey makes his confession too late and Eppie prefers the confiding love of Silas.

In D. H. Lawrence's *Sons and Lovers* the story of the day gets told to the mother:

The children, alone with their mother, told her all about the day's happenings, everything. Nothing had really taken place in them until it was told to their mother. But as soon as the father came in, everything stopped. He was like the scotch in the smooth, happy machinery of the home. And he was always aware of this fall of silence on his entry, the shutting off of life, the unwelcome. (ch. iv)

Lawrence is alive to the significance of the telling, which makes things 'really take place', imprinting events and establishing value. Sometimes in other writers this repetition of event is private, as when Anne Elliot, in *Persuasion*, needs solitude after the agitated joy of her reunion with Wentworth, or when Turgenev's Irina, in *On the Eve*, seeks solitude to meditate on her unidentified feelings for Insarov, or when Gide's Edouard in *The Counterfeiters* has to write down the story of the day in the 'pocket mirror' of his journal, unable, like the Morel children, to 'feel that anything that happens . . . has any real existence' until it gets told. As Lawrence emphasizes, the confirmations of our private narratives in record and reverie are also made when we talk to our intimates and the fall of silence which greets Morel's homecoming is a hideous denial of a common need. Mrs Morel is observed with a truth that pierces more sharply than the novelist may have realized, as she drives wedges between father and children while appearing to build bridges:

> 'Now you'd better tell your father when he comes in,' said Mrs Morel. 'You know how he carries on and says he's never told anything.'
> 'All right,' said Paul. But he would almost rather have forfeited the prize than have to tell his father. (ch. iv)

The son's telling is restrained and unspontaneous and the father's responses are stiff, brief, becoming inarticulate. The forced dialogue is worse than silence. As Lawrence says, 'conversation was impossible between the father and any other member of the family'. His explanation follows: 'He was an outsider. He had denied the God in him'.

Morel's God is not beyond resurrection and Morel can enter into the life of 'his own people' when he is happily at work. His energies are shown as he makes and mends things and also in the telling of stories. Like Odysseus and Robinson Crusoe, he makes things and tales. The happy telling and listening is clearly self-analysed in the context of that stilted little report organized by Mrs Morel. Morel tells the story of his day to his children. It is what he knows and has feeling for, it is his life. He can tell because he is asked, with love:

> Meantime Arthur, still fond of his father, would lean on the arm of Morel's chair, and say:
> 'Tell us about down pit, daddy.'
> This Morel loved to do.

'Well, there's one little 'oss—we call 'im Taffy,' he would begin. 'An' he's a fawce un!'

Morel had a warm way of telling a story. He made one feel Taffy's cunning.

'He's a brown un,' he would answer, 'an' not very high. Well, he comes i' th' stall wi' a rattle, an' then yo' 'ear 'im sneeze.

' "Ello, Taff," you say, "what art sneezin' for? Bin ta'ein' some snuff?"'

'An' 'e sneezes again. Then he slives up an' shoves 'is 'ead on yer, that cadin'.

' "What's want, Taff?" yo' say.'

'And what does he?' Arthur always asked.

'He wants a bit o' bacca, my duckey.'

This story of Taffy would go on interminably, and everybody loved it.

Or sometimes it was a new tale.

'An' what dost think, my darlin'? When I went to put my coat on at snap-time, what should go runnin' up my arm but a mouse.'

(ch. iv)

The story is also a ritual, a serial telling solicited and encouraged with love. It is not a performance by one narrator but a communion, and a real conversation. Morel's story is told in vivid fragments, with those imaginative gifts which Lawrence might well appreciate, 'a warm way of telling' and the imaginative ability to show and feel the individuality of the animals. Affection is alive in Morel's attitude to his story and his listeners and with it we see that vitality which first made Gertrude Coppard feel stirred by his stories of the pit to imagine 'the life of the miners, hundreds of them toiling below earth and coming up at evening!' The story-telling in *Sons and Lovers* reveals the degeneration of a marriage. The story of the day is the story of the life. It breaks that deadly silence, it joins the father 'to his own people', and it spontaneously communicates his story, his imagination, and his love. Like Mrs Gaskell, Fontane and Dickens, Lawrence knows that stories are sometimes the only ways of telling people our secrets while preserving secrecy or privacy. In *Sons and Lovers* Morel's tales show precisely how Lawrence's tale is more trustworthy than the artist who said many years later that he wished he had given his father a better showing.

Virginia Woolf's *To the Lighthouse* resembles *Sons and Lovers* in using a painter, not a novelist, for its portrait of the artist. Even when novelists make such displacements, for disguise, variation and experiment, the narrative imagination emerges with great vitality somewhere in the novel. Characters in novels offer spirited examples of narrative imagination, even if they are not professional story-tellers, or not even artists at all. Arthur Seaton, the hero of Alan Sillitoe's *Saturday Night and Sunday Morning*, is a great teller of wild, teasing and funny stories, which show his energy and his love, particularly for the children he tells them to. Mrs Ramsay is not an artist, putting her creative energy into being a wife and mother, but Lily Briscoe, who finds the word, let alone the story, hard to utter, the urgency of the moment always 'missing its mark', has to learn to remember and understand experience in narrative terms. She only finishes her picture with the aid of Mrs Ramsay's kindly ghost, after she has moved from paint into story to recall and try to imagine the past and thereby to will not only the completion of her own painting but of the journey to the lighthouse, which Mrs Ramsay had once willed. The story ends with the last brush-stroke but also with the laying down of the novelist's pen. The novel's last full stop brings brush and pen together after vision and fatigue.

Just as Lily has to exercise her narrative imagination, so Mr and Mrs Ramsay need and use stories in their relations with each other, their children, and their friends. Mr Ramsay's mode of thinking tends to be rational and discursive but like Leslie Stephen, whose ghost he preserves as Lily's picture preserves Mrs Ramsay's, he is a great admirer of novelists and especially Scott. He reads *The Antiquary* while his wife reads Shakespeare's sonnet, 'From you I have been absent in the spring', and likes to think that they are reading on their own, away from all the others. But the reading of husband and wife is detached as well as intimate. After looking up from the page to his wife, Mr Ramsay returns to Scott and Balzac with the thought that 'the whole of life did not consist in going to bed with a woman'. Liking to underrate his wife's powers of mind he assumes that she probably does not understand what she is reading, but they are both good readers with strong individual responses like most of Virginia Woolf's reading people. Mrs Ramsay feels that the sonnet is like a magnet attracting to it all the odds and ends of the day, leaving her mind swept clean while it lay 'suddenly entire shaped in her hands, beautiful and reasonable, clear and complete, the essence sucked out of life and held rounded here—the sonnet'. The poem and the novel stir a large affective response in them both. She feels eased and rid of the day's debris, also wanting to be left alone for a while, but at last emerging from solitude and privacy to tell him that Paul and Minta are engaged and to make a random joke. She thinks that she wants him to say something, 'anything will do'. He responds to the tragic events of Steenie's drowning and Mucklebackit's grief with delight and vigour and she responds to Shakespeare dreamily, her mind 'going up and down, up and down with the poetry'. The story of those parts of the day they have not shared presses to be told and in her mind she runs through everything that has happened since she had last seen him alone, dressing for dinner, the moon, Andrew holding his plate, depression, birds, sofa, children awake, something she made up about Tansley waking them, and Paul's wash-leather watch case. She picks out the story of the engagement. The mutual narrative is brief and random, not directly concerned with the responses to their books but drawing vitally from it. He feels the surge of her habitual pessimism and she feels his rebuke through the asperity in his voice when he says, 'You won't finish that stocking to-night'. She accepts his meaning and is glad of it, then feels his desire for her to say that she loves him. She cannot say it but in a moment of great happiness accedes to the request indirectly, 'Yes, you were right. It's going to be wet to-morrow'. Virginia Woolf goes further than Lawrence in revealing the subliminal communion of feeling through silences, looks and inflections of the voice which attach themselves to arbitrary or random words and stories. 'You were right', speaks her acquiescence. The story of our feelings cannot always be altered and substitutes have to be found.

Everyday narrations are as symbolic as works of literature and the stories we tell may be randomly chosen or tangentially related to our personal life. They may attach and express an emotion, since a community of feeling can make do with anything, as Mrs Ramsay feels. The stories people tell in novels tend to be significant in form, feeling and content. Virginia Woolf said in her diary that 'the sea is to be heard all through' *To the Lighthouse*, and *The Antiquary*, the novel Mr Ramsay is reading in defiant admiration of Scott's 'strength and sanity, his feeling for straightforward simple things', is about endurance, work, grief, death by drowning, the family, the difficult loves of parents and children, a fisherman and his wife. One of the other prominent stories[2] in *To the Lighthouse* is also about a fisherman and his wife.

The Grimms' fairy-story links together many of the inner and outer happenings in the first section, 'The Window'. It is the key image of mother and child which casts its benign shadow in the last section ('The Lighthouse') to solve and complete Lily's composition, and help her to remember and imagine the Ramsays' story. In the first attempt at the painting, mother and child have been reduced to a purple triangular shape, despite Mr Carmichael's objection to the non-representational abstraction. The shape resembles the image of the wedge of darkness which Virginia Woolf uses to represent Mrs Ramsay's relaxed return to self after the strenuousness of loving. The novelist, like Lily, represents her state of mind through the image which takes on fresh resonance from the darkness between the beams of light from the lighthouse. Because she is a novelist and concerned with representation of more than mood and feeling, she takes great pains to show Mrs Ramsay with her son fully and naturalistically, through surface as well as symbol. The presentation of mother and child is not unlike the scene between husband and wife, being also a communion which works implicitly and indirectly. Mrs Ramsay's love for James is powerfully uttered in the story she reads to him. The reading also allows her, like the private reading of the Shakespeare sonnet, to come and go, give and reserve. It demands only part of her mind and her attention, behaving, as she tells us with considerable explicitness, like a bass which every now and then moves up into the melody.

The story of 'The Fisherman and his Wife' functions in several ways. Its relevance need not be laboured: its subjects are marriage, ambition, success, frustration, man, woman, class, life, death and the sea. Even its interweaving of prose and verse is right in a novel which contains so much quotation. Waves and storm move through the story as through the novel and the sense of the sea's threat is strong and plain in both. The bass moves up into the melody on one occasion to make explicit the relevance of theme:

'But the father of eight children has no choice...' Muttering half aloud, so he broke off, turned, sighed, raised his eyes, sought the

---

[2] Another important sea-story which recurs throughout the novel is Cowper's 'The Castaway'.

figure of his wife reading stories to the little boy; filled his pipe. He turned from the sight of human ignorance and human fate and the sea eating the ground we stand on, which, had he been able to contemplate it fixedly might have led to something; and found consolation in trifles so slight compared with the august theme just now before him that he was disposed to slur that comfort over...

The story his wife is reading to the little boy is also about human ignorance and human fate and the sea eating the ground we stand on. Virginia Woolf has chosen her tale with particular care to keep the sound of the sea going, but many of the stories we read or tell our children deal magically and delightedly with common themes. I doubt if George Eliot was quite so compositionally aware as Virginia Woolf of the relation of microcosm to macrocosm when she made Mary Garth choose the story of Rumplestiltskin to tell at the Vincys' Christmas party, in *Middlemarch*. If one wants to press the relevance, the parallels are there: money, marriage, promises, class, ambition, names, but any number of other fairy-stories would do almost as well. If we want to insist on the sound of the sea, as in *To the Lighthouse*, the choice will be more restricted, but ambition, class, marriage, fear and death are likely to crop up frequently in fairy-tales and folk-tales. The important thing about the reading of 'The Fisherman and his Wife' is surely its combination of solace and realism. Mr Ramsay finds consolation in the sight of his wife reading after he has stood on the spit of land which the sea is slowly breaking up. She reads the story to James in order to console him for his father's rational prediction that the trip to the lighthouse will have to be put off because the glass is falling. The dismaying hardness of Mr Ramsay's truth is softened by Mrs Ramsay's fairy-tale but its fantasy and make-believe do not erase a truth and offer a lie. She presents the same truth about the perils of mortal expectations in an enchanting story which distracts, consoles, but still faces reality. It offers the child the storm within its peace, as Mrs Ramsay later covers the pig's skull in the nursery with her shawl. What more can we do for our children without telling lies?

The story encloses the mother and her child in its magic circle. It is interrupted, as stories often are. After she makes her usual effort to answer her husband's demand for reassurance, to sink back exhausted, James feels that the 'twanging' of his father's feelings have disturbed the simplicity and good sense of his relations with his mother and urges her back to their story. Later on, his sister Cam dashes in and lingers briefly, attracted by the word 'flounder'. Mrs Ramsay tells her to stay or go and feels her own affinity with James. At one moment, ashamed by the knowledge that she needs admiration, she feels she must devote herself to the story but she does not concentrate on it wholly. The familiarity and ease of narration leave her room for other thoughts and feelings and for observations of the people outside the window where they are sitting.

Mrs Ramsay doesn't ever attend so much to the actual story as to the listening boy. At times the resonance of the story is only too plain to the reader, who doesn't even need to go back to Grimm, since the quotation is lavish:

> When she read just now to James, 'and there were numbers of soldiers with kettle-drums and trumpets,' and his eyes darkened, she thought, why should they grow up and lose all that? He was the most gifted, the most sensitive of her children. But all, she thought, were full of promise.

She has already thought of him becoming a judge but does not attend to the fate of the wife's ambitions told in the story. Neither mother nor child thinks of the story as symbolic or relevant, their relation to it being ironically and movingly innocent. When she reads the final description of the sea at its most outraged ('mountains trembled, rocks rolled into the sea, the sky was pitch black'), she decides to finish the last few lines of the story even though it is nearly bed-time. We are aware of the final darkness in the inset story and of the changing light in the garden of the novel. There is a fisherman out there too, with sea and rocks:

> Andrew had his net and basket. That meant he was going to catch crabs and things. That meant he would climb out on to a rock; he would be cut off. Or coming back single file on one of those little paths above the cliff one of them might slip. He would roll and then crash. It was growing quite dark.

The ground bass is undisturbed and she 'did not let her voice change in the least as she finished the story'. The one bit of the Grimms' tale (in Margaret Holt's translation) which seems to be changed by Virginia Woolf is the last sentence: 'And there they are still living to this day'. Mrs Ramsay's version reads 'And there they are living still at this very time', but she speaks those last words after she shuts the book, 'as if she had made them up herself, looking into James's eyes'. The mother allows the child to take in the impact of that marvellous ending, but as she looks into his eyes she sees 'the interest of the story' die away and 'something else take its place; something wondering, pale, like the reflection of a light, which at once made him gaze and marvel'. It is only for the space of the story that she can distract the child from his longing to go to the lighthouse, though its duration in the space of the novel is extended in feeling, action and analysis. It seems to occupy much time but also to be over too quickly.

Those outside the window cannot hear the story but they watch. Lily Briscoe reduces the mother and child to a triangular shape, Carmichael sees a classical form and ideal of maternity, William Bankes gazes in a rapture, which Lily, watching him watch, sees as love:

> It was love, she thought, pretending to move her canvas, distilled and filtered; love that never attempted to clutch its object; but, like the love which mathematicians bear their symbols, or poets their phrases, was meant to be spread over the world and become part of the human gain. So it was indeed. The world by all means should have shared it, could Mr Bankes have said why that woman pleased him so; why the sight of her reading a fairy tale to her boy had upon him precisely the same effect as the solution of a scientific problem, so that he rested in contemplation of it, and felt, as he felt when he had proved something absolute about the digestive system of plants, that barbarity was tamed, the reign of chaos subdued.

'Anything will do.' This may be admired as an insight into the stories we tell to our nearest and dearest and as an insight into the symbolism of art. Almost anything, though not quite anything, would do for the story Mrs Ramsay tells James to illustrate her protectiveness and love, her loose but assured hold on the text, and her delight in his delight, as his ruined tomorrow is briefly forgotten. Since Virginia Woolf is writing rhetorically, facing reader as well as characters, the story also functions as an appropriate symbol and resonant part of the novel. The story within the story which is told to James or to Mr Ramsay is carefully pinned to the larger narrative which is told to us. Like Proust, Virginia Woolf insists on the arbitrariness of the vehicle, in love or memory, and so makes use of the random or opaque event.

Proust uses the unreleased spring in the mysterious trees[3] and Virginia Woolf offers the list of things Mrs Ramsay could tell her husband. What is needed by the listener within the novel is any piece of news that is spoken by the willing voice and heard by the waiting ear. Virginia Woolf is also creating for the listener outside the novel continuity of feeling, as the chosen item of the engagement, which Mr Ramsay hears without surprise so that its impact is suitably muted, provokes her pessimism and his distaste for that pessimism. Any of the other details about the children would have done equally well to release her pessimism. What the 'anything' conveys is a moment of desired communication which cannot remain as a moment but goes on, impelled by the continuity of narrative, out of harmony into discord. The discord is silent because the narratives of intimates do not need to be complete, but it is no less disturbing for the silence. Harmony is restored in the final choice of another story, his prediction of rain and her hope for the journey. She joins memory with prediction, to tell indirectly and casually her sense that his general optimism is probably right by accepting local pessimism about the weather. The vehicle for her loving acquiescence could have been 'anything', but the novelist's story is shaping the character's story, and so Mrs Ramsay chooses the lighthouse. Virginia Woolf most brilliantly combines the arbitrariness of love's narrations with the total demands of her novel's form.

Indirect stories will do for familiar lovers who know each other's themes, style and conventions. The indirect story may also express a timidity, inhibition, awe or passion. T. S. Eliot describes art's imaginative joining of the sound of the typewriter, Spinoza, being in love and the smell of cooking. Such energy of conjunction and synthesis is released by passion as well as art; the lover and the poet are equally able to make experiences compact. As Lear surveys the universe, he can tell only the one story of filial ingratitude. Donne's joyful lovers concentrate the whole of life within their bed, dismissing the past before they met as prelude or dream.

The narrative of love tends to fall into two kinds: the pure and simple declaration, 'I love you', and the indirect telling. The first occurs naturally enough, in literature or life, when love is news. Such good news may take the form of a lyric declaration of feeling but if it is an imaginative passion, not an appetite which needs no past or future, it

[3] See above p. 91.

will possess a narrative urge, remaking past and engrossing future. What William James called the specious present is nowhere more sharply visible than in such narratives of love which eagerly seize memory and anticipation. The embrace is sooner or later broken off to make room for the ever-interesting story of how it came about and what will happen next.

History and fantasy are necessarily present in different proportions in different love stories. Jane Austen provides a perfect model for the story which spreads eagerly over past and future. Emma's knowledge of her own feeling and of Knightley's has come with such piercing surprise that his narrative of the past is urgently needed by them both:

> This one half hour had given to each the same precious certainty of being beloved, had cleared from each the same degree of ignor-ance, jealousy, or distrust.—On his side, there had been a long-standing jealousy, old as the arrival, or even the expectation, of Frank Churchill.—He had been in love with Emma, and jealous of Frank Churchill, from about the same period, one sentiment having probably enlightened him as to the other. It was his jealousy of Frank Churchill that had taken him from the country.—The Box-Hill party had decided him on going away. He would save himself from witnessing again such permitted, encouraged attentions. —He had gone to learn to be indifferent.—But he had gone to a wrong place. There was too much domestic happiness in his brother's house; woman wore too amiable a form in it; Isabella was too much like Emma—differing only in those striking inferiorities, which always brought the other in brilliancy before him, for much to have been done, even had his time been longer. He had stayed on, however, vigorously, day after day—till this very morning's post had conveyed the history of Jane Fairfax. (*Emma*, ch. xlix)

This story also involves a candid history of the speculations of the past, open confession and confidence erase secrets and false fantasy and passionately embrace the future. Such a future is implicitly easy for such lovers in such a society, their difficulties practical and real but not too painful. The future is more difficult for Catherine and Klesmer in George Eliot's *Daniel Deronda*. These lovers have known for some time about their mutual feelings but he has been held back by social, she by sexual pride. Their joint declaration is impelled by

Klesmer's fury at the condescensions of Mr Bult, 'expectant peer' and 'esteemed party man'. The story trembles on the brink of its telling while they talk of other things. He softly and abstractedly plays his own setting of Heine's 'Ich hab' dich geliebt und liebe dich noch', but music is not explicit enough and the story has to be told. He makes the declaration about past and present, she the brave leap into the story of the future in one of the most delicate proposals of marriage made by a woman in fiction:

'Well, at least one man who has seen women as plenty as flowers in May has lingered about you for your own sake. And since he is one whom you can never marry, you will believe him. That is an argument in favour of some other man. But don't give yourself for a meal to a minotaur like Bult. I shall go now and pack. I shall make my excuses to Mrs Arrowpoint.' Klesmer rose as he ended, and walked quickly towards the door.

'You must take this heap of manuscript, then,' said Catherine, suddenly making a desperate effort. She had risen to fetch the heap from another table. Klesmer came back, and they had the length of the folio sheets between them.

'Why should I not marry the man who loves me, if I love him?' said Catherine. To her the effort was something like the leap of a woman from the deck into the lifeboat.

'It would be too hard—impossible—you could not carry it through. I am not worth what you would have to encounter. I will not accept the sacrifice. It would be thought a *mésalliance* for you, and I should be liable to the worst accusations.'

'Is it the accusations you are afraid of? I am afraid of nothing but that we should miss the passing of our lives together.' (bk. iii, ch. xxii)

In *Much Ado about Nothing* Beatrice and Benedick find it hard to tell the story of their love. Their restraint is particularly moving because untypical, understandable as the tongue-tied reticence of bold and eloquent talkers rebuked by passion. They have needed the encouragement, if not the whole inspiration, of the pleasant slanders of Hero and Margaret and they also need the provocation of intensity borrowed from a crisis in other lives. The shameful disgrace of Hero in the chapel forces them to break their silence and tell each other their story. The telling is supported by the solemnity and urgency which makes banter blasphemous and candour decorous. They are also helped by being pressed into the service of other people, their own feeling helpfully subdued to the occasion and the time. The inhibitions of play finished, they speak with seriousness, openness, and affection:

> BENEDICK. Surely I do believe your fair cousin is wronged.
>
> BEATRICE. Ah! how much might the man deserve of me that would right her.
>
> BENEDICK. Is there any way to show such friendship?
>
> BEATRICE. A very even way, but no such friend.
>
> BENEDICK. May a man do it?
>
> BEATRICE. It is a man's office, but not yours.
>
> BENEDICK. I do love nothing in the world so well as you: is not that strange?
>
> BEATRICE. As strange as the thing I know not. It were as possible for me to say I loved nothing so well as you; but believe me not, and yet I lie not; I confess nothing, nor I deny nothing. I am sorry for my cousin.
>
> BENEDICK. By my sword, Beatrice, thou lovest me.
>
> (IV. i. 262–78)

The clashes of wit are almost gone, though some echoes connect the present awe with past levity. The past is implicit also in the wonder, 'is not that strange?'. After declaration, love is immediately put to the test in the violence of 'Kill Claudio', eloquent not only of the loyalty and anger of the particular occasion, but intensely expressive of the extremity, totality and irrationality of a lover's imperative. The story of these lovers is told through someone else's story and with an appropriate passion which makes us feel that it could not very well be told in any other way. The obliquity can be admired as dexterous dramatic shift from comic to serious feeling, from flirtatious boldness to loving shyness, and it is a stroke of artifice which instructs us in the need and nature of imagination. Benedick is the perfect teller and listener, for he is willing to act as well as tell and listen. The exchange is rare in its congeniality.

In the last section of *War and Peace*, 'The French at Moscow', two other lovers exchange their difficult stories of the past. Peter comes to learn about his friend's death and wonders if Andrew has died in irritability or peace. His urgent desire to know breaks through Maria's reluctance to tell her story and eventually creates the freedom of intense sympathy: 'his questions and the interest he took in them, his voice trembling with emotion, persuaded her to retrace by degrees the scenes which she hardly dared call up for herself'. Peter's listening is analysed in all its emotional complexity. He feels eager to know about Andrew, fitfully embarrassed, and 'conscious that every word he spoke, and everything he did, lay open to a judge whose opinion was the most precious in the world to him'. As he responds to Maria's story, 'What, then, had he to fear in death?', he turns spontaneously to Natacha, his eyes filling with tears as he says, 'How happy it was for him that you should have met once more!' The genuine questions of sympathy break down her silence. Her story is also analysed in its medium of feeling. The initial tension and effort gradually give way to the release of free confidence:

> Peter, as he listened, was thinking neither of Prince Andrew nor of death, nor of what she was saying. He was conscious only of intense pity for the pain it must be to her to call up the grief of the past; but Natacha was impelled by an irresistible impulse. She mingled the most trivial details with the most sacred feelings, told the same scenes again and again, and did not seem to know how to stop.
>
> (bk. xvi, ch. cxxvi)[4]

She stops only when there is an interruption, leaving hurriedly, 'And that is all—that is all...'. Peter wonders about the nature of her pain and Maria begs him to stay to supper, adding, 'This is the first time... that she has spoken of him'.

At supper it is Peter's turn to tell his story. Tolstoy registers the aftermath of the previous confidences, which have left the three people feeling that awkwardness which commonly ensues after a serious intimate conversation. There is relief and restored energy as well as awkwardness, and as they all try to think about ending the painful silence the womens' eyes shine 'with revived joy in living, and an unconscious admission that grief is not eternal, but may still give place to happiness'. Maria's invitation, 'Will you have a little brandy, count?' is enough 'to chase the shadows of the past', and is followed by her invitation to Peter to tell the story of his survival, of 'how he managed to live' through the siege.

The long, detailed drama of his telling and their listening beautifully balances and reverses the relationships of the previous chapter. Once again Tolstoy follows minutely the course of a dynamic interaction of

[4] The translation used is that of the Everyman edition.

feeling. Maria's friendly interest about the 'perfect romance' is answered by his amused observation, 'Things have been invented about me that I never saw in my dreams... I find myself a person of interest, and I do not mind it at all. . . . My friends vie with each other in asking me to their houses, and telling me all the detail of my captivity as they have imagined it'. This gently ironic response to the exaggerations of possessive gossip makes a strong contrast to the halting and reticent story of his wife's solitary death, and his response of shock and pity, even though they were 'not a model couple'. Once more there is difficulty about telling the story of the past, accompanied by a sense that some things have to be said in order to be put behind.

Now it is Peter's turn to be led on by sympathy and interest. Like the narratives of Natacha and Maria, his story comes out bit by bit. Painfully, slowly, but gathering impetus, it moves from irony into deeper feeling:

> ... allowing himself to be led on by their questions, he gave them a full account of all his adventures. He spoke at first with that light irony that tinged all his opinions of others and of himself; but by degrees the remembrance, still so vivid, of the sufferings and the horrors he had witnessed gave his speech the genuine and reticent emotion that is natural in a man who goes back in memory to the scenes of acute interest in which he has taken part. (bk. xvi, ch. cxvii)

A common movement of memory, especially the recollection of shocking events, is made individual and characteristic. Peter's story-telling is expressive of his peculiar moral style. He finds the detail of the rape difficult to relate and tries also to leave out his own good actions. Natacha senses the gaps and tries to get them filled in. If his goodness of heart is impressed on the narrative, so too is the sympathy of the listener, which is not generalized sympathy with the awful experiences but a particular knowledge of the story-teller attaching her to what is said as to what is unsaid:

> Natacha, with her elbow on the table and her chin resting on her hand, followed every detail with varying expression. Her eyes, her exclamations, her brief questions, all showed that she was fully entered into the real meaning of what he endeavoured to make them understand; nay, better still, the hidden sense of much that he could not utter in words. The episode of the rescue of the child and of the

woman whom he had tried to defend—the immediate cause of his being taken prisoner—he related in these words:

'It was a horrible sight; children deserted or left to perish in the flames—one was saved before my very eyes. Then the women, and soldiers snatching away their dresses and even their ear-rings—' he coloured and paused. 'And just then a patrol came along and arrested the peasants and all who were not plundering, myself among them.'

'You are not telling the whole story,' said Natacha interrupting him. 'You would certainly have...have done some good action.'

(bk. xvi, ch. cxxvii)

Peter passes from shyness and reticence to openness and freedom. As he recounts the events, pacing up and down, expressing his affection, and telling what he learnt from 'that guileless soul who could neither read nor write', he tells the story of 'the hapless creature's illness and death' in a voice 'quivering with emotion'. He is listener and narrator.

The course of feeling here, as in *To the Lighthouse*, is observed in a conversation. The telling and listening create a permanent change in the relationship between two people. The relationship is that of narrator and listener but a third person, Princess Maria, is listening and also observing what is going on. She is interested in Peter's story but even more interested in the thought that Peter and Natacha are falling in love. Telling and listening to stories, whatever the subject, can be the occasion of an unspoken conversation of sympathy between the speaker and the listener and may therefore take place in a public conversation. Tolstoy observes that Peter's narration changes the experience, or rather, brings out 'new meaning', and his generalization about woman's listening role, derived partly from social observation and partly from his misogyny, should not obscure the insight:

He himself had never seen his adventures in the light in which they now appeared. They bore a new meaning for him; and as he narrated them to Natacha he felt the keen pleasure which comes of the sympathy, not of a clever woman whose sole object is to assimilate what she hears and to enrich the stores of her little brain, but of that of a true woman who possesses the faculty of bringing out and taking in all that is best in a man. Natacha, though unconsciously, was all attention. Not a word, not a shade of tone, not

> a glance, a thrill, or a gesture escaped her; she caught his sentences half-spoken, as it were in the air, and treasured them in her heart, divining the mysterious travail that had taken place in his soul.
>
> (bk. xvi, ch. cxxvii)

The final proof of love comes as Peter decides that he would not wish away the terrible past. Its acceptance involves the acceptance of the future for them both, 'While there is life there is happiness'.

Under the nourishing condition of love's congeniality, warmth and understanding, we can tell our stories. If the lover can resemble the artist, the artist resembles the lover in curiosity and care, and outdoes him in impartiality. Of all the many narrators within novels, perhaps none combines caring with impartiality more zealously than Conrad's Marlow. 'Of all my people,' said Conrad, 'he's the one that has never been a vexation to my spirit. A most discreet, understanding man...' ('The Author's Note', 1917, prefaced to *Youth*).

If Marlow did not vex his author, he has caused the critics vexation. Conrad did not respect those critics who found Marlow's energetic narratives implausible; he produced arguments in favour of men's ability to talk and listen for hours on end, in the tropics, the temperate zones and the Houses of Parliament. More profound than this superficial answer to a superficial objection is the insight of the narrator-listener in *Heart of Darkness*. He distinguishes the ordinary sailor's yarn, which has 'a direct simplicity, the whole meaning of which lies within the shell of a cracked nut', from Marlow's stories which 'contain their meaning... not inside like a kernel but outside, enveloping the tale which brought it out only as a glow brings out a haze, in the likeness of one of those misty halos that sometimes are made visible by the spectral illuminations of moonshine'. In other words, Marlow is the true artist, whose form is created by his feeling. Conrad makes this plain enough by appending an illustration to the image of the misty halo: Marlow suddenly produces the key image of the book, as he sees that England has once also been 'one of the dark places of the earth'. He announces motif and meaning.

Marlow is talking about himself. Much criticism of Conrad seems to have wasted its spirit in a confusion between the background and the foreground of these intricate, subtle stories. Marlow finds Kurtz because he too wants to explore the darkness, though restrained by the rules and cautions of reason. The discovery of Kurtz involves him in some measure of compromise and the narrator who detests lies ends his narration with the story of his necessary lie. Kurtz is, moreover, wholly condemned for his expedition into the heart of darkness. The darkness in which Kurtz finally finds horror is death but the image links death with the degradations of savagery. Kurtz's report is a story told by the extremity of irrational imagination to the rational Marlow who has held back from such experience. But Marlow also nearly dies and the imagery and feeling of his story draw a parallel and a distinction between Kurtz and himself. His wrestle with death he describes as 'the most unexciting contest you can imagine. It takes place in an impalpable greyness, with nothing underfoot, with nothing around, without spectators, without clamour, without the great desire of victory, without the great fear of death, in a sickly atmosphere of scepticism' (*Heart of Darkness*). He finds with some humiliation that he has no horror to report of this greyness and feels the moderate man's imaginative envy of the extremist. Kurtz 'had summed up—he had judged', and Marlow's opinion that Kurtz is remarkable is a judgement passed on damnation by neutrality. He feels he has lived through Kurtz's extremity and can remember it better than his own. His report of that experience, however, cannot always be made truthfully.

Marlow is the imaginative but rational man regarding the irrational destructiveness of uncontrolled imagination. He is also the imaginative man whose moral faith has held, because of luck, accident, effective illusion, or for other reasons he cannot wholly explain. Critics have regretted such uncertainty, but this is like wanting Sancho Panza to be Don Quixote or Partridge to be Tom Jones. To be sure, Don Quixote and Tom Jones are never guilty of cowardice. Lord Jim's possibly deluded yet saintly heroism, marked by the heroic title, has something in common with Don Quixote's. The listener in *Heart of Darkness* speaks ironically but truly of Marlow's 'inconclusive experiences'. He also feels regret when Marlow says that he knows they don't want to hear his personal story. But this personal story is just what they do want to hear in *Heart of Darkness*, as in *Youth* and *Lord Jim*. Conrad knows that the imaginative narrator only tells what moves, bewilders and tests him. His are adventures of the spirit, like those of James's Strether or Rowland Mallet. He is less involved in the action than James's spectators but he is not entirely inactive. He seeks out his men and his places, asks questions, and invests faith, hope, or moral curiosity. Like Proust's Marcel, he tests memory in narrative, while speaking with more detachment as a spectator, whose imagination plays strenuously on other people's more violent engagement with life. Like Kurtz, Jim goes further than Marlow, so trying those beliefs Marlow has not put to such dangerous tests. Jim's experience may be conclusive for him, though since his ghost is silent, we cannot be sure. But Marlow is like the artist who batters his imagination against an unyielding experience.

Marlow would understand but not take part in a cult of derangement. (He might even accept a censorship, though probably not.) He speaks so highly of the truth that we feel his distaste for the compromise involved in following Kurtz, even at a distance:

> I would not have gone so far as to fight for Kurtz, but I went for him near enough to a lie. You know I hate, detest, and can't bear a lie, not because I am straighter than the rest of us, but simply because it appals me. There is a taint of death, a flavour of mortality in lies,— which is exactly what I hate and detest in the world—what I want to forget. It makes me miserable and sick, like biting something rotten would do. Temperament, I suppose. Well, I went near enough to it by letting the young fool there believe anything he liked to imagine as to my influence in Europe. I became in an instant as much of a pretence as the rest of the bewitched pilgrims. This simply because I had a notion it somehow would be of help to that Kurtz whom at the time I did not see—you understand.
>
> *(Heart of Darkness*, ch. i)

Critical impatience has been roused by Marlow's candour about those other lives which we have to admit into our investigations of morality and meaning, but cannot wholly understand. The grey and tepid scepticism is present in *Lord Jim* as in *Heart of Darkness*. At the end of *Youth*, Marlow asks his listeners an honest question, phrased in the crude style which has not always been popular:

> 'By all that's wonderful, it is the sea, I believe, the sea itself—or is it youth alone? Who can tell? But you here—you all had something out of life: money, love—whatever one gets on shore—and, tell me, wasn't that the best time, that time when we were young at sea; young and had nothing, on the sea that gives nothing, except hard knocks—and sometimes a chance to feel your strength—that only— what you all regret?'

The listeners nod:

> ...the man of finance, the man of accounts, the man of law, we all
> nodded at him over the polished table that like a still sheet of brown
> water reflected our faces, lined, wrinkled; our faces marked by toil,
> by deceptions, by success, by love; our weary eyes looking still,
> looking always, looking anxiously for something out of life, that
> while it is expected is already gone—has passed unseen, in a sigh,
> in a flash—together with the youth, with the strength, with the
> romance of illusions.

Conrad is tackling the paradox of the contemplative narration, its
disengagement, its scepticism, and the inconclusiveness of its negative
capability. Imagination follows Jim into the destructive element but has
to draw back or it could not tell its story. *Lord Jim* reports on the
experiments of romantic imagination, which cannot push through
into successes until it has known failure, whose cowardice alone can
plumb and prove courage. *Lord Jim* is filled with listeners whose
listening defines Marlow's enterprise, and his passivity.

There are the unimaginative men, like Brown, whose failures
confirm the fineness of Jim's vision but whose resemblance to his
situation is fatally tempting:

> When he asked Jim, with a sort of brusque despairing frankness,
> whether he himself—straight now—didn't understand that when
> 'it came to saving one's life in the dark, one didn't care who else
> went—three, thirty, three hundred people'—it was as if a demon
> had been whispering advice in his ear. 'I made him wince,' boasted
> Brown to me. 'He very soon left off coming the righteous over me.
> He just stood there with nothing to say, and looking as black as
> thunder—not at me—on the ground.' He asked Jim whether he had
> nothing fishy in his life to remember that he was so damnedly hard
> upon a man trying to get out of a deadly hole by the first means
> that came to hand—and so on, and so on. And there ran through
> the rough talk a vein of subtle reference to their common blood, an
> assumption of common experience; a sickening suggestion of
> common guilt, of secret knowledge that was like a bond of their
> minds and of their hearts. (*Lord Jim*, ch. xlii)

This establishes Jim's activity as a listener. By understanding he
acts, forgives and fatally trusts. Marlow's trust is smaller and less costly.

There is the man of honour, the French lieutenant with enough stake in the story to care to know, but whose intellectual sympathy is touchily withdrawn in moral pride. He knows that man is *né poltron* but uses the knowledge to confirm his own unshakeable courage, 'It would be too easy otherwise'. He leaves immediately at Marlow's suggestion of 'taking a lenient view':

> ' "I am glad to see you taking a lenient view," I said. "His own feeling in the matter was—ah!—hopeful, and..."
>
> 'The shuffle of his feet under the table interrupted me. He drew up his heavy eyelids. Drew up, I say—no other expression can describe the steady deliberation of the act—and at last was disclosed completely to me. I was confronted by two narrow grey circlets, like two tiny steel rings around the profound blackness of the pupils. The sharp glance, coming from that massive body, gave a notion of extreme efficiency, like a razor-edge on a battle-axe. "Pardon," he said, punctiliously. His right hand went up, and he swayed forward. "Allow me...I contended that one may get on knowing very well that one's courage does not come of itself (*ne vient pas tout seul*). There's nothing much in that to get upset about. One truth the more ought not to make life impossible...But the honour—the honour, monsieur!...The honour...that is real—that is! And what life may be worth when"...he got on his feet with a ponderous impetuosity, as a startled ox might scramble up from the grass..."when the honour is gone—*ah ça! par exemple*—I can offer no opinion. I can offer no opinion—because—monsieur—I know nothing of it." '
>
> (ch. xiii)

Unlike this listener, Marlow cannot walk out. The artist must not be deafened by the code of honour in the attempt to understand. Conrad shows the painfulness of listening (and sometimes of telling) as forcefully as Homer and Virgil.

There is the crowd of easy, armchair listeners:

> 'Talk! So be it. And it's easy enough to talk of Master Jim, after a good spread, two hundred feet above the sea-level, with a box of decent cigars handy, on a blessed evening of freshness and starlight that would make the best of us forget we are only on sufferance here and got to pick our way in cross lights, watching every precious minute and every irremediable step, trusting we shall manage yet to

go out decently in the end—but not so sure of it after all—and with dashed little help to expect from those we touch elbows with right and left. Of course there are men here and there to whom the whole of life is like an after-dinner hour with a cigar; easy, pleasant, empty, perhaps enlivened by some fable of strife to be forgotten before the end is told—before the end is told—even if there happens to be any end to it.' (ch. v)

One of them is finally picked out as privileged to hear the end of Marlow's story, his listening, his response, and his telling:

> 'You alone have showed an interest in him that survived the telling of his story, though I remember well you would not admit he had mastered his fate. You prophesied for him the disaster of weariness and of disgust with acquired honour, with the self-appointed task, with the love sprung from pity and youth. You had said you knew so well "that kind of thing," its illusory satisfaction, its unavoidable deception.' (ch. xxxvi)

Unlike this listener, Marlow accepts the experience beyond the known rules, conventions, and order of civilization.

Marlow is like Nick Carraway, Scott Fitzgerald's narrator in *The Great Gatsby*, also a man with too much sympathy, a man who attracts confidences, but a man with his own life which sometimes presses hard as he goes on listening:

> 'Oh yes. I attended the inquiry,' he would say, 'and to this day I haven't left off wondering why I went. I am willing to believe each of us has a guardian angel, if you fellows will concede to me that each of us has a familiar devil as well. I want you to own up, because I don't like to feel exceptional in any way, and I know I have him—the devil, I mean. I haven't seen him, of course, but I go upon circumstantial evidence. He is there right enough, and, being malicious, he lets me in for that kind of thing. What kind of thing, you ask? Why, the inquiry thing, the yellow-dog thing—you wouldn't think a mangy, native tyke would be allowed to trip up people in the verandah of a magistrate's court, would you?—the kind of thing that by devious, unexpected, truly diabolical ways causes me to run up against men with soft spots, with hard spots, with hidden plague spots, by Jove! and loosens their tongues at the sight of me

for their infernal confidences; as though, forsooth, I had no confidences to make to myself, as though—God help me!—I didn't have enough confidential information about myself to harrow my own soul till the end of my appointed time. And what I have done to be thus favoured I want to know. I declare I am as full of my own concerns as the next man, and I have as much memory as the average pilgrim in this valley, so you see I am not particularly fit to be a receptacle of confessions. Then why? Can't tell—unless it be to make time pass away after dinner.' (ch. v)

This receptivity is a condition of art and particularly of the novelist's art. Conrad's triumph, like that of Joyce, is to relate the advantages, disadvantages, strengths and weaknesses of the artist's imagination to the trials of mind outside art. He wants to test moral faith in the ideal, to understand the meaning of those dreams, codes and standards which seem to be both necessary and fallible:

> Why I longed to go grubbing into the deplorable details of an occurrence which, after all, concerned me no more than as a member of an obscure body of men held together by a community of inglorious toil and by fidelity to a certain standard of conduct, I can't explain. You may call it an unhealthy curiosity if you like; but I have a distinct notion I wished to find something. Perhaps, unconsciously, I hoped I would find that something, some profound and redeeming cause, some merciful explanation, some convincing shadow of an excuse. I see well enough now that I hoped for the impossible—for the laying of what is the most obstinate ghost of man's creation, of the uneasy doubt uprising like a mist, secret and gnawing like a worm, and more chilling than the certitude of death—the doubt of the sovereign power enthroned in a fixed standard of conduct. (ch. v)

Marlow recognizes his own condition in Jim, as he did in Kurtz:

> Was it for my own sake that I wished to find some shadow of an excuse for that young fellow whom I had never seen before, but whose appearance alone added a touch of personal concern to the thoughts suggested by the knowledge of his weakness—made it a thing of mystery and terror—like a hint of a destructive fate ready for us all whose youth—in its day—had resembled his youth? (ch. v)

This sympathy reflects that involvement of the artist which is as dangerous and as essential as his detachment. Marlow's withdrawal is made utterly clear when we see the more desperate needs of Jim, who is also a narrator, though only a listener on that one fatal or fortunate occasion when he listens to Brown. Like Marlow, Jim needs to talk in order to understand, but he also needs something more practical, to send back a message to the world of ordinary, decent men. Jim needs Marlow to carry back his message, though he dies of course before he can replace his nothing with something.

Marlow carries back an ambiguous message. How could it be otherwise? The cost has to be heavy, or the romantic ideal would not be sufficiently under trial. It is typical of Marlow's scepticism that he should give almost, but not quite, the last word to doubt:

> 'But we can see him, an obscure conqueror of fame, tearing himself out of the arms of a jealous love at the sign, at the call of his exalted egoism. He goes away from a living woman to celebrate his pitiless wedding with a shadowy ideal of conduct. Is he satisfied— quite, now, I wonder? We ought to know. He is one of us—and have I not stood up once, like an evoked ghost, to answer for his eternal constancy? Was I so very wrong after all? Now he is no more, there are days when the reality of his existence comes to me with an immense, with an overwhelming force; and yet upon my honour there are moments, too, when he passes from my eyes like a dis- embodied spirit astray amongst the passions of this earth, ready to surrender himself faithfully to the claim of his own world of shades...' (ch. xlix)

The very last word is Stein's. It seems reasonable to give a concluding prominence to fatigue, age and the preparation for death. These will be the last words of any artist and the most he can do is to make that marginal gesture to faith, waving 'his hand sadly at his butterflies'. But the last image leaves the question open. Is Jim like the butterfly, his feet in the dirt, his flight necessarily depending on the sacrifice of the girl? Or is he unlike the butterfly, choosing only shadow? Marlow's ques- tions, like Lear's,[5] indicate scrupulously his author's sense that the imagination cannot solve but must try to appreciate the difficulties of being human.

[5] Winifred Nowottny, 'Questions in Lear', *Shakespeare Survey*, 10 (1969).

The good teller and the good listener are loving and truthful, aware of each other, as parents and children, friends and lovers, courteous strangers, novelists and readers. They use speech and silence but are never certain that the telling or the hearing has been perfect. The truthful narrative may have to take an interrogative form.

PART TWO

Authors

6
Charles Dickens

Most men, you may observe, speak only to narrate; not in
imparting what they have thought, which indeed were often
a very small matter, but in exhibiting what they have undergone or seen, which is a quite unlimited one, do talkers
dilate. Cut us off from Narrative, how would the stream of
conversation, even among the wisest, languish into detached
handfuls, and among the foolish utterly evaporate! Thus, as
we do nothing but enact History, we say little but recite it,
nay, rather, in that widest sense, our whole spiritual life is
built thereon. For, strictly considered, what is all Knowledge
too but recorded Experience, and a product of History; of
which, therefore, Reasoning and Belief, no less than Action
and Passion, are essential materials?
(Thomas Carlyle, 'On History', 1830)

Telling stories within stories is a very old narrative convention, and
Dickens was well acquainted with the intricate Chinese boxes of *The
Arabian Nights* and the episodic journey novels of Smollett and
Fielding whose travellers' tales are strung irregularly on their narrative
thread. But we do not have to go to literary sources to account for
Dickens's stories within stories. To proliferate and vary one's form
is self-evidently gratifying, a virtuoso performance which we find
not only in fiction, but in plays within plays, characters who perform
many roles, and all the forms of internal parody and self-parody. Just
as a dramatist tries to squeeze in as many histrionic opportunities as
possible, so a great story-teller naturally seizes every chance to tell a
story. Dickens's novels are full of travellers' tales, confessions, lies,
reports, warnings, autobiographies, tall stories, anecdotes, narrative
jokes, books, readings and fairy-tales. Even in his early novels,
however, the tales are given internal point and function. Without
their rather clumsy inset stories, *Pickwick Papers* and *Nicholas Nickleby*
would not only lose narrative padding but some definition and
contrast. Even these stories are self-reflective, though less so than
the briefer and more brilliant anecdotes which have much to tell us,

implicitly and explicitly, about Dickens's awareness of narrative forms, in art and outside art.

His most brilliant story-tellers are either totally and professionally in command, detached, dazzling and polished, or totally and un-professionally out of control, involved, naïve and floundering. The early professionals include Jingle, both the Wellers, and the unforget-table Bagman, who is brought in simply to draw the long bow once and for all. Each has his own style. The several variations on the tall story in *Pickwick Papers* are combined and contrasted: what better foil for Jingle's terse and telling telegrams, each with a theme designed for the individual consumer and swiftly adapted through the dashing stylized structures, than Sam Weller's good-humoured slow-moving set-pieces about the man devoured by his sausage machine or the man who died defending crumpets, which pile up their effects slowly to reach heights of the incredible from which everyone except the credulous Pickwickian must topple? (Sam, of course, has his own curt style also.) The inefficient story-tellers tell as much about narrative art: Mrs Nickleby's total unawareness of the effect on her listeners is expressive not only of self-aggrandizing intent and self-deflating effect, but of that sheer stupidity which commits all the narrative sins, rambles, forgets, stumbles and misses the point. Of course, the uncontrolled joke is as funny as the con-trolled, the unawareness of the bad story-teller providing its own amusement and the whole structure firmly controlled, one stage back, by Dickens. It would be hard to choose between Jingle's tale of Don Bolaro Fizzgig and the public fountain and Mrs Nickleby's daft reminiscences of an infallible cure for the common cold. Happily, we don't have to. Dickens's story-tellers reflect his own variety of narrative styles: he too commands terseness, dash, verblessness, sob-stuff, formal set-pieces, informal stragglings, simplicity, intricacy, wit, plainness, exaggeration, understatement, excess, irony, garrulous-ness and reserve, nightmare and lucid vision. Not only do his story-tellers extend and develop his narrative virtuosity in a way previously unsurpassed in the English novel (Fielding and Sterne seem to be the closest competitors, though working within a much smaller range), but their forms of narrative draw our attention to the nature of his story-telling, and to story-telling in general.

Dickens's story-tellers often use story in order to manipulate people, as story-tellers frequently do. Ancient Mariners all, for better or for worse, they are made to show a moral and a psychological reason for their styles and stories. Jingle is in the business for money and the speed and stereotype of his narrative sales-talk draw attention to his cynicism and proficiency. But the style is the man, and one of the novel's triumphs is Dickens's conversion of Jingle's form for the expression of a change of heart. When Pickwick meets him in the Fleet, Jingle still goes on telling his brief and tall tales, but this time the professionalism is stoical, the morbidity personal, the fantasy real. Jingle finds that truth is as nasty as his lies. Pickwick finds that the con-man can staunchly go on with the dashing style, feebly and appealingly, but still a joker. The bizarre details and jerkiness come into their own:

> 'Spout—dear relation—uncle Tom—couldn't help it—must eat, you know. Wants of nature—and all that.'
> 'What do you mean?'
> 'Gone, my dear sir—last coat—can't help it. Lived on a pair of boots—whole fortnight. Silk umbrella—ivory handle—week—fact —honour—ask Job—knows it.'

The laconic style too gains new meaning in the eloquent appeal of brave understatement:

> '...Inquest—little bone-house—poor prisoner—common neces-saries—hush it up—gentlemen of the jury—warden's tradesmen— keep it snug—natural death—coroner's order—workhouse funeral —serve him right—all over—drop the curtain.' (ch. xlii)

Dickens permits Pickwick to draw his conclusions from the 'accustomed volubility' which he rightly reads as assumed 'reckless-ness'. The style is preserved, in a brilliant and touching decorum which allows it to move into a new register with new experience. Jingle never stops telling stories, never changes the form, but the story itself is a new one.

Like Homer and Samuel Beckett, whose characters narrate for dear life, Dickens creates story-tellers who tell in order to survive. Another Ancient Mariner whose medium for self-advertisement and self-aggrandizement is incorrigibly narrative, is Mrs Gamp. Her two chief characters, Mr Gamp, possibly drawn from life, and Mrs Harris, offspring of self-devoted and elastic creativity, are as stylized as Jingle's telegraphese. Her stories stop when Mrs Harris is challenged by that shrewd if over-literal critic, Betsey Prig, and then finally given a new role and new life in the real detective drama. Mrs Gamp, Jingle, Sam Weller and the medical students are all marvellous instances of Dickens's comic morbidity, but each is an individual, distinct and different in moral and psychic life. Sairey Gamp's aggressive, exhibitionist and demanding stories, while perfectly in tune with character, profession and value, resemble her creator's. They reflect the grotesque, grisly, zany, comedy of the Dickens world and refract its darkness and light, comedy and tragedy. Her harshness, maudlin sentiment and black comedy about childbed pains, death, deformity and drink exist at a remove from her author's profundity, pathos and social criticism, but contribute to it. Story-tellers with hearts can make excellent use of story-tellers who are heartless:

> 'True! Don't I know as that dear woman is expecting of me at this minnit, Mr Westlock, and is a-lookin' out of window down the street, with little Tommy Harris in her arms, as calls me his own Gammy, and truly calls, for bless the mottled little legs of that there precious child (like Canterbury Brawn, his own dear father says, which so they are) his own I have been, ever since I found him, Mr Westlock, with his small red worsted shoe a' gurglin' in his throat, where he had put it in his play, a chick, wile they was leavin' of him on the floor a-looking for it through the 'ouse and him a-choakin' sweetly in the parlour!' (*Martin Chuzzlewit*, ch. xlix)

Self-flattering gush and ingratiating buttonholing are brilliantly done: if Dickens mightn't quite have appreciated Oscar Wilde's crack about needing a heart of stone not to laugh at Nell, it is worth remembering that small red worsted shoe. The sentimental tale like this one or the gruesome anecdote about the six-and-twenty blessed little strangers brought on prematurely by steam engines, show Dickens's use of outrageous story-telling, which extends his powers and licence. Dickens is one of the most extravagant fantasists in English fiction and there are extremes of wild humour which he can reach only through narrative impersonations. The rewards of such impersonation are complex: Mrs Gamp's stories, like Jonas's terrible dreams, are in character. They are relentlessly businesslike, spuriously and drunkenly lachrymose, anti-male, sexual, morbid, funny, demanding and unbelievable. In a similar way, the very different material of Jonas's nightmare about trying to make the door secure with iron plates and nails that 'broke, or changed to soft twigs, or what was worse, to worms, between their fingers' is not only perfectly right for the character and for the psychology of dreaming, but contributes an extra dimension of horror to the novel. Dickens's story-tellers allow him to produce effects and to move into reaches where his own narrative, unaided, dare not go.

Mrs Gamp, Jonas Chuzzlewit, Jingle and the Wellers, are not simply narrative agents. They are part of a great network of narrative through which Dickens creates character. Dickens's fiction is rooted in the realization of the story-telling in all our waking and sleeping lives. Dickens's story-tellers do more than reflect and reflect on his self-consciousness and virtuosity as a novelist; they also expose and analyse the narrative nature of life outside fiction. Extravagance and plainness, incoherence and lucidity, boasting and modesty, revelation and restraint, are seen as literary modes, but not only as literary modes. In Dickens's exploitation of narrative for moral expression, in Jingle, the Wellers, Mrs Gamp, or Mrs Nickleby and David Copperfield, we see his grasp of the moral significance of the stories people tell. He knows that good and bad stories may be told by good and bad people, that the equations are not simple: your good story-teller need not be your good man, though the co-presence of Jingle and the Wellers ensures that we don't fall into the trap of assuming that the brilliant story-teller is necessarily a bad man.

Dickens is not usually associated with restraint, but because the novels are so filled with garrulous narrators the occasional presence of the repressed story makes itself powerfully felt. We do not see Dombey's memories and desires, apart from the exceptional episode of the railway journey after Paul's death and that is not a narrative but a lyric presentation in which Dombey's passions select images but don't arrange themselves in story form. Perhaps Dombey's avoidance of story is significant: he can only identify partially, can only fix on the destructiveness of the railway, not its path of enlightenment. Here and elsewhere, he can only select from the past and the future. To tell the story would be to bring in his daughter, amongst other undesirable elements. Another repressed narrative is crucial in *Hard Times*. Louisa Gradgrind wants to tell her father about her reluctance to marry Bounderby but because he has repressed the story-telling and story-listening of childhood she can only make enigmatic statements, lyric rather than narrative, about the fires of

Coketown. When at last she can tell her story, after she runs away from her husband, it is almost too late. People cannot always tell their secrets and the reticence may be destructive, walling us off from each other, inhibiting love and help. To exchange stories is to confess, to commit, to communicate. In *Great Expectations*, as in *Dombey and Son* and *Hard Times*, the change of heart is shown through a great release of story-telling. Pip tries to get Jaggers to listen to his story, but Jaggers, the wary barrister who knows that narrative is evidence and may be used against us all, tries not to listen. However, Pip wins, and forces him to hear. The result is morally moving and psychologically complex. The impulse to listen is closely linked with the impulse to tell; and after Jaggers becomes an un-professional listener, out of the sympathy which makes and is made by the listening, comes his own story. Its form is complicated. Like Jingle, he can't change his style, but he can change his theme. His style remains forensic, and his repeated and stereotyped 'Put the case' underlines the formality and provisional caginess of his narrative. The story of Estella's mother is told fully, despite the guard of its rhetoric. But the story about someone else often permits us to tell our own story, and in one or two hints and glimpses we see that Jaggers too has his personal history, that he has dreamed, has loved, and has lost. The reticence is speaking. Jaggers picks up Pip's thoughtless words about the 'poor dreams' and repeats them, making clear that they are his, as they are everybody's. The story that is not told is revealed, sufficiently, through the resonant taciturnity and caution of the professional narrative. Like Jaggers's other feelings, his dreams have not been utterly destroyed. When he washes the professional life from his hands, it is because there is something more to the man than the office and the court where the story of the heart dare not be told. He tells the story in which he has been moved by sympathy and pity for Miss Havisham and Estella's mother and at the same time, movingly because laconically, he tells the story that cannot be fully told, of his own 'poor dreams'. Pip and the reader are made to realize that he is neither the kind of listener nor the kind of story-teller we had taken him to be. A revelation about plot becomes a revelation about character.

As Dickens knew so well, the secret life presses hard. It may come out by reticent implication, or in skilful disguise. The enigmatic story which is perhaps closest to Dickens's own habitual modes of fantasy is that told by Little Dorrit to Maggy. It is a fairy-tale of her own composition. Dorrit, like many fictitious characters who tell stories to children, is moved by love, patience and generosity. Dorrit, Esther, Tom Pinch, Sissy Jupe and David Copperfield all read, read aloud, or tell the stories Dickens loved, fairy-tales from *The Arabian Nights*, *Don Quixote* and the eighteenth-century narratives (the last suitably censored—David is a child's Tom Jones). But all these people tell their stories differently. Tom Pinch reads to the unreformed Martin Chuzzlewit in order to send him to sleep, in what may perhaps be a source for the terrible captive story-telling of Dickens's own novels at the end of Evelyn Waugh's *A Handful of Dust*. Sissy's early story-telling with her father is another image and instance of the education of feeling and wonder which has been shut out of the Gradgrind nursery. Steerforth is a listener whose life might have been changed had he told David the story he kept to himself as he uneasily gazed into the fire (a gaze he shares with Louisa Gradgrind and Lizzie Hexam), and early in the novel it is he who makes David begin his narrative career by re-telling the stories in the dormitory, thus encouraging not only the beginnings of a novelist's career, but that dreamy, romantic 'story-telling in the dark' which is an important strain in David Copperfield and his education. David in the end has to learn to listen before he can truly tell, has to come out of the dark.

Little Dorrit reveals Dickens's grasp of the function of story-telling in many ways. She tells the story to Maggy, adult in years but a child in need and taste. Like many a story, it is told for the teller as well as for the listener; like many a story told to a child, it is improvised, using a traditional form but adapting itself to the expressed and unexpressed needs of the listener and the teller. As Dickens says at the beginning of *The Chimes*, 'it is desirable that a story-teller and a story-reader should establish a mutual under-standing as soon as possible'. The relation between Dorrit and Maggy draws on their already established understanding, in which Dorrit tenderly and sensitively mothers the retarded woman, in a role-reversal which avoids condescension or sentimentality. It is a relationship of telling and listening rather like Paul Dombey's vision-ary communication to Toots. Dickens was clearly fascinated by such contrasts and communions. Dorrit tells the tale to order, and Maggy requires two things which most listeners need, a personal stake in the story and the delight of fantasy:

'Now, Little Mother, let's have a good 'un!'

'What shall it be about, Maggy?'

'Oh, let's have a Princess,' said Maggy, 'and let her be a reg'lar one. Beyond all belief, you know!'

Little Dorrit considered for a moment; and with a rather sad smile upon her face, which was flushed by the sunset, began:

'Maggy, there was once upon a time a fine King, and he had everything he could wish for, and a great deal more. He had gold and silver, diamonds and rubies, riches of every kind. He had palaces, and he had—'

'Hospitals,' interposed Maggy, still nursing her knees. 'Let him have hospitals, because they're so comfortable. Hospitals with lots of Chicking.' (bk. i, ch. xxiv)

The emotions of teller and listener are made plain, Dorrit beginning with the sad smile and Maggy plainly enjoying the vicarious pleasures of the chicken and baked potatoes, chuckling and hugging her knees in that grotesque but affectionate comic touch which is one of Dickens's own devices for avoiding condescension. We gradually observe the personal involvement of the teller, as well as the more openly demanding listener; Dorrit creates her central character, the 'poor little tiny woman', and contradicts Maggy's gloss of 'A old woman', by explaining, perhaps seeing for the first time, that she has to be not old but 'quite young'. The functions of the interruptions are masterly. Dickens no doubt first learnt to admire the dramatization of narrative in *The Arabian Nights* and *Tom Jones*. Maggy's listening doesn't quite match the subtlety we find in the classical interruptions of Partridge, whose refusals to give the Man of the Hill his undivided attention tells us much about aesthetic manners and matters, but like Partridge, and like Dickens's own Toots, she questions and comments to present the daily unromantic world outside the fairy-tale. Like them, she insists on that unromantic world's appetite for romance. Maggy wants the story to be beyond all belief but she helps to earth its fantasy. She also emphasizes Dorrit's rapt and solitary needs in imagination. We tell stories lovingly to the children but gratify also the listener within ourselves. Maggy's hints are carefully placed. She emphasizes Dorrit's identification within the young heroine and subsequently brings out the sex of the shadowy 'Some one who had gone on to those who were expecting him':

'Some one was a man then?' interposed Maggy.

Little Dorrit timidly said yes, she believed so, and resumed...

We see the ambiguous sunset blush deepen on Dorrit's face, and when the story is over, 'she interposed her hand to shade it'. The story she has told half-abstractedly has revealed and not revealed the story of her hidden love for Clennam, and her desire to keep it secret out of love and modesty. It has been the story of Little Dorrit herself, uttered, like Jaggers's 'poor dreams', reticently, in release and relief. Dickens knew about telling in order not to tell too much, as he knew about the combination of dream and reality.

Little Dorrit comes very close to her creator but it would be a mistake to identify Dickens with any one of his many story-tellers. He tells the story of dreaming but he is also the chronicler of the everyday narrative, trying at times to tell it as it really is. Amongst the many sober chroniclers in Dickens, whose realism contrasts with the sentimental fantasy of Little Dorrit and the unpunctuated verve of Flora Finching ('you will be surprised to hear that he proposed seven times once in a hackney-coach once in a boat once on a donkey at Tunbridge Wells and the rest on his knees') is Esther Summerson, elevated with David and Pip to the professional status of a major narrator of the novel. Esther shares her narrative with the powerful public present-tense of the novel's other narrator and Dickens quietly shows the beginning of her personal, confidential and reminiscent story-telling in solitude and need. What Esther wants is something most people want, someone to listen to the story of the day. Her listener is a doll and, like the reader of *Bleak House*, it can't interrupt the story that has to be told. Dickens does not give a very elaborate analysis of the artists in his artist-novels, but he takes care to ground their narrative urge in early need, impulse and habit. David, Esther and Pip are three lonely children. The stories they tell, like the stories they read, are rooted in the experience of solitude. David's reading habits are encouraged by hurt and loneliness, his story-telling is demanded and organized by his friend and patron. Moistened by raspberry shrub, he thinks of himself as a latter-day Scheherazade. Pip is one of the most sympathetic liars in Dickens; urged into story-telling by rapacious listeners, he tells the fantastic and delicious tales of the meal in the coach, which surpass even the bizarre facts of Satis House. If we insist on hearing stories, we may force the teller into telling such real whoppers, as he tries to satisfy curiosity and disguise humiliation. Pip goes on telling himself stories, much urged by the stories other people want to hear or to tell, about themselves and about society. Esther—a coy and less attractive narrator—practises her narrative observations on the doll, telling her the secrets of the repressed child, the hopes of the over-conscientious child, and the chronicle of the observant child:

> And so she used to sit propped up in a great arm-chair, with her beautiful complexion and rosy lips, staring at me—or not so much at me, I think, as at nothing—while I busily stitched away, and told her every one of my secrets.

> My dear old doll! I was such a shy little thing that I seldom dared to open my lips, and never dared to open my heart, to anybody else. It almost makes me cry to think what a relief it used to be to me, when I came home from school of a day, to run upstairs to my room, and say, 'O you dear faithful Dolly, I knew you would be expecting me!' and then to sit down on the floor, leaning on the elbow of her great chair, and tell her all I had noticed since we parted. I had always a noticing way...(*Bleak House*, ch. iii)

Dickens always knows why his listeners listen, why his story-tellers tell. Both the sober realists and the extravagant fantasists in his stories about story-telling possess understandable, common, human needs. They listen and tell in order to preserve, to bear, to keep secrets, to understand life, to share it and to transform it through the efforts of narrative imagination.

7
Thomas Hardy

While waiting I shall tell myself stories, if I can.
(Samuel Beckett, *Malone Dies*)

The crucial narrative is nowhere more apparent than in the novels of Hardy. All his plots declare the importance of telling or of not telling stories. *Tess of the d'Urbervilles* begins with the fatal story of the d'Urberville ancestry, which goes to Sir John's head and ruins his family. The antiquarian parson rightly begins to doubt his wisdom as soon as he gives in to the impulse to tell the story of his discovery. Tess finds it hard to tell Angel her history and the telling is fatally obstructed and delayed. Jude listens to Phillotson's plans to go to Christminster, which instigate his own hard-working dream. It is later strengthened by the teasing lies of Physician Vilbert, the grotesquely vivid gossip of the carter, the bits of information from the clever old hunchbacked woman who is a great reader. The child's mind is fed with knowledge and fantasy and the man's life grows. When the Widow Edlin casts back her mind to the past, on the intended wedding eve of Sue and Jude, it is to recollect such a gruesome example of marriage that the lovers take fright. Their first meeting was brought about by aunt Druscilla's warning of the ill-fated Fawley's tale. Hardy makes his plots out of the narrative forms we all use. His crises and climaxes turn on confidence, confession, warning, encouragement, revelation, history, and on reticence, lies, secrets and silence. What is told, and what is withheld make up the comic or tragic pattern of his people, whose destinies are woven by a story-teller particularly alert to the dangerous power of memory and fantasy and to the difficulty of telling our friends and lovers enough, but not too much or too little, of our own story.

The greater part of the talk in Hardy's novels is narrative, because it cannot be discursive. His characters are often too simple to reflect or analyse. Feelings and behaviour often have to be explained in stories, but because these stories are created for their tellers by a master of language and psychology they usually act like powerful narrative poems, compressing and implying passions and motives. Wordsworth used narrative in this way in *Lyrical Ballads*, where it allows him to answer intellect by feeling, for instance in 'We are Seven', in a way that leaves little room for the superior meditations and analysis of the discursive intellect. The child's pure and insistent story, is left appropriately in the ascendant. A similar effect is often found in the stories used by Hardy. In *The Woodlanders*, Mr Melbury explains to some of his wondering neighbours why he has given his daughter Grace a superior education. This is a crucial narrative because it explains the impetus which creates the whole action. It is also an appropriate narrative. The uneducated man formulates his feelings by recounting their origin, not by analysing or reasoning. The story is self-explanatory in its moving content and its unanswerable argument:

> 'I heard you wondering why I've kept my daughter so long at boarding-school,' said Mr Melbury, looking up from the letter which he was reading anew by the fire, and turning to them with the suddenness that was a trait in him. 'Hey?' he asked with affected shrewdness. 'But you did, you know. Well now, though it is my own business more than anybody else's, I'll tell ye. When I was a boy, another boy—the pa'son's son—along with a lot of others, asked me "Who dragged Whom round the walls of What?" and I said, "Sam Barret, who dragged his wife in a wheeled chair round the tower when she went to be churched." They laughed at me so much that I went home and couldn't sleep for shame; and I cried that night till my pillow was wet; till I thought to myself—"They may laugh at me for my ignorance, but that was father's fault, and none o' my making, and I must bear it. But they shall never laugh at my children, if I have any; I'll starve first!" (ch. iv)

Two of his most delicate stories, *Under the Greenwood Tree* and *The Trumpet-Major*, end with a similarly implicit recognition, of the secrecy of human lives. Simple-hearted Dick Dewy, in *Under the Greenwood Tree*, has mistaken one unimportant piece of frankness for what he calls 'entire confidence', and looks forward to that lovers' heaven of total candour:

> 'It has won me to tell you my every movement since then. We'll have no secrets from each other, darling, will we ever?—no secret at all.'

'None from today,' said Fancy. 'Hark! what's that?' (pt. v, ch. ii)

After her carefully literal reply, the less simple-hearted Fancy changes the subject, turning to the song of the nightingale which can tell no tales. As she thinks of the secret she will never tell, the mocking but innocent bird-song reminds us, by not being human, that human nature is like this. It sounds an appropriately unverbal goodbye to all the secrets and confessions of the book, in an acceptance of the limitations of honeymoon honesty too good-tempered and sturdy to be ironic. Anne Garland, in *The Trumpet-Major*, gratefully listens to John Loveday's last loving lies about the fickleheartedness of soldiers, and Bob Loveday merrily tells his brother that she has agreed to marry him at last. Hardy knows that neither brother's future is really a future but only part of a dead past, that the happy and the unhappy expectations have long since crumbled, that this is the story-telling and secrecy of ghosts.

Under the Greenwood Tree and *The Trumpet-Major* combine two kinds of story-telling, private and public. Hardy's method is to place the personal act of narrative imagination within the public chronicle. People tell themselves and each other the truths, half-truths, lies and fantasies by which we all live, but Hardy constantly reminds us of the context of such individual narratives. He is interested in secrecy and in revelation. Our personal stories about the past and the future are seen as part of history, and to be historical is to be dead. Hardy joins the inner narrative with public records, old men's reminiscences, newspaper cuttings and memoirs, so that the individual story-teller, brimming over with a sense of his own importance, is put in his place, definitely, considerately and tenderly. Hardy's novels are highly original novels of memory, being reminiscent narratives infused with the melancholy of the act of reminiscence. Wordsworthian though he is in some ways, nothing could be less like Wordsworth's memorial consolations than Hardy's sad shafts of recollection. Wordsworth, George Eliot and Proust redeem the passage of time by the ordering and memorial process of art, by its ability to bind and collapse events in time, thus reviving and celebrating time. Hardy cannot be persuaded that such revival is possible, except in fits and starts. Even while he draws on parish chronicle and gossip's memory to create the illusion that time past is time present, he insists on a regular interruption of the historic present by the real present. Since that too has vanished by the time the book is finished, the reader's reception of this melancholy is indeed resonant.

The only other novelist who comes close to Hardy's un-Proustian attitude to time is Beckett, in all his passionate refusals to praise such a fragile, deceptive and unreliable power as memory. Hardy is decidedly less anguished than Beckett about memory, having no doubts about its imaginative strength and ignoring its sleights of hand and its dotages, but for him too there is no question of celebrating those spots of time which make even the desert evergreen for Wordsworth and Proust. Even when he lingeringly and affectionately remembers an idyllic moment in the personal or communal life, he is inclined to look hard both at the past and at the memory which recalls it. In his verse, the voice of recollection sometimes trembles with bitterness and regret as he weaves memory, anticipation, memory of anticipation and anticipation of memory, particularly in the poems written after the death of his first wife. The memories in the novels look back less wryly, their rational sadness accepting that there has to be a limit to our lament for our mortality.

In *The Trumpet-Major* we observe the story-telling of hopes, desires, plans, fears and sacrificial lies, private and national. It is a historical novel recalling urgent anticipation and expectation. It would be possible to describe *Middlemarch* in similar terms, as a novel about characters in the past looking to the future, but there are very few occasions when George Eliot makes much of the pastness of her characters' sense of futurity. She tells us that many of them are still alive at the time when the novel is being read. She wants us to derive a possible hopefulness even from human frustration and failure. She reminds us with dry regret that the hopes for Reform in 1832 were more enthusiastic than they can be in the late 1860s. But unlike Hardy she never turns her characters into ghosts. Still, it was not for nothing that he, like her, called himself a meliorist, and there is certainly nothing pessimistic about his recognition of the deadness of past desires and fantasies. Apart from *Tess of the d'Urbervilles* and *Jude the Obscure*, Hardy's novels are usually very goodhumoured in their stoicism. Many of his characters, particularly the minor ones, are endowed with his own resilience and tolerance. We see them looking back to times when they looked forward, but making no hysterical or violent wishes to live in some other universe. The very stones, bridges, steps and arches in *The Trumpet-Major* are worn and pitted by the years. The people conceive plans, dream, choose, fear, take precautions and make sacrifices, as weather, lights, clocks and calendars visibly and audibly tick time away. But they behave, as we mostly do behave, as if they had plenty of time, as if time were something to kill, not something killing, as if the future were something to be carefully considered and created. While they prepare for invasion, or for marriage, or for work, each minute's motion of feeling vividly present, their chronicler shows us openly how he is changing the lights in order to bring out his people's solidity or to show their ghostly transparency. The soldiers sing, and Hardy tells us how they all died. Anne Garland is terrified by the 'new and shining' pikes standing against the church wall, but Hardy chronicles the subsequent fates of the pikes as they decay, as they are stolen and carried off, as they are degraded to the status of rakestems and pick-handles, right up to the time of his writing.

Hardy's reminiscent fiction about a past or a changing world is peopled with reminiscent characters. His nostalgia is too well seasoned to rot into sentimentality. His characters possess a matter-of-fact though perfectly sensitive acceptance of the passage of time. They tell their nostalgic stories, but they are hardly ever simply nostalgic, as are many characters in Dickens, Thackeray[1] and George Eliot who, like their omniscient authors, are given to sighing over the past. Even in the nostalgically lyric lament of 'During Wind and Rain', Hardy seems to be aware of the selective powers of the sentimental imagination, and in his novels, where he is free to ring the changes on many different attitudes of recollection and where the critical spirit has full play, he dramatizes the types of memory in such a way as to analyse and express his sense of the values of the narrative imagination, inside and outside art.

Walter Benjamin has suggested that story-telling has come to an end and it is of course literally true that the custom of public story-telling no longer exists in our society. Hardy's story-tellers often narrate in routines and rituals that have passed away. There is only one professional story-teller, Ethelberta, in Hardy's novels, but there is a traditional place and a demand for formal and informal story-telling at weddings, funerals, dances and parties, in inns, at work, by the fire, in

---

[1] Though Thackeray is well aware that nostalgia is a dangerously self-indulgent, dimming emotion, and tries to inoculate his sentiments with irony and satire, the effect of his reminiscence is usually an intense regret for the dear dead past.

the dark. Even though Hardy is celebrating such rituals of narrative art through his story-tellers, the moral force of narrators and narrations persuades us that his interest in the narrative imagination is not restricted to the art of fiction or even to the social rituals of public story-telling. His interest is not primarily social or technical, but ethical. The moral imagination expressed, positively and negatively, in Hardy's reminiscent characters, is scarcely of a kind that can die out. It involves efforts, successes, or failures in understanding, ordering and loving. Story-telling is valued in Hardy, as an activity of mind and heart. His story-tellers are bound neither by the past or the future. After George Eliot it is heartening to meet Hardy's ability to imagine people who look back without turning into pillars of salt. His novels are the sadder for the presence of such people, since there is usually some pain in the contemplation of 'the ruins of past purpose'.

In *The Trumpet-Major* Hardy kills the story of the future in many ways but most violently and decorously in the last sentence which takes John Loveday out of the door on to the battlefield and into his grave, in the very last movement of the novel's pendulum swing of 'seventy or eighty years'. Hardy also kills the story of the past with equal force. For a novelist who was a historian, he showed courage and insight in making Tess refuse the history lessons so helpfully offered by Angel Clare:

> 'Never mind about the lords and ladies. Would you like to take up any course of study—history, for example?'
>
> 'Sometimes I feel I don't want to know anything more about it than I know already.'
>
> 'Why not?'
>
> 'Because what's the use of learning that I am one of a long row only—finding out that there is set down in some old book somebody just like me, and to know that I shall only act her part; making me sad, that's all. The best is not to remember that your nature and your past doings have been just like thousands' and thousands', and that your coming life and doings 'll be like thousands' and thousands'.'
>
> (*Tess of the d'Urbervilles*, ch. xix)

Tess's reasons for rejecting history are peculiar to her situation, since she and her family have been wrecked by a story of the past, but she is recognizing in a justifiably desperate way that sad sameness of human life which Hardy often contemplates with equanimity. He is one of the few novelists who can not only look back at the past calmly but with a deep and various understanding of what that act can entail. He resembles Timothy Fairway in *The Return of the Native*, who contemplates his past, and that of others, with remarkable steadiness:

'Ah, well; he was looking for the earth some months afore he went. At that time women used to run for smocks and gown pieces at Greenhill Fair, and my wife that is now, being a long-legged slittering maid, hardly husband-high, went with the rest of the maidens, for 'a was a good runner afore she got so heavy. When she came home I said—we were then just beginning to walk together—"What have ye got, my honey?" "I've won—well I've won—a gown piece," says she, her colours coming up in a moment. 'Tis a smock for a crown, I thought; and so it turned out. Ay, when I think what she'll say to me now without a mossel of red in her face, it do seem strange that 'a wouldn't say such a little thing then... However, then she went on, and that's what made me bring up the story. "Well, whatever clothes I've won, white or figured, for eyes to see or for eyes not to see" ('a could do a pretty stroke of modesty in those days), "I'd sooner have lost it than seen what I have. Poor Mr Yeobright was took bad directly he reached the fairground, and was forced to go home again." That was the last time he ever went out of the parish.' (ch. v)

In *The Woodlanders* Hardy has his own fine explanation of the time-span he chooses for his retrospective fiction. To cast back to the near past allows the reminiscent novelist to draw on real reminiscences:

The house was of no marked antiquity, yet of a well-advanced age; older than a stale novelty, but no canonized antique; faded, not hoary; looking at you from the still distinct middle-distance of the early Georgian time, and awakening on that account the instincts of reminiscence more decidedly than the remoter, and far grander, memorials which have to speak from the misty reaches of mediaevalism. The faces, dress, passions, gratitudes, and revenges of the great-great-grandfathers and grandmothers who had been the first to gaze from those rectangular windows, and had stood under that keystoned doorway, could be divined and measured by homely standards of to-day. It was a house in whose reverberations queer old personal tales were yet audible if properly listened for; and not, as with those of the castle and cloister, silent beyond the possibility of echo. (ch. iv)

Hardy can use the strength of memory to define the strength of fantasy. Fitzpiers is driven by isolation and ennui to construct his circumstantial but impossible dream of love, with scenes and dialogues in which Grace turns out to be mistress of the manor, and Hardy reflects that a deeply-rooted sense of the past preserves us from too great a susceptibility to rootless and powerful fantasies:

> Winter in a solitary house in the country, without society, is tolerable, nay, even enjoyable and delightful, given certain conditions; but these are not the conditions which attach to the life of a professional man who drops down into such a place by mere accident. They were present to the lives of Winterborne, Melbury, and Grace; but not to the doctor's. They are old association—an almost exhaustive biographical or historical acquaintance with every object, animate and inanimate, within the observer's horizon. He must know all about those invisible ones of the days gone by, whose feet have traversed the fields which look so grey from his windows; recall whose creaking plough has turned those sods from time to time; whose hands planted the trees that form a crest to the opposite hill; whose horses and hounds have torn through that underwood; what birds affect that particular brake; what bygone domestic dramas of love, revenge, or disappointment have been enacted in the cottages, the mansion, the street or on the green. The spot may have beauty, grandeur, salubrity, convenience; but if it lacks memories it will ultimately pall upon him who settles there without opportunity of intercourse with his kind. (ch. xvii)

Hardy is one of the few novelists to say and show much of the importance of living in the present, without leaning too hard on either the story of the past or the story of the future. Since the form of fiction is especially well-endowed in memory and fantasy, tradition and desire, it tends to be engrossed with those narrative forms. A *Bildungsroman* like *Middlemarch* or *A Portrait of the Artist as a Young Man* may divide its action almost entirely between recollection and anticipation, and say very little about living in the present. But living in the present is something Hardy praises and explains with exceptional clarity. *The Mayor of Casterbridge* ends with a remarkable picture of a human being refusing to dwell too much in the past or the future. Elizabeth-Jane Farfrae could easily have been bound by the last will and testament of Michael Henchard but Henchard did not intend to bind her, and she knows it. She takes him at his word and accedes to his wish not to be remembered, at least not with pain and remorse:

> What Henchard had written in the anguish of his dying was respected as far as practicable by Elizabeth-Jane, though less from a sense of the sacredness of last words, as such, than from her independent knowledge that the man who wrote them meant what he said. She knew the directions to be a piece of the same stuff that his whole life was made of, and hence were not to be tampered with to give herself a mournful pleasure, or her husband credit for large-heartedness.
>
> All was over at last, even her regrets for having misunderstood him on his last visit, for not having searched him out sooner, though these were deep and sharp for a good while. From this time forward Elizabeth-Jane found herself in a latitude of calm weather...
>
> (ch. xlv)

It is hard to imagine Louisa Gradgrind, Gwendolen Harleth or Isabel Archer ceasing to feel deep sharp regrets and living so freely and thankfully in the present. Henry James sometimes seems to hover on the verge of realizing that a historical imperative can be as destructive as moral amnesia, as in Isabel Archer's image of the fragility of preciousness,[2] but as a rule his characters are even more time-bound than George Eliot's. Hardy knows that life goes on, that regret for the past, however 'deep and sharp', must come to an end. Elizabeth-Jane's dispassionate and wise refusal to live in the past is of a piece with her moderate gratitude for the present, and her cautious expectations of the future:

> That she was not demonstratively thankful was no fault of hers. Her experience had been of a kind to teach her, rightly or wrongly, that the doubtful honour of a brief transit through a sorry world hardly called for effusiveness...(ch. xlv)

She actually has an answer to the problem of living without paying too heavy a debt either to past or future:

[2] *The Portrait of a Lady,* ch. liii.

...the finer movements of her nature found scope in discovering to the narrow-lived ones around her the secret (as she had once learnt it) of making limited opportunities endurable; which she deemed to consist in the cunning enlargement, by a species of microscopic treatment, of those minute forms of satisfaction that offer themselves to everybody not in positive pain...(ch. xlv)

Making the most of our own minute forms of critical satisfaction, we may admit that Hardy does not always make his novels out of this remarkable adjustment to the present, but is, like his fellow-Victorians, often concerned with people in positive pain. Elizabeth-Jane's great discovery is seen to be central to the novel only at its end; it is a discovery of content which comes after loss and hardship, and it contrasts violently with the time-hauntedness of other characters in the novel. The wife-selling is a crucial event whose consequences explode in the future. The time-bound characters try to live in the present, but fail. As they try to make amends, adjustments, and new plans, they tell each other stories about the past and the future. The stories sometimes seem misleadingly candid in appearance, like Michael Henchard's ready public explanations of his vow of abstinence and Susan's explanation to Michael that she couldn't live happily with Newson once she discovered that the selling was neither solemn nor binding. Henchard, Susan and Lucetta are not reserved or reticent, but tend to withhold something crucial when they appear to be most frank and confiding. Even Leopold Bloom, who at the end of the Blooms' day tells Molly so much, withholds one or two things, and Hardy only endows characters with complete candour if they have nothing worth hiding.

In *The Mayor of Casterbridge*, the story-telling about the past mostly consists in half-truths, half-tellings and silences. Susan tells Elizabeth-Jane and Michael Henchard only a part of the truth about the past, though she completes her story sooner than she intended in the carelessly sealed letter which Henchard carelessly opens. Lucetta tells significantly different versions of her story to Elizabeth-Jane, Farfrae and Henchard. The characters show that familiar mixture of disclosure and reticence, candour and silence, which marks those letters to Miss Lonelyhearts about other people's problems, those veiled confidences where pronouns replace proper names, and those truncated versions of the whole truth which allow us relief in telling while still keeping something of our secrets. But *The Mayor of Casterbridge* is not only concerned with incomplete and frustrated narrative exchange. On one occasion it shows the freedom we traditionally feel when we confide in the stranger in the train. Farfrae is Henchard's ideal listener. He is a stranger, he is only passing through Casterbridge, he seems congenial, detached and well disposed, and he turns up conveniently just at the moment when the various strands of Henchard's past have become inconveniently knotted. Henchard's isolation and his practical need make him turn to Farfrae, saying: 'But, damn it all, I am a lonely man, Farfrae; I have nobody else to speak to; and why shouldn't I tell it to 'ee?' (ch. xii).

Farfrae is first indifferent, then concerned, then willing to advise: 'Can ye no' take her and live with her, and make some amends?' (ch. xii). His genuine feeling comes out in a sympathetic comparison, as he links their lives, 'Ah, now, I never feel like it', which deepens further into a sympathy for what lies beyond 'his simple experiences', eventually moving on to some feeling for the melancholy situation of the two women. The experience is articulated and appreciated in the last sincere and formal exchange, Henchard saying gratefully that he feels some relief, Farfrae saying warmly, 'And I am sorry for ye!'. What the reader has observed, the teller and the listener also understand.

The telling and the listening join the feelings of the two men. Strangers come closer to each other and cease to be strangers, getting to know each other by the exchange of stories. Even Farfrae's laconic references to his own life convey a little about his reserve, inexperience and candour. The need to tell and listen is commonly recognized in Victorian fiction and there are times and circumstances in which the story-teller in search of a listener feels, like the lover requiring an object, that anything will do. For Esther Summerson, it is a doll, for Little Dorrit, it is Maggy, for Paul Dombey, it is Toots. Sometimes a dumb or stupid listener is easier than a sensitive and clever one, but Dickens's desperate children would really like someone better. Like Dickens, Hardy is interested in the relationships created through story-telling, and in this novel he generally prefers incomplete or thwarted communication. The conversation between Henchard and Farfrae is rare in its communion but success is partly there as a prologue to failure and separateness. It is usually dangerous to confide in Casterbridge. Newson confides frankly in Henchard, and is misled in return. Susan confides in an acquaintance in Canada, discovers that she was wrong to feel bound to Newson, and her settled life is disrupted. This is not the only novel in which confidences don't work well. Tess feels encouraged to confide in Angel when he confides in her, not reckoning with the double standard in sexual confession. Sue Bridehead is an intelligent and candid woman who torments her men by telling them too much. Hardy knows that we can get to know each other by telling and listening, but he knows that story-telling is a difficult and dangerous business.

He also knows that it can be used for deceit and gain, but he is not much better at showing deception, lies and false performance than at gossip and scandal. *The Hand of Ethelberta* is about a professional career in story-telling which is forced upon Ethelberta by a society in which honesty is unprofitable. Like Stendhal's Julien Sorel, Thackeray's Becky Sharp and Gissing's Godwin Peake, Ethelberta decides on an elaborate deception in order to survive and succeed. Using Hardy's own ability to put aside romantic zest, Ethelberta sets aside affection and sincerity to get money and status, first by a profession, then by marriage. What is interesting, though insufficiently undramatized, is the relation between the personal story-telling and the false and spell-binding public story-telling, which she optimistically hopes may break the restrictions of family reading. (One of her reviewers observes that we have had novel-reading in public and now have novel-telling.) The public story-telling succeeds only temporarily, because of its novelty, and because she has earned enough notoriety as a poet to draw the public to her readings in the hope of some pungent revelation of the innermost events of her life. Eventually the self-revelation comes about, for Ethelberta decides to turn fiction into truth, and when tactlessly requested to perform at a dinner-party, embarks on the extraordinary story of her own life, which breaks down to merge into the present as she wins a listener for a husband. There is not much in the story which shows Hardy's ability to psychologize narrative. Ethelberta's performances in life and art work together effectively; we are told that both are aspects of her imaginative power, and she can't move from one room to another without making an interesting story of it. Hardy also glimpses the possibility of life being affected by performance,[3] so that what she does in life prepares and fits her for the

---

[3] For a fuller and more subtle example we can go to Thackeray's treatment of the sentimental self-corruption of Pendennis and Blanche Amory in *Pendennis*.

professional narration, which in its turn enables her to tell a story for gain in personal relations:

> It was in performing this feat that Ethelberta seemed first to discover in herself the full power of that self-command which further onward in her career more and more impressed her as a singular possession, until at last she was tempted to make of it many fantastic uses, leading to results that affected more households than her own. A talent for demureness under difficulties without the cold-bloodedness which renders such a bearing natural and easy, a face and hand reigning unmoved outside a heart by nature turbulent as a wave, is a constitutional arrangement much to be desired by people in general; yet, had Ethelberta been framed with less of that gift in her, her life might have been more comfortable as an experience, and brighter as an example, though perhaps duller as a story. (ch. xvi)

Hardy observes Ethelberta's three sources of inspiration: in childhood romancing where reality and fiction are mingled; in Eastern story-telling, public, romantic, and lucrative; and in the verisimilitude of Defoe, Ethelberta's proclaimed model for a fiction related as truth, in the right tones and in the right language. 'I am going to talk De Foe on a subject of my own', she tells Christopher Julian. Unfortunately the reference to Defoe shows up the absence in her of a language of feeling which in Hardy's best novels colours and characterizes the story-telling. Ethelberta's public stories are not put into words. The brief extract from a rehearsal before her brothers and sisters deceives Christopher Julian, but is ludicrous in style and content. Hardy even misses the opportunity of distinguishing the final true story from the earlier fictions, and it almost looks as if the novel is about its own wooden and implausible narrative pot-boiling. There was no doubt a certain pleasure for the author in making wry jokes about the public's fickleness, the writer's need for money, and the automatic biographical speculations of the reviewers. But *The Hand of Ethelberta* unfortunately shows what might have been his self-conscious and most formal analysis of story-telling arrested at the stage of an unimpassioned idea. His dry suggestion that Ethelberta's performance has more art than inspiration is all too resonant.

Yet Hardy can show perfect telling and listening, and show it perfectly. It is to be found amongst his minor characters, the choric story-tellers. He makes lavish use of these onlookers who see so much of the game, from the survivors in *Jude the Obscure*, Arabella and the Widow Edlin, to the great choric characters like Timothy Fairway, Robert Penny, Michael Mail and Reuben Dewy, but none of them is omniscient or influential. They provide a singular commentary on the main action less by reflection and analysis than by the moral quality of their imagination. Their story-telling is sometimes a commentary on the main action, sometimes uninvolved in it, but always casts revealing lights or shadows.

The best dispassionate narration comes in *Under the Greenwood Tree*, a good-tempered and untragic idyll. The story-telling is often freely anecdotal, accumulating local history in splendid self-contained jokes and grotesque reminiscence to reveal certain tendencies of Hardy's narrative imagination with particular incisiveness. One thing is certain, Hardy is no good at showing the *mauvaise langue*. His characters tell their stories with charity, enthusiasm, some moderate pride in their story-telling, and an almost total absence of back-biting. When Michael Mail tells his most musical 'circumstance' of chewing fried liver and lights in the Three Mariners in time to the brass band outside, Mrs Dewy objects to the coarse taste of the story and her husband, one of the most cheerful and resilient of Hardy's husbands, responds neatly to reflect his author's lack of sententious fuss:

> 'Well, now,' said Reuben, with decisive earnestness, 'that sort o' coarse touch that's so upsetting to Ann's feelings is to my mind a recommendation; for it do always prove a story to be true. And for the same reason, I like a story with a bad moral. My sonnies, all true stories have a coarse touch or a bad moral, depend upon't. If the story-tellers could ha' got decency and good morals from true stories, who'd have troubled to invent parables?' (ch. xiii)

This attitude to morality is very commonly found in Hardy's stoutly sane story-tellers and listeners, though of course there is a sense in which their anecdotes are parables too, of a highly imaginative kind and illustrating a highly imaginative morality. What they are interested in is life, which may be expected to be coarse or immoral. Toughness and tolerance is found not only in the choruses. In *The Trumpet-Major*, Bob Loveday responds irritably to his brother's news that Matilda, his betrothed, is a well-known camp-follower, saying that she would have been good enough for him, and he might never have found out. In *The Mayor of Casterbridge*, when Newson is told that Henchard has lied about Elizabeth-Jane's death, he remarks with great good temper that the lie wasn't so bad, and 'not ten words'. When Hardy tries to use the dangers of malignant story-telling, he does so weakly and undramatically. In *Desperate Remedies*, Owen and Cytherea Graye are supposed to be driven out of their home town by what is described as 'the shadow of a cloud' of public talk, but the only actual excerpt given is feeble: 'Rashness; they would have made a better income in Hocbridge, where they are known! There is no doubt that they would' (ch. i). The gossip is described rather than shown, and Hardy falls back significantly on grotesque visual impressions of the malignant talkers, instead of imagining their words, tones, and feelings:

> Their few acquaintances passed them hurriedly. Ancient pot-wallopers, and thriving shopkeepers, in their intervals of leisure, stood at their shop-doors—their toes hanging over the edge of the step, and their obese waists hanging over their toes—and in discourses with friends on the pavement, formulated the course of the improvident, and reduced the children's prospects to a shadow-like attenuation. The sons of these men (who wore breastpins of a sarcastic kind, and smoked humorous pipes) stared at Cytherea with a stare unmitigated by any of the respect that had formerly softened it. (ch. i)

There are convincing comments on the response to gossip, such as a remark on the difference between individual bad opinion and a collective exchange of ideas. A hundred people, he reflects, may know 'our skeleton-closet's whereabouts' but what is 'distressing to the nerves' is collective chat. This thin and vague rendering of collective opinion is not just the result of immaturity in *Desperate Remedies*, because the same deficiency is found in the more thoroughly and profoundly imagined *The Mayor of Casterbridge*. Here Hardy speaks strongly of 'a miasmic scandal' which ends in the skimmity-ride for Lucetta, and he seems to be taking considerable pains to do better this time with a rendering of the social group of evil talkers. They are a seedy lot who frequent Mixen Lane and drink in the inn called Peter's Finger; amongst them are ex-criminals and a landlady who has been to gaol. But once Hardy gets close to imagined individuals, even characters meant for typicality, he becomes vague about the details of backbiting. The general trend of talk moves indeed towards tolerance, praise, and friendly generosity. Two members of the crew of drinkers are a poacher and an ex-keeper, and as Hardy uses them to invoke a shady past, his tones rise into irrepressible life. The past itself, the poacher's skill, and the cleverness of the keeper's wife, are enjoyed, the enjoyment taking Hardy's typical form of amused appreciation. Nothing could be less like miasmic scandalizing than this:

> 'Dos't mind how you could jerk a trout ashore with a bramble, and not ruffle the stream, Charl?' a deposed keeper was saying. ' 'Twas at that I caught 'ee once, if you can mind?'
> 'That can I. But the worst larry for me was that pheasant business at Yalbury Wood. Your wife swore false that time, Joe—O, by Gad, she did—there's no denying it.'
> 'How was that?' asked Jopp.
> 'Why—Joe closed wi' me, and we rolled down together, close to his garden hedge. Hearing the noise, out ran his wife with the oven pyle, and it being dark under the trees she couldn't see which was uppermost. "Where beest thee, Joe, under or top?" she screeched. "O—under, by Gad!" says he. She then began to rap down upon my skull, back and ribs, with the pyle till we'd roll over again. "Where beest now, dear Joe, under or top?" she'd scream again. By George, 'twas through her I was took!' (ch. xxxiv)

After this conversation which shows so inefficiently the unsavouriness of the low company, it is not surprising that the opening of Lucetta's letters and the planned skimmity-ride, 'I say, what a good foundation for a skimmity-ride', is feeble too. Where Hardy's plot demands malicious gossip and scandal, he tries to show it, but the necessary backbiters turn out to be kind souls and good hearts in disguise. Even the skimmity-ride is engagingly described as 'the funniest thing under the sun!'. The Casterbridge choir is shocked at Henchard's request that they sing the one hundred and ninth psalm because it is so comminatory that they can't believe that the psalmist knew what he was doing when he wrote it. Their dislike of calumny in art is characteristic of Hardy's strength in charity and weakness in defamation.

The characters in *The Mayor of Casterbridge*, where public opinion is so crucial, speak tolerantly, and wellwish more than they backbite. Mrs Stannidge objects to Farfrae's courtship of Elizabeth-Jane ('and he a pillow of the town') but this is brief and feeble compared with Christopher Coney's spirited defence:

> 'No, ma'am, no wonder at all. 'Tis she that's a stooping to he— that's my opinion. A widow man—whose first wife was no credit to him—what is it for a young perusing woman, that's her own mistress and well-liked? But as a neat patching up of things I see much good in it. When a man have put up a tomb of best marble-stone to the other one, as he've done, and weeped his fill, and thought it all over, and said to hisself, "T'other took me in; I knowed this one first; she's a sensible piece for a partner, and there's no faithful woman in high life now";—well, he may do worse than not to take her, if she's tender-inclined.' (ch. xliii)

Even though Coney's defence of Elizabeth-Jane begins with criticism of Farfrae, this is slight and does not last long. Hardy is far from being sloppily tolerant and he does not want us to see Coney, or anyone else in his crowd-scenes, as priggishly charitable. He follows the defence of Farfrae's second marriage with a reminder that we must not weigh it too heavily, since the defenders are typically interested in looking out for festive occasions and are really very superficial in their interest in their fellow-men:

> Thus they talked at the Mariners. But we must guard against a too liberal use of the conventional declaration that a great sensation was caused by the prospective event, that all the gossips' tongues were set wagging thereby, and so on, even though such a declaration might lend some 'éclat' to the career of our poor only heroine. When all has been said about busy rumourers, a superficial and temporary thing is the interest of anybody in affairs which do not directly touch them. It would be a truer representation to say that Casterbridge (ever excepting the nineteen young ladies) looked up for a moment at the news, and withdrawing its attention, went on labouring and victualling, bringing up its children, and burying its dead, without caring a tittle for Farfrae's domestic plans. (ch. xliii)

Even in this novel, where rumour changes lives, Hardy tries to persuade us that gossip is seldom very malignant or powerful. The memory of the crowd is often weak: the unforgettable furmity-woman says she would not have remembered anything so banal as a wife-selling if Henchard had not returned to give her the message for

Susan. Village gossip is faintly shown and seldom made influential, unlike the gossip in George Eliot's *Scenes of Clerical Life* or *The Mill on the Floss* or *Middlemarch* where the lives of the Bartons, Maggie Tulliver and Philip Wakem, are transformed by idle talk and gossip, where marriages are made and unmade by what the town says, where even a kind man like Caleb Garth hastens to dissociate himself from Bulstrode at the first breath of scandal. George Eliot may have had good personal reasons for her strong feelings about gossip, but whatever the reasons behind Hardy's charity, charity it certainly is.

His choric narrators are benevolent and he takes great pains to make sure that their tolerance is individualized in all its aspects of humour, compassion and imaginative praise. It is not an automatically switched-on charity, never a priggish, sententious or cloistered virtue, but clearly seen to emerge from the trials of hard experience. The two main speakers in the chorus of Casterbridge, Christopher Coney and Solomon Longways, are delighted and amazed by Farfrae's song of national sentiment, remarking on their own entire lack of feeling for their 'ain countree.' These worthies, 'only too prone to shut up their emotions with caustic words', briefly summarize Casterbridge as:

'. . . a old, hoary place o' wickedness, by all account.' Tis recorded in history that we rebelled against the king one or two hundred years ago, in the time of the Romans, and that lots of us was hanged on Gallows Hill, and quartered, and our different jints sent about the country like butcher's meat; and for my part I can well believe it.'
(ch. viii)

Christopher Coney adds his observation that:

'. . . it wasn't worth your while on our account, for, as Maister Billy Wills says, we be bruckle folk here—the best o' us hardly honest sometimes, what with hard winters, and so many mouths to fill, and God-a'mighty sending his little taties so terrible small to fill 'em with. We don't think about flowers and fair faces, not we—except in the shape o'cauliflowers and pigs' chaps.' (ch. viii)

Such candid, rough but generous self-depreciation is a characteristic tone in Hardy's choric story-tellers. They all have qualification for wise commentary in the ability to distinguish knowledge from hearsay, and a disqualification for gossip, which grows by being unscholarly in references and extravagant in its claims to knowledge. Hardy's story-tellers also weigh rights and wrongs, to create a careful balance-sheet. Though the direction of their feelings is unmistakably benign, they do not sentimentalize human conduct any more than they sentimentalize the past. When they tell stories of the dead, they speak traditionally in terms of praise, but a praise so passionate, precise and particular, that the sense of the complete human being rises astonishingly from the brief anecdote. The chorus is made up of working people, their wit native or traditional, their arts those of conversation and anecdote. The story-telling is collective and oral, but individual biographers stand out within the group which sustains, constructs, inspires, and confirms the history and the biography. They imprint their identity on the mind and typify the stoicism and humour of a class: perceptive, conservative, grim and caustic.

Timothy Fairway plays a more prominent solo part in *The Return of the Native* than any other member of Hardy's narrative chorus. He is in the prime of life, able to look back, as we have seen, with a certain ripeness and coolness on his courting days. He seems never to have been a green hopeful like Dick Dewy and one of his best stories makes it plain that his caustic scepticism started early:

> 'Ah, Humph, well I can mind when I was married how I zid thy father's mark staring me in the face as I went to put down my name. He and your mother were the couple married just before we were, and there stood thy father's cross with arms stretched out like a great banging scarecrow. What a terrible black cross that was—thy father's very likeness in en! To save my soul I couldn't help laughing when I zid en, though all the time I was as hot as dog days, what with the marrying, and what with the woman a-hanging to me, and what with Jack Changley and a lot more chaps grinning at me through the church window. But the next moment a strawmote would have knocked me down, for I called to mind that if thy father and mother had had high words once, they'd been at it twenty times since they'd been man and wife, and I zid myself as the next poor stunpoll to get into the same mess... Ah—well, what a day 'twas!' (ch. iii)

When we meet him on Egdon Heath, the heat of youth has cooled, but Hardy makes it clear that he is still an active man, fond of food and even fonder of drink, liable to seize the hefty Susan Nunsuch and whirl her into a wild dance with a light-hearted but resonant reminder of the past, 'you and I will have a jig—hey, my honey?—before 'tis quite too dark to see how well-favoured you be still, though so many summers have passed since your husband, a son of a witch, snapped you up from me'. When Christian Cantle complains of being rebuffed in a marriage proposal, Fairway is laconically appreciative:

> 'Not encouraging, I own,' said Fairway. ' "Get out of my sight, you slack-twisted, slim-looking maphrotight fool," is rather a hard way of saying "No." But even that might be overcome by time and patience, so as to let a few grey hairs show themselves in the hussy's head.' (ch. iii)

The same poker-faced teasing and sympathy is implicit in his brief, terrible ghost story about the little boy who saw the red ghost and his good-natured cynicism about giving the supposed newly-weds a song: 'When folks are just married 'tis as well to look glad o't, since looking sorry won't unjoin 'em.'

He is part of a brilliantly contrasted group, which includes the endearing, feeble, effeminate Christian Cantle, and the flighty old fool, Grandfer Cantle. The Cantles tell their stories with a well-meaning, dim perfection and a vivid language, unable to see the unflattering implications. Timothy interprets, explains and moves into his own virtuoso performances, marked by control, intelligence, and an ability to see precisely what the story means, even if it is a story against himself. He is capable of the tough and disarming enjoyment of putting himself down. A combination of criticism and self-deflation is part of the charm and surprise of his stories. He criticizes institutions and individuals implicitly, bringing to the story-telling and listening his sympathy and praise. It is he who ensures the reader's appreciation of the odd charms of Grandfer Cantle and his youngest son, and he is sincerely apologetic when one of his stories provokes Christian to identify himself as the man no woman would have. His story-telling is marked by proverbs, condensed anecdotes and histories, 'Aesop's fables in a sentence'.[4] 'No moon, no man', confirms the gloomy diagnosis of Christian Cantle's lack of manly powers.

Fairway can stand as the type of Hardy's strong and intelligent story-tellers. He chronicles the past without sighing for it, but in a comic form that neighbours elegy. His narrative tone is too appreciative for cynicism, too thorough for idealism, too enthusiastic for stoicism

---

[4] This is the Reverend Mr Irwine's phrase in *Adam Bede*.

but too courageously committed for irony. He is a mirror for the author, as Marlow is for Conrad, but standing at an oblique angle to the action. One the one occasion when he plays an important role in exposition, as he tells the story of Mrs Yeobright's forbidding of the banns, Hardy writes an appreciation of his personal qualities as narrator, which cunningly breaks up and disguises the block of exposition. We get a vivid sense of the scene, the group, and Timothy himself:

'I not only happened to be there,' said Fairway, with a fresh collection of emphasis, 'but I was sitting in the same pew as Mis'ess Yeobright. And though you may not see it as such, it fairly made my blood run cold to hear her. Yes, it is a curious thing; but it made my blood run cold, for I was close at her elbow.' The speaker looked round upon the bystanders, now drawing closer to hear him, with his lips gathered tighter than ever in the rigorousness of his descriptive moderation.

' 'Tis a serious job to have things happen to 'ee there,' said a woman behind.

' "Ye are to declare it," was the parson's words,' Fairway continued. 'And then up stood a woman at my side—a-touching of me. "Well, be blasted if there isn't Mis'es Yeobright a-standing up," I said to myself. Yes, neighbours, though I was in the temple of prayer that's what I said. 'Tis against my conscience to swear and curse in company, and I hope any woman here will overlook it. Still what I did say I did say, and 'twould be a lie if I didn't own it.'

'So 'twould, neighbour Fairway.'

' "Be blasted if there isn't Mis'ess Yeobright a-standing up," I said,' the narrator repeated, giving out the bad word with the same passionless severity of face as before, which proved how entirely necessity and not gusto had to do with the iteration. 'And the next thing I heard was, "I forbid the banns," from her. "I'll speak to you after the service," said the parson, in quite a homely way—yes, turning all at once into a common man no holier than you or I. Ah, her face was pale! Maybe you can call to mind that monument in Weatherbury church—the cross-legged soldier that have had his arm knocked away by the schoolchildren? Well, he would about have matched that woman's face, when she said, "I forbid the banns." '

The audience cleared their throats and tossed a few stalks into the fire, not because these deeds were urgent, but to give themselves time to weigh the moral of the story.

'I'm sure when I heard they'd been forbid I felt as glad as if anybody had gied me sixpence,' said an earnest voice—that of Olly Dowden, a woman who lived by making heath brooms, or besoms. Her nature was to be civil to enemies as well as to friends, and grateful to all the world for letting her remain alive.

'And now the maid have married him just the same,' said Humphrey.

'After that Mis'ess Yeobright came round and was quite agreeable,' Fairway resumed, with an unheeding air, to show that his words were no appendage to Humphrey's, but the result of independent reflection. (ch. iii)

Timothy's stories individualize him, but also create a sense of community. His narrative arises naturally from the flow of conversation, commenting, recalling and picking up naturally from other people's remarks and immediate events.

He is usually not telling the main story, but dozens of small stories that create a moral environment for the central action. Details about him are given: he has a firm figure, is a polite guest, arriving late, in time for things to have settled down, is sharply interested in people, and caustically not displeased with life. He has taken everything into his wide glance, without repugnance. As a story-teller he shows similar firmness, energy, enjoyment, and confident consideration for his listeners and his subjects. He is sufficiently pleased with his own powers to exercise them decisively, but never obnoxiously, like some of Dickens's exhibitionist narrators. Hardy does not show story-tellers who are bores or con-men, and his best tellers are sufficiently powerful for their pleasure in story-telling to be thoroughly justified. But despite the personal character of the narration, its impact is essentially social. Fairway narrates for his supper at Wildeve's house and at Mrs Yeobright's Christmas party. Wildeve's thinly disguised boredom reflects on his own selfish spirit. Fairway is happily and courteously holding forth in celebration of past and present, praising Mr Yeobright in a good wedding-guest's story. It is not an exclusive narrative, but makes room for the collaboration of Sam the turf-cutter. At times the narrative becomes a duet, and as it freely quotes public opinion, there is the sense that the benign Timothy is speaking on behalf of a benign community:

'Well,' said Timothy Fairway, feeling demands upon his praise in some form or other, ''tis a worthy thing to be married, Mr. Wildeve; and the woman you've got is a dimant, so says I. Yes,' he continued, to Grandfer Cantle, raising his voice so as to be heard through the partition, 'her father (inclining his head towards the inner room) was as good a feller as ever lived. He always had his great indignation ready against anything under-hand.'

'Is that very dangerous?' said Christian.

'And there were few in these parts that were upsides with him,' said Sam. 'Whenever a club walked he'd play the clarinet in the band that marched before 'em as if he'd never touched anything but a clarinet all his life. And then, when they got to church door he'd throw down the clarinet, mount the gallery, snatch up the bass viol, and rozum away as if he'd never played anything but a bass viol. Folk would say—folk that knowed what a true stave was—"Surely, surely that's never the same man that I saw handling the clarinet so masterly by now!" '

'I can mind it,' said the furze cutter. ' 'Twas a wonderful thing that one body could hold it all and never mix the fingering.'

'There was Kingsbere church likewise,' Fairway recommenced, as one opening a new vein of the same mine of interest....

'He used to walk over there of a Sunday afternoon to visit his old acquaintance Andrew Brown, the first clarinet there; a man good enough, but rather screechy in his music, if you can mind?'

' ''A was.'

'And neighbour Yeobright would take Andrey's place for some part of the service, to let Andrey have a bit of a nap, as any friend would naturally do.'

'As any friend would,' said Grandfer Cantle, the other listeners expressing the same accord by the shorter way of nodding their heads.

'No sooner was Andrey asleep and the first whiff of neighbour Yeobright's wind had got inside Andrey's clarinet than everyone in church felt in a moment there was a great soul among 'em. All heads would turn, and they'd say, "Ah, I thought 'twas he!" One

Sunday I can well mind—a bass viol day that time, and Yeobright had brought his own. 'Twas the Hundred and thirty-third to "Lydia"; and when they'd come to "Ran down his beard and o'er his robes its costly moisture shed," neighbour Yeobright, who had just warmed to his work, drove his bow into them strings that glorious grand that he e'en a'most sawed the bass viol into two pieces. Every winder in church rattled as if 'twere a thunderstorm. Old Pa'son Williams lifted his hands in his great, holy surplice as natural as if he'd been in common clothes, and seemed to say to hisself, "O for such a man in our parish!" But not a soul in Kingsbere could hold a candle to Yeobright.'

'Was it quite safe when the winder shook?' Christian inquired.

He received no answer, all for the moment sitting rapt in admiration of the performance described. As with Farinelli's singing before the princesses, Sheridan's renowned Begum Speech, and other such examples, the fortunate condition of its being forever lost to the world invested the deceased Mr. Yeobright's *tour de force* on that memorable afternoon with a cumulative glory which comparative criticism, had that been possible, might considerably have shorn down. (ch. v)

The story is mobile, yet keeps a unity. It describes the dead man in a memorial anecdote which praises praise. It is a sensitive appreciation of a man and his skills, like a good funeral oration or obituary, the appreciation finding a solemn conclusion in the reply to Christian's question, 'D'ye think he had great pain when 'a died?': 'O no—quite different. Nor any pain of mind. He was lucky enough to be God A'mighty's own man.' This is a story-telling compounded of ritual and individual art.

Hardy formalizes history and values. He exhibits not only the tolerance and traditions of the community in which Eustacia and Wildeve and Clym live, with frustration and friction, but also the rebellion against such stability. We feel the need Clym has to put down his old roots again into its rich and stable strength, the impatience of Eustacia and Wildeve. Timothy is created to display a simple, straightforward, undemanding life, without tragic problems, without rebellion, and one which adjusts to the inescapable pains of aging and disillusionment. His story-telling is a medium for Timothy's generous imagination and participation. He has a stability and a limitation which the other characters cannot share, but he has art and intelligence also. It would be hard to think of a more appropriately quiet and implicit way of handling an admirable minor character's life. When George Eliot attempts the same thing, as with Caleb Garth, she finds it necessary to analyse and praise explicitly. But Timothy's still yet stirring life is expressed wholly in the stories he tells, chiefly about other people, but with scope for direct and indirect autobiography. This disengagement is revealing. Mrs Gaskell and George Eliot also piece together people's lives in a natural-seeming, slow and quiet way. The story of Miss Matty in *Cranford* is gradually accumulated through the stories and secrets she tells to Mary. Bartle Massey, a minor character in *Adam Bede*, is given substance by a shadowy past modelled with deliberate sketchiness through what is, and what is not, disclosed. Hardy's way is to put his piecemeal narrative into his choruses, where it acts as a frame or foil for the more momentous and fully realized lives of other people, and reveals itself with a dignified and suitable reticence. The background story of ordinary lives is not anonymous but highly representative, stretching suggestively into past and future, but not in a sad line like that of the imagined ancestresses of Tess. Timothy's is a warm yet caustic story of warm yet caustic survivors. The rambling stories are deceptively wayward, both within themselves and as a series strung together by incident, occasion and character. The story of Timothy Fairway and other characters of his kind makes an obverse pattern to the main pattern, an essential part of the whole fabric, though only fully visible when we closely scrutinize each stitch. George Eliot adopted Wordsworth's image of 'the underwood' from *The Excursion* as a motto for her tales of small people in *Adam Bede*, but she knows that Adam is 'not an average man'. Other characters, like Bartle Massey and Mrs Poyser, show her artist's eye for the imaginative powers possessed by so-called ordinary people. Hardy shows even more firmly, more reticently, and more obliquely, that no one is ordinary. I do not want to exaggerate the reticence; Timothy Fairway, Michael Mail and the Pennys are instances of people quietly created through their anecdotes, but the choruses also contain conspicuous grotesques, like the Cantles, Joseph Poorgrass, and Thomas Leaf. I would hesitate to use the word 'caricature' for these persons who are given such complete relationship with the whole community of character.

It is tempting to generalize about Hardy's narrators. Yet what is true of *The Return of the Native* is not true of *Jude the Obscure*, where the conflict of rebellion and conformity is treated differently, and where much less approval extends to sheer survival in such characters as Arabella and Vilbert. The triumph of *The Return of the Native* lies in its comprehension of the restless and tragic lives of Eustacia, Wildeve and Clym, and its equal comprehension of the untragic people who are not stupid, but who survive to enjoy life, like Elizabeth-Jane, though with even smaller gratifications. Their refusal to be tragic finds potent and properly understated expression in all those funny and solemn stories about love, marriage, courtship, death and growing old. This is the narrative of low demand and common sense, but neither the demand nor the sense is underrated. The result is a steady unpathetic portrayal of the process of history and destiny. We do not often feel in Hardy the presence of what Henry James finds necessary to fiction, the ministrations of fools to the intensities of others.[5] Hardy mixes wise men with his choruses of fools, and he is tender even of folly.

This tenderness is at its most impressive in the story-telling of *Under the Greenwood Tree*, where the community choir—chorus in both senses—is particularly and variously gifted in narrative power. This community values story, and employs it with zest and variety. The tone is sometimes sharp, as with Mrs Penny's story about her Midsummer-eve vision of her future husband:

> 'And a thing I never expected would come to pass, if you'll believe me, came to pass then,' continued Mrs Penny. 'Ah, the first spirit ever I see on a Midsummer-eve was a puzzle to me when he appeared, a hard puzzle, so say I!'
>
> 'So I should have fancied,' said Elias Spinks.
>
> 'Yes,' said Mrs Penny, throwing her glance into past times and talking on in a running tone of complacent abstraction, as if a listener were not a necessity. 'Yes; never was I in such a taking as on that Midsummer-eve! I sat up, quite determined to see if John Wildway was going to marry me or no. I put the bread-and-cheese and beer quite ready, as the witch's book ordered, and I opened the door, and I waited till the clock struck twelve, my nerves all alive and so strained that I could feel every one of 'em twitching like bell-wires. Yes, sure! and when the clock had struck, lo and behold

[5] The preface to *The Portrait of a Lady* (New York edition, 1913).

I could see through the door a *little small* man in the lane wi' a shoemaker's apron on.'

Here Mr Penny stealthily enlarged himself half an inch.

(pt. i, ch. viii)

The whole situation is imagined: the polite and easily ignored murmurs of Spinks, the discomfort of Penny, his expostulation: 'You needn't be so mighty particular about little and small!', and the over-confident rounding off, 'I've fancied you never knew better in your life; but I mid be mistaken', ignored as his wife lets her eyes 'stay idling on the past scenes just related, which were apparently visible to her in the centre of the room.' The stories are frequently stories told about marriage by the elders and Dick Dewy does from time to time feel surprised by the common theme of love's mortality, though blind to its implications. Experience tells its stories to innocence, but innocence is a bad listener.

They are often professional stories, like Penny's about the family foot of John Woodward's drowned brother, where the pain of death is neatly displaced by the shoemaker's ruling interest. In this group are also the many stories about music, which establish the skill, knowledge and enthusiasm of the choir. They relate through anecdote a history of parish music, like the stories of the coming of organs and the passing of serpents. Each instrument gets its story and the accounts of the icicle of spit on the clarinet and the parson's barrel-organ lead to the celebration of strings by the four string players, and the chorus of praise for 'such a divine thing as music'. The set of stories is itself a narrative harmony. Hardy gets great good humour out of these stories, which are usually excellent jokes, but he also uses them to establish the character and importance of the Mellstock Quire, and to establish particularly their tolerance and good nature.

Praise is even more emphatic in this novel than in *The Return of the Native* and though it is always sung in matter-of-fact tones, the matter-of-factness only serves to ground the praise more firmly in real life. Stories rise naturally from the doings of the characters. The stories of praise are often stories told in celebration of the history and use of objects, like Fancy Day's shoe and its family resemblance to her father's last, and the cider-barrel which Reuben Dewy has such trouble in opening. The very cider gets a story and the history of its making takes Reuben back to two kinds of apples and a particular place in an orchard. The story of the barrel is another example of speaking well of the dead, in this case, the remarkably tolerant praise of an unscrupulous seller, Sam Lawson, who sold the cask to Reuben, by telling a good story:

> 'This is a' old cask, and the wood's rotted away about the tap-hole. The husbird of a feller Sam Lawson—that ever I should call'n such, now he's dead and gone, poor heart!—took me in completely upon the feat of buying this cask. "Reub," says he—'a always used to call me plain Reub, poor old heart!—"Reub," he said says he, "that there cask, Reub, is as good as new; yes, good as new. 'Tis a wine-hogshead; the best port-wine in the commonwealth have been in that there cask; and you shall have en for ten shillens, Reub,"—'a said says he—"he's worth twenty, ay, five-and-twenty, if he's worth one; and an iron hoop or two put round en among the wood ones will make en worth thirty shillens of any man's money, if—..."' (pt. i, ch. ii)

Once more, the narration is collective. Mrs Dewy is scornful about her husband's gullibility and he makes an oblique but plainly offensive reply in agreement, which causes Michael Mail to tide over a 'critical point of affairs' with the distracting story about a nod to an auctioneer which brought him an unwanted 'feather-bed, bolster, and pillers'. Goodwill is present in the tactful turn of the stories and also in the underlying assent which is entirely lacking in moral fuss. Sam Lawson is praised, being dead, by the name 'poor heart', or 'poor old heart', and the story of his barrel, which specifies all the hoops Reuben has had to make for it, ends with a choric praise:

> 'Ah, Sam was a man,' said Mr Penny, contemplatively.
> 'Sam was!' said Bowman.
> 'Especially for a drap o' drink,' said the tranter.
> 'Good, but not religious-good,' suggested Mr Penny.
>
> (pt. i, ch. ii)

A remarkable feature of Hardy's story-telling is the way one tale breeds another, as if the community recognized narration as a ritual necessity. So the community pours forth its benign autobiography. Every object and every event has its propensity for narrative expression. Narrators quote and build on other stories. Timothy Fairway tells the tale of Mrs Yeobright's approbation of her husband, and so adds a vital detail to her character. The criticism of Eustacia is brightened by the appreciative forecast of the good fortune of her future husband. Hardy's story-tellers are good men, and their sprightly and potent characters, their ironic but tolerant sympathies are expressed and implied in their stories.

Perhaps the most impressive appearance of the social psychology and morality of Hardy's ritual narratives is in the last sight we get of the story-telling community in *Under the Greenwood Tree*. In the final chapter, Hardy creates a highly formal image of story-telling, as traditionally performed by the older people who sit under the beech-tree while the young ones dance. As always the sense of time and experience is strong and the physical scene thoroughly imagined, in gesture, motion and forms:

> Here the gaffers and gammers whose dancing days were over told stories of great impressiveness, and at intervals surveyed the advancing and retiring couples from the same retreat, as people on shore might be supposed to survey a naval engagement in the bay beyond; returning again to their tales when the pause was over. Those of the whirling throng who, during the rests between each figure, turned their eyes in the direction of these seated ones, were only able to discover, on account of the music and bustle, that a very striking circumstance was in course of narration—denoted by an emphatic sweep of the hand, snapping of the fingers, close of the lips, and fixed look into the centre of the listener's eye for the space of a quarter of a minute, which raised in that listener such a reciprocating working of face as to sometimes make the distant dancers half wish to know what such an interesting tale could refer to.
>
> (pt. v, ch. ii)

The stories are told for the occasion, rising from the memory of similar occasions in the past, told in courtesy, congratulation, celebration. Deaths usually invoke celebration and praise in Hardy's novels, marriages tend to summon up an unromantic contrast between past and present. One of the lesser members of the Mellstock Quire is the feeble but willing Thomas Leaf, who hopefully turns up on important occasions, to be criticized but tolerated and protected by his more gifted fellows. They apologize for him, introduce and explain him, and generally permit him to take a place in their community, without sentimentality but with generous sentiment. Leaf arrives in 'a long smock-frock of pillow-case cut and of snowy whiteness' to ask if he can come to the wedding and, despite a certain rough reproach, 'we've got no room for 'ee, Leaf' from the tranter, and 'fie upon 'ee for prying' from old William, they let him come: 'His looks are rather against en, and he is terrible silly; but 'a have never been in jail, and 'a won't do no harm.' He receives the tribute and the invitation with gratitude and, like a good guest, makes his contribution to the ritual story-telling under the beech. Like all Hardy's fools and weaklings, his silliness has a certain grace, composed of good-will, sweetness, trust and enthusiasm. These graces mark his story, which is a tactful contribution to the ritual story-telling, and a kindly optimistic contribution to the matter-of-fact memories of past weddings, and their consequences of too many children and too little money. Thomas Leaf's story is perfectly timed and placed:

'Yes, that it can!' said the impulsive voice of Leaf, who had hitherto humbly admired the proceedings from a corner. 'It can be done—all that's wanted is a few pounds to begin with. That's all! I know a story about it!'

'Let's hear thy story, Leaf,' said the tranter. 'I never knew you were clever enough to tell a story. Silence, all of ye! Mr Leaf will tell a story.'

'Tell your story, Thomas Leaf,' said grandfather William in the tone of a schoolmaster.

'Once,' said the delighted Leaf, in an uncertain voice, 'there was a man who lived in a house! Well, this man went thinking and thinking night and day. At last, he said to himself, as I might, "If I had only ten pound, I'd make a fortune." At last by hook or by crook, he got the ten pounds!'

'Only think of that!' said Nat Callcome satirically.

'Silence!' said the tranter.

'Well, now comes the interesting part of the story! In a little time he had made that ten pounds twenty. Then a little time after that he doubled it, and made it forty. Well, he went on, and a good while after that he made it eighty, and on to a hundred. Well, by-and-by he made it two hundred! Well, you'd never believe it, but— he went on and made it four hundred! He went on, and what did he do? Why, he made it eight hundred! Yes, he did,' continued Leaf in the highest pitch of excitement, bringing down his fist upon his knee with such force that he quivered with the pain; 'yes, and he went on and made it A THOUSAND!'

'Hear, hear!' said the tranter. 'Better than the history of England, my sonnies!'

'Thank you for your story, Thomas Leaf,' said grandfather William; and then Leaf gradually sank into nothingness again.

(pt. v, ch. ii)

It is a bad story, lacking form and point, an excellent example of a lame attempt by the omniscient teller to excite his listeners. Like all foolish narrators, Thomas calls attention to variation and tension where there is none, imagining that his listeners feel as interested as he does, but unable to create that interest. His story is pathetically full of monotony and anti-climax, rather than sound and fury. It is a version of the 'shaggy-dog story',[6] where surprise lies in the frustration of surprise. Hardy uses the pointlessness of it for his own imaginative purposes, to instruct us in the ways of listening with generous love. The unsympathetic listener is rebuked, as in the performance of the rustics in *A Midsummer Night's Dream*, but Hardy's presiding spirits, Reuben Dewy and grandfather William, are even better than Duke Theseus at showing how hosts and listeners should attend to poor but honest entertainment. *The Trumpet-Major* ends with Hardy's implicit reminder of the Duke's words, 'The best in this kind be but shadows', and Thomas Leaf's story elicits the tactful, kindly vote of thanks from two of Thomas Hardy's accomplished story-tellers, who really know that it is the thought that counts.

If we remember the comedy as well as the solemnity of the telling, it seems clear that Thomas Hardy uses Thomas Leaf to declare that a poor story may be the precious life-blood of a human spirit. But the novel does not end with a story. Its conclusion reminds us of human separateness and secrecy, with Dick's honeymoon hope for complete candour, Fancy's evasiveness, and the bird's wordless incapacity for lying. Hardy takes us to the very verge of human telling and listening.

[6] See Samuel Hynes's introduction to his edition of *The Great Short Works of Thomas Hardy* (New York, 1967).

8
James Joyce

I. DUBLINERS

Joyce's Dubliners move through their nights and days, telling stories
to themselves and to each other. However mean their existence,
however thin their feelings, however numb their reflections, they are
never so paralysed as to be incapable of narrative. Their language and
symbolism may be feeble, second-hand or banal, but the form,
function and individuality of their stories prove that they are imagined
as imaginative. They tell over the past and sketch out the future. They
exchange overt or covert confessions, pleas and defences. The most
lightly sketched characters make some effort to survive, and even to
grasp meaning, through memory or expectation, while many of them
are capable of fervent and energetic lies, dreams, projects, boasts,
anecdotes, reminiscences, aspirations, fantasies, confidences and
disclosures. Many of them are great talkers, telling stories to communicate, help, deceive, cheer, cadge, show off or beg. Others are
stammering, inarticulate, silent. Through each of the stories in
Dubliners runs the story-telling of that private and public life which
forms the narratives of yesterday, today and tomorrow.

The boy in the first three stories, 'The Sisters', 'An Encounter' and
'Araby', has a febrile imaginative activity, strong in imagery as well as
narrative, stimulated by sexual dreams, religious stories and popular
fiction. The less educated inner narratives of Eveline and the two
gallants are similarly creative in enterprise, also searching past and
future in a desperate attempt to survive, also lit by brighter fires than
have ever warmed actual experience, also attempting the hard work of
relating memory and fantasy, struggling to make sense of their lives,

and even decency. 'The Boarding House' is made up of competing and combating stories of a mother's plan, the lovers' memories, and their confessions and expectations. Bob Doran and Polly Mooney are tiny but precisely particularized figures, Polly in her capacity for absent-minded abstraction, Bob in his timid response to the memory of Jack Mooney's threat 'that if any fellow tried that sort of a game on with *his* sister he'd bloody well put his teeth down his throat, so he would'. Each of them has an individual memory of the common past, Polly's 'unperturbed', 'secret' and 'amiable', Bob's clearly described as 'the patient memory of the celibate'. To imagine story-telling is to imagine particular feeling, as well as common form.

Feeling less, but always feeling something, Maria in 'Clay' painstakingly remembers, expects a little, hopes for the best. In 'Counterparts', 'Ivy Day in the Committee Room' and 'Grace', incident is largely composed of the narratives of social conversation: rambling or dashing anecdotes, lies, inflations, dishonest eloquence, sentimental tales, boasts and praises, sermons and ballads. In the two stories in which narrative is only implicitly present, 'After the Race' and 'A Mother', action turns on the bathos, sourness and vanity of dreams of brilliance, at home or abroad. In the subtle compressions of growth and vision of 'A Little Cloud', 'A Painful Case' and 'The Dead', the imaginations of Chandler, Mr Duffy and Gabriel Conroy grope towards the enlargements of hope, desire, aspiration, love, memory, succeeding and failing to work out the story of their own inner lives and its relation to other people's private or public stories. The story of yesterday and the day before yesterday is all too alive in the chronicle of Dublin's mean streets and alcoholic dreams, and the stories told in the truthful and untruthful myths, songs and ballads of Ireland or England have a part to play in encouraging, defining, elevating and deflating the private story-telling. While the Dubliners live, they talk and tell, and after they are dead they become parts of other people's stories, like Parnell, Emily Sinico, and Michael Furey.

Dublin is a centre of moral paralysis but its people are not quite paralysed. Feeble and frail, like Wordsworth's tramps, children and old people, or Beckett's paralytics and travellers, they never entirely lose narrative's momentum because they tell in order to live. Narrative is for them like conversation, the art form of the very poor. 'Poor' has to include the poor in spirit as well as the poor in pocket, though in Joyce the two poverties often, if not invariably, coincide. Only in 'The

Dead' is there anything approaching discursive thought and even there it is the collision of Gabriel's fantasy and Gretta's secret memory which clarifies and completes the earlier debate and analysis. Narrative is not the only form of art available but it is almost the only form of thought. It often appears in poetic form, the more trippingly, nostalgically and flauntingly for its rhyme and music, but the poetry of *Dubliners* is a narrative poetry, the unsentimentalized narrative of a generally banal folk-art. Story is the medium of the most reduced and poverty-stricken communion with the self and with others, very much as it is in *Lyrical Ballads*, where the little girl in 'We are Seven' puts down the mature and rational adult story of death by her loving pragmatism; where even the idiot boy makes a minimal report of experience:

> And thus to Betty's question, he
> Made answer, like a traveller bold,
> (His very words I give to you,)
> 'The cocks did crow to-whoo, to-whoo,'
> 'And the sun did shine so cold.'
> —Thus answered Johnny in his glory,
> And that was all his travel's story.
>
> ('The Idiot Boy', 457–63)

The *Lyrical Ballads* locate glory in the energy and individual truthfulness of these minimal stories, and while Joyce's spirit in *Dubliners* is not a mocking one, his stories are closer to George Eliot's early *Scenes of Clerical Life* than to the Wordsworthian celebrations of simplicity. The place of *Dubliners* in Joyce's work is very like that of *Scenes of Clerical Life* in George Eliot's. Like her, Joyce is defining, rebuking and pitying a provincialism which has formed him but which he has outgrown. Like her, he tries his paces in a short canter before the long and arduous gallop. Like her, he tries an experiment which is only possible for him on the small scale of the story. There the resemblance ends. *Dubliners* commands feeling and rhetoric, *Scenes of Clerical Life* uncertainly proffers compassion and solemnity. George Eliot creates Amos Barton, as unimaginative as a decent man can be. He is feeble in speech, insight and the understanding of himself and everyone else, but his author peers protectively round his limitations, imploring us to embrace his humanity. Amos's style is one of scrupulous meanness but George Eliot's unscrupulous eloquence overflows with articulate energy. When Joyce creates the language of Maria's meagre goodwill and repression, the coarseness of Lenehan and Farrington, and the kindly solecismsof Eliza Flynn, the priest's sister, it is without aid or addition. We are contained and restricted by the limits of their style and their imagination. Through brilliant feats of *erlebte Rede*[1] Joyce puts us directly to the test, making us encounter the poor in spirit by letting them speak and think for themselves. In scrupulously avoiding a contrast between his style and theirs, or his sensibility and theirs, he teaches us not to condescend.

As he knew, such restraint laid him open to the charge of caricature; since his style of scrupulous meanness involved a mimicry of meanness, scrupulously unaccompanied by authorial commentary, it could be mistaken for satire. Hence Frank O'Connor's complaint that Joyce denied his characters autonomy and presented them critically, from the outside. It is true that the satirist often implies criticism through the comic distortion of character but this is not Joyce's way. He risks taking us to the very verge of satire but refuses to cross over. His art is too infused with individual feeling to be justifiably mistaken for satire. A distaste for sentimentality forces silence upon him and the materials of *Dubliners* encourage the reserve, shyness, coolness and invisibility, which were to be used for other purposes in his later fiction. *Dubliners* is neither immature nor tentative but remarkably restrained and comprehensive. The characters are left to speak haltingly for themselves, but are so far from being caricatures as to be felt as creative human beings, observed from the inside, presented through their individual imaginative lives. 'Creative' may seem a strong word for the imaginative flutterings of some of the Dubliners but each has his imagination.

Despite the heavy irony of its title, 'Two Gallants' does not offer a caricature of Lenehan and Corley, who pursue their dreary little gallantries, coarsely and greedily, as desperate men. Lenehan is shown as a barfly, who talks himself into the round of drinks by his 'stock of stories, limericks and riddles'. We first meet him as he listens to Corley's boastful narrative about the girl, and the impression they make is that of two greedy, grubby and fatigued creatures, living exhaustingly and exhaustedly on their wits and their coarse charms. Lenehan's inner life constitutes the chief channel of interest and

---

[1] For discussion of the useful concept of *erlebte Rede* or the free indirect style, see Randolph Quirk, *Charles Dickens* (Durham, 1959) and C. Bally, 'Le style indirect libre en français moderne', *Germanisch-Romanische Monatschrift*, iv (1912).

continues throughout the story, as he takes the three passive roles of listener, patient loafer, and sharer in his friend's extracted share of the slavey's earnings. But however tarnished his mind and life, its inner action is intense. As he wanders through the streets, too tired even to respond to the women's glances, too dry of brain and throat 'to speak a great deal, to invent and to amuse', worn out by 'shifts and intrigues', his fantasy-life is dispirited. But its pattern is familiar. His response to the music of the harp is automatic but alive, for his feet beat the melody and his fingers twiddle the variations. Similarly, his fancy is alive and though its language is tired and banal, its imagery that of cheap journalism, an inner life is presented, engaged in the actions of recalling past, invoking desirable and undesirable futures and imagining Corley with his girl: 'In his imagination he beheld the pair of lovers walking along some dark road; he heard Corley's voice in deep energetic gallantries and saw again the leer of the young woman's mouth'. His attentive memory serves his fantasy. He has nothing to do but recall and recast his life, and however styleless, it is kept alive by narrative efforts:

> He would be thirty-one in November. Would he never get a good job? Would he never have a home of his own? He thought how pleasant it would be to have a warm fire to sit by and a good dinner to sit down to. He had walked the streets long enough with friends and with girls. He knew what those friends were worth: he knew the girls too. Experience had embittered his heart against the world. But all hope and not left him. He felt better after having eaten than he had felt before, less weary of his life, less vanquished in spirit. He might yet be able to settle down in some snug corner and live happily if he could only come across some good simple-minded girl with a little of the ready. ('Two Gallants')

The narrative imagination of Chandler in 'A Little Cloud', is, by comparison, rich, elaborate, intense and literary. He has got the wife, home and family of Lenehan's fantasy, but in addition he also possesses something like a poet's sensibility, together with the ability to recognize it. Little Chandler's imagination is energetically and complicatedly inventive, finding forms for his feelings of pity and melancholy. Joyce's capacity to individualize fantasy-life shows itself brilliantly in Chandler's whimsicality: just as he unbared the dreary generalities of Lenehan's domestic dreams, so he stops us pitying

Little Chandler too much. Joyce makes it plain that he would have been negligible as a poet, only too well equipped for the weak flutters of fancy in the Celtic twilight. He also is not wholly satirized for Joyce shows his inner life and his capacity for feeling, as self-indulgence makes him strike the child but love and sense make him shrink from the stroke in remorse.

Maria has nothing of Chandler's dubious gifts of style and fancy, nor of Lenehan's sensuous and vivid fantasy. She lacks their complex ability to look before and after, and then to look before in the light of looking after. But as if to make up for her imaginative weakness, Joyce endows her with a benevolence they lack. Maria's impulse is more benign but her mind smaller. She is perhaps the minimally endowed character in *Dubliners*, her language mean, banal, repetitive, but she is presented compassionately rather than ironically. She is herself capable of motions of compassion and generosity, and receives a little compassion as well as cruelty within the story. Despite the flickering feebleness of her imaginative style, it can encompass comparison and evaluation as she remembers:

> She was very fond of that purse because Joe had brought it to her five years before when he and Alphy had gone to Belfast on a Whit-Monday trip. In the purse were two half-crowns and some coppers. She would have five shillings clear after paying tram fare. What a nice evening they would have, all the children singing! Only she hoped that Joe wouldn't come in drunk.
>
> ...she thought of how she used to dress for mass on Sunday morning when she was a young girl...
>
> She arranged in her mind all she was going to do and thought how much better it was to be independent and to have your own money in your pocket. She hoped they would have a nice evening. She was sure they would but she could not help thinking what a pity it was Alphy and Joe were not speaking. They were always falling out now but when they were boys together they used to be the best of friends: but such was life. ('Clay')

Joyce's feeblest characters are presented through their rudimentary narratives. Some of them speak a blank or borrowed language, incompetent or vague in imagery, but each tells his own story, making slight or strong gestures of narrative imagination. The characters also tell stories to each other. In 'Eveline' Eveline's lover and father tell rival stories. Frank re-tells his sailor's yarns and traveller's tales which evoke an exotic hope of distant shores and her father offers a ghost story, appropriately pulling her back to dust, duty and dullness, where the ghost of her mother, who also told Eveline her story of duty, in her way, defeats the fantasies of the living. There is no clear-cut right or wrong about her decision, for she keeps a promise to the dead on behalf of the living. To keep it is to choose a kind of life (as well as a death) and to choose it after another life has been carefully and painfully imagined. The choice is active and genuine and made through the comparative fantasies of past and present. If Joyce is suggesting that the possible future is a nasty deception on Frank's part, as Hugh Kenner suggests in *The Pound Era*, the choice would be uninteresting and her mind more paralysed than these analyses seem to indicate:

> Her father was becoming old lately, she noticed; he would miss her. Sometimes he could be very nice. Not long before, when she had been laid up for a day, he had read her out a ghost story and made toast for her at the fire. Another day, when their mother was alive, they had all gone for a picnic to the Hill of Howth. She remembered her father putting on her mother's bonnet to make the children laugh.
>
> Her time was running out but she continued to sit by the window, leaning her head against the window curtain, inhaling the odour of dusty cretonne. Down far in the avenue she could hear a street organ playing. She knew the air. Strange that it should come that very night to remind her of the promise to her mother, her promise to keep the home together as long as she could. She remembered the last night of her mother's illness; she was again in the close dark room at the other side of the hall and outside she heard a melancholy air of Italy. The organ-player had been ordered to go away and given six-pence. She remembered her father strutting back into the sickroom saying:
>
> —Damned Italians! coming over here!
>
> As she mused the pitiful vision of her mother's life laid its spell on the very quick of her being—that life of commonplace sacrifices closing in final craziness. She trembled as she heard again her mother's voice saying constantly with foolish insistence:
>
> —Derevaun Seraun! Derevaun Seraun!

She stood up in a sudden impulse of terror. Escape! She must escape! Frank would save her. He would give her life, perhaps love, too. But she wanted to live. Why should she be unhappy? She had a right to happiness. Frank would take her in his arms, fold her in his arms. He would save her. ('Eveline')

Eveline's conflict of story is inward-looking but it involves what other people have imagined and narrated. 'A Little Cloud' also turns on a conflict of imaginations. Little Chandler's story is a response to Gallaher's boast:

Ignatius Gallaher puffed thoughtfully at his cigar and then, in a calm historian's tone, he proceeded to sketch for his friend some pictures of the corruption which was rife abroad. He summarised the vices of many capitals and seemed inclined to award the palm to Berlin. Some things he could not vouch for (his friends had told him), but of others he had had personal experience. He spared neither rank nor caste. He revealed many of the secrets of religious houses on the Continent and described some of the practices which were fashionable in high society and ended by telling, with details, a story about an English duchess—a story which he knew to be true. Little Chandler was astonished.

—Ah, well, said Ignatius Gallaher, here we are in old jog-along Dublin where nothing is known of such things.

—How dull you must find it, said Little Chandler, after all the other places you've seen!

—Well, said Ignatius Gallaher, it's a relaxation to come over here, you know. And, after all, it's the old country, as they say, isn't it? You can't help having a certain feeling for it. That's human nature... But tell me something about yourself. Hogan told me you had... tasted the joys of connubial bliss. ('A Little Cloud')

His own story is terribly brief, 'I was married last May twelve months', his timidity easily put down by Gallaher's stories which are as elaborate as they are banal. He is confused by 'the adventure of meeting Gallaher after eight years, of finding himself with Gallaher in Corless's surrounded by lights and noise, of listening to Gallaher's stories and of sharing for a brief space Gallaher's vagrant and triumphant life'. But like Eveline he is recalled, unenthusiastically but not too ignobly, to the dull daily life. After the heady combination of Gallaher, whiskey, his revived poetic aspirations and a final Byronic inspiration have so upset him that he hits his wailing baby, he is recalled by the feeling for the child's reality, 'if he had died'. Joyce renders these lives so scrupulously that more than meanness emerges.

The single human being and the relationship of friends, lovers, rivals or allies are presented in terms of the narrative imagination. Joyce's stories deal with public as well as private life and he knows that narrative is a group activity. His rendering of social life depends much on the acts of story-telling. Like the stories we tell ourselves, the ones we tell in public are also a mixture of truths and lies. Joyce can hardly ignore the native gift of narration, the boast, blarney, lie, tall story and joke, but he uses it to analyse the variety and hierarchy of the social group, the public pecking-order. In 'Grace', Martin Cunningham is by far the best story-teller, authoritative, commanding, controlled and eloquent. The unreliability of his stories and his facts only emphasizes the social authority of the man. The whole group is constructed around Cunningham's lead. When he speaks, often in the uncompromising and exclusive anecdote, the structure of listening is plain:

> —65, catch your cabbage!
>
> Everyone laughed. Mr M'Coy, who wanted to enter the conversation by any door, pretended that he had never heard the story. Mr Cunningham said:
>
> —It is supposed—they say, you know—to take place in the depot where they get these thundering big country fellows, omadhauns, you know, to drill. The sergeant makes them stand in a row against the wall and hold up their plates.
>
> He illustrated the story by grotesque gestures.
>
> —At dinner, you know. Then he has a bloody big bowl of cabbage before him on the table and a bloody big spoon like a shovel. He takes up a wad of cabbage on the spoon and pegs it across the room and the poor devils have to try and catch it on their plates: 65, *catch your cabbage*. ('Grace')

When Kernan eventually gets in his shuffling and stuttering story, we are aware of Cunningham waiting and prompting:

> —I heard him once, Mr Kernan continued. I forget the subject of his discourse now. Crofton and I were in the back of the . . . pit, you know . . . the—

—The body, said Mr Cunningham.

—Yes, in the back near the door. I forget now what. . . O yes, it was on the Pope, the late Pope. I remember it well. Upon my word it was magnificent, the style of the oratory. And his voice! God! hadn't he a voice! *The Prisoner of the Vatican*, he called him. I remember Crofton saying to me when we came out—...(ibid.)

M'Coy can only get his entry by pretending not to know the anecdote. Fogarty, the polite and quite well-informed grocer, corrects some of Cunningham's shakier assertions about *Lux upon Lux* and the cardinals who voted against papal infallibility, but is helpless to thwart the flow and form of the splendid story, with its concluding *Credo*. Cunningham is to return with his generosity and tact rather more prominent in *Ulysses*. His aggressive proficiency in narrative is unchanged as he snatches Bloom's story on the way to Paddy Dignam's funeral. Joyce observes character and social life in terms of a struggle for power. To tell a story is to ask a lot of the attentiveness, concentration and silence of one's fellows. Poaching, preaching, flattery and solicitation all form part of the social story-telling. The content of the stories in 'Grace' shows something of the importance and triviality of the religious life, through social and psychological analysis of a masculine group. The woman brings in the tray, but says nothing.

In 'Counterparts', a pecking order is reversed. Farrington's crude inner life is shown in imaginative activity, as it prepares a social performance which will not only be an impressive boast but will reverse the roles endured in his office life. He has transformed his loose-tongued, stupid impertinence, which was followed by an abject apology, into a proud memory which encourages and prepares him for his final assertiveness towards his son. In imagination he works himself up through the pride of performance to a deluded self-belief and a real brutality:

The man passed through the crowd, looking on the spectacle gener-ally with proud satisfaction and staring masterfully at the office-girls. His head was full of the noises of tram-gongs and swishing trolleys and his nose already sniffed the curling fumes of punch. As he walked on he preconsidered the terms in which he would narrate the incident to the boys:

—So, I just looked at him—coolly, you know, and looked at her.

Then I looked back at him again—taking my time, you know. *I don't think that that's a fair question to put to me*, says I.

Nosey Flynn was sitting up in his usual corner of Davy Byrne's and, when he heard the story, he stood Farrington a half-one, saying it was as smart a thing as ever he heard. ('Counterparts')

In 'Ivy Day in the Committee Room', the conversation is trivial and sentimental, the story which Mr Henchy tells about Edward VII showing the facile sentiment which betrays the old Parnellite ideal:

—Parnell, said Mr Henchy, is dead. Now, here's the way I look at it. Here's this chap come to the throne after his old mother keeping him out of it till the man was grey. He's a man of the world, and he means well by us. He's a jolly fine decent fellow, if you ask me, and no damn nonsense about him. He just says to himself: *The old one never went to see these wild Irish. By Christ, I'll go myself and see what they're like.* And are we going to insult the man when he comes over here on a friendly visit? Eh? Isn't that right, Crofton?

('Ivy Day in the Committee Room')

At the end, after allegiances and alliances have shifted through the flow of conversation and story, Hynes sings his ballad. It may be facile in sentiment, too, but despite the banality of its limping verse it does truly praise Parnell, recalls his dream, attacks his slanderers, and celebrates Ivy Day:

'He dreamed (alas, 'twas but a dream!)
Of Liberty: but as he strove
To clutch that idol, treachery
Sundered him from the thing he loved.

Shame on the coward caitiff hands
That smote their Lord or with a kiss
Betrayed him to the rabble-rout
Of fawning priests—no friends of his.' (ibid.)

The popping Guiness corks are comic and trite but Hynes and O'Connor are moved, and there is a lull in the drinking. A ritual has been performed, to focus and revive genuine feeling. A story has been told with sufficient sincerity and response:

Mr Hynes sat down again on the table. When he had finished his recitation there was a silence and then a burst of clapping: even Mr Lyons clapped. The applause continued for a little time. When it had ceased all the auditors drank from their bottles in silence. (ibid.)

Similarly, in 'Clay', although Maria's sexual repressions and bad memory make her leave out the second verse of 'I dreamt I dwelt in marble halls', her beerfogged brother Joe and the rest of the family are too 'nice' to mention the mistake and there is a high point of conclusion for her and for them. The sentiment is insipid, the language banal, the story not fully told, and the sympathetic listening, as so often in Joyce's Dublin, is warmed and lubricated by alcohol. All the same, the social occasion is gripped and shaped by the song and the response. A ritual has been genuinely, if feebly, enacted. The result is bathetic, but not null. Her dreams are given an utterance. Joyce knows that sentimental verse and song may elicit a real feeling.

Narrative is crucial to the creation of individuals, relationships and social life. It is also crucial in each story, as theme, subject and action. The epiphanies of *Dubliners* are essentially narrative, revelations being made through the bad, good, partial, complete, false and true telling of a story. In many of the stories the action itself is precipitated by a narrative. His own fantasy and his friend's boast push Chandler into frustration and fury. Stupidity loosens Farrington's tongue, drink and dishonesty turn his humiliated memory into a boast and make him vulnerable to the further humiliation of losing the game of physical prowess. This could easily have been a simple story about the compensatory shifts in a pecking-order, but what Joyce shows is not just the encounter between Farrington and his boss but the transformation of the encounter into a story. This is what brings about the transient success which pushes him into aggression. In the stories of 'A Mother', 'The Boarding House' and 'After the Race' the empty and pitiable happenings are precipitated by corrupt and corrupting day-dreams, frustrated and successful.

Story creates or is created by the action. Sometimes the action consists of a narrative, incompletely, inadequately or only gradually pieced together by characters and reader. 'Two Gallants' begins *in medias res* as Lenehan laughs appreciatively at what Corley has been saying. We do not fully understand what has been said until the very end of the story. We are suspended during Lenehan's waiting and wondering, which we half-understand, to share the gross triumph when the gold coin gleams eloquently in Corley's revealing palm. Our delay in understanding the story of the two gallants coincides with the suspended story within the story and the final surprise triggers off an explosive shock. The story we are eventually told is the meaning and nature of this gallantry. The title partakes of the fine repression of the whole story. In 'Counterparts', the inner story which is depressingly revealed is the self-assertive fantasy of Farrington's cock-pride, its brutality and emptiness.

'Ivy Day in the Committee Room' and 'Clay' work through similar concluding revelations of meaning, though their ritual climaxes are less depressing, offering something thin or vapid but better than nothing. The narrative epiphany is not always or wholly dispiriting. The marble halls of Maria's ballad are preferable to the deathly clay, even though they are only made of Victorian imitation marble. The popular ballad is banal but offers some outlet for the feeling of little imaginations. But Joyce sometimes places the life-stories of his characters against more formal and literary narratives. After the mock-Dantesque structure of 'Grace', where the first fall down the lavatory steps is infernal, the talk by the bedside purgatorial, and the last sermon paradisal, the final depreciation is startling. The religious life does not rebuke the dreary worldliness of these Dubliners, having sold out to Mammon. Father Purdon's sermon tells a lie about serving Christ and Mammon to complete the exposure of a religious life which is nearly paralysed but has enough spirit left to reveal its dishonesty in an appropriate language:

> Jesus Christ was not a hard taskmaster. He understood our little failings, understood the weakness of our poor fallen nature, understood the temptations of this life. We might have had, we all had from time to time, our temptations: we might have, we all had, our failings. But one thing only, he said, he would ask of his hearers. And that was: to be straight and manly with God. If their accounts tallied in every point to say:
> —Well, I have verified my accounts. I find all well. ('Grace')

Mr Kernan's cure is itself contaminated. Grace is being sold at a discount.

Joyce's stories are often stories of disorder and the end of 'Grace' disappoints any hope for a paradisal promotion from this inferno or purgatory. Where we might have found order, lies profound disorder.

Joyce's habit was to provide most accurately for the literary needs of each character and class in order to invoke a distinction between expectation and exultation, however tawdry, and the anti-climax or dreariness of ordinary life. Unlike Cervantes and Flaubert, Joyce does not insist strongly on the unrealities of literature or the deficiencies of everyday life, but rather uses literature to define and explain the powers of fantasy. The first three stories of childhood all turn on the specious contrast between romantic dream, aided and partly formed by not very good literature, and the reality of life.[2] And life sometimes turns out to confirm the wildness of literary fantasy. The dream of strange customs in 'The Sisters' is not contrasted with dull reality but with a history of madness, sacrilege, paralysis and death. The boy's romantic Persian dream is less sinister and disturbing than the broken chalice and confessional laughter. Fiction's truth shows a truth which is stranger and stronger than fiction's fiction. In 'Araby' the intense turmoil of vanity and guilt are revealed through the trivial bazaar which is so unlike Araby, and romance is not so much discredited as redefined. Just as Catherine Morland finds her adventure in Northanger Abbey, so the boys in 'An Encounter' find an adventure more unpleasant and threatening than anything offered in the clean adventure stories of the Wild West or the American detective stories 'traversed from time to time by unkempt fierce and beautiful girls'. The boy is hungering for 'wild sensations, for the escape which those chronicles of disorder alone seemed to offer', and finds himself listening to a chronicle of disorder and frightened by wild sensations. Joyce is not writing a narrative of anti-climax but transmuting literary sources into the terms and tones of the known environment. Even in the genuine anti-climax of 'A Little Cloud', where the reading of Byron is interrupted by the crying baby, the weighting is by no means entirely on the side of the romantic poet.

What the boy discovers in 'An Encounter' is the nature of his environment, the kind of adventure and sensation typical of Dublin. He discovers it through the encounter with the pervert, whose aggression takes a narrative form. His obsessed sadistic reverie is a fantasy, spoken raptly to the sexual object, attempting a pathetic but alarming rape in words. As it frightens the boy, it offers the reader clear explanation of what the man 'had been doing' and eventually gives the

[2] See Harry Stone, ' "Araby" and the Writings of James Joyce', *Antioch Review* (Fall, 1965).

boy too an unpleasant enlightenment. Some of the sexual fantasies in *Ulysses* and some of Joyce's letters to Nora make it clear that the literary forms of sexual address had a particular interest for him. The active pornography of 'An Encounter' is brilliantly particularized in its personal absorption and attack, finely placed after the literary discussion about Scott and Bulwer Lytton:

> He began to speak on the subject of chastising boys. His mind, as if magnetised again by his speech, seemed to circle slowly round and round its new centre. He said that when boys were that kind they ought to be whipped and well whipped. When a boy was rough and unruly there was nothing would do him any good but a good sound whipping. A slap on the hand or a box on the ear was no good: what he wanted was to get a nice warm whipping. I was surprised at this sentiment and involuntarily glanced up at his face. As I did so I met the gaze of a pair of bottle-green eyes peering at me from under a twitching forehead. I turned my eyes away again. ('An Encounter')

The boy's awakening but controlled agitation are as carefully observed as the rhapsodic feeling of the reverie. The free indirect style renders the moralizing, monotonous and tumescent brooding of sexual reverie:

> He said that if ever he found a boy talking to girls or having a girl for a sweetheart he would whip him and whip him; and that would teach him not to be talking to girls. And if a boy had a girl for a sweetheart and told lies about it then he would give him such a whipping as no boy ever got in this world. He said that there was nothing in this world he would like so well as that. He described to me how he would whip such a boy as if he were unfolding some elaborate mystery. He would love that, he said, better than anything in this world; and his voice, as he led me monotonously through the mystery, grew almost affectionate and seemed to plead with me that I should understand him. (ibid.)

The man's attention to the listener and his own pleasure is marked as Joyce says, 'with care and precision'. As the boys run away, terrified now by ignorance and half-knowledge, it is a mystery in every sense of the word which has been exposed for them and for the reader.

Many of the stories are stories of encounters in which we meet the life outside ourself, as strangers tell us their stories. Their ways of telling—the marvellously various mean styles of *Dubliners*—are as important as their subject matter. The story within the story is the story of other people's mystery and each story in *Dubliners* is an adventure story and a detective story. The detection is made through listening and telling. In the very simplest stories, it is only the reader who understands the full story and the revealed meaning of such laconic titles as 'Two Gallants', 'The Sisters', 'An Encounter', and 'Ivy Day in the Committee Room'. As the stories of these lives accumulate, we read Joyce's whole chapter of Ireland's moral history.

'The Sisters' is a clear model of a story about narrative disclosure. The boy listens to the stories told by the adult world about the mystery of death, condescendingly, fragmentarily, pruriently. Old Cotter used 'to be rather interesting, talking of faints and worms' but has become boring with 'his endless stories about the distillery'. He and the boy's uncle discuss the death of Father Flynn. The boy's aunt responds conventionally, 'God have mercy on his soul', and the boy hides his response from Cotter's scrutinizing black eyes. His hints about impressionable children join with the news of the death to haunt the boy's dreams. Gossip and dream are observed carefully, as social and emotional events, but the emphasis of the story is placed on incomplete knowledge. The mystery of the priest haunts first the gossip and then the dream, 'the heavy grey face of the paralytic' suggestively murmurs its desire to confess, smiling, with 'lips...moist with spittle'. The boy dreams that his listening is a kind of absolution.

The next effort of narrative is made by the boy's memory, provoked by his sense that it was strange and irritating not to feel in 'a mourning mood'. By an act of will he summons the past, remembering the dislocated and superficial stories of the priest, 'about the catacombs and about Napoleon Bonaparte' and about the mystery of the priesthood. When he tries to remember the end of his dream, it has disappeared. Each stage of story-telling is frustrated until we read the ritual discussion of the dead between the aunt and the priest's sisters. The boy listens as his aunt's, 'Ah, well, he's gone to a better world', and her ritual question about the death elicit Eliza's account of its peace and beauty. The original version of 'The Sisters' says explicitly that the aunt was a 'gossip, a harmless one', but the final version omits these words and makes the gossip entirely implicit. The aunt's final promptings are also toned down from a specific reference to the chalice and the effect on the priest's mind to the vaguer, 'I heard something'. The talk of the wake allows the story to arise naturally, working back from the narrative of the death to the narrative of the life. Stimulated by sips of sherry, Eliza tells her rambling tale while her sister Nannie sleeps. The crux of the story comes after Eliza falls into a deep reverie, the story coming out with a brooding, introspective allusiveness, 'It was the chalice he broke... That was the beginning of it. Of course, they say it was all right, that it contained nothing, I mean. But still... They say it was the boy's fault'. This is followed by the last image of Father Flynn, 'wide-awake and laughing-like to himself', in his confession-box. After the story she pauses to listen. The story of the recent dead evokes the nervous stillness but the boy knows that the end of the story is death, 'the old priest was lying still in his coffin as we had seen him, solemn and truculent in death'. The story is told haltingly, ungrammatically and repetitively, to avid listeners, with love and care. No ill is spoken of the dead man whose secret is out at last. History can replace gossip. The boy has known the priest but not his story. The homely, malapropistic narrative of Eliza Flynn tells the whole truth about the things that had so fascinated him, about decay, nastiness, illness, and the stories of the priestly duties. The boy thinks of the man's end, in another box, 'an idle chalice on his breast'. It is the boy—who resembles Stephen Dedalus if not James Joyce—who completes the story with the movingly formal and resonant ending. The telling is as important as the listening. In death and life the priest was cared for by his sisters and it is their life we feel also as we listen to the story and the silence.

The inset stories within the stories of *Dubliners* are almost always slowly unfolded private histories. The secret life is revealed explicitly or implicitly. The revelation usually elicits the whole shape of the story, its completion coinciding with the conclusion. The two finest stories tell of the revelation being made to a lover and a husband. The story releases and reveals the life of the teller and at last the life of the listener. Mr Duffy's feeling for Emily Sinico's life is slowly brought into his consciousness and his conscience. His repressed awareness is released by a bad story, an inappropriate story, though a very common story. The newspaper report of an inquest, with its squalid details of drink and suicide and its crudity of statement, reminiscent of Arnold's 'Wragg is in custody',[3] is so harsh and matter-of-fact that it pushes Duffy's resistance into a full look at the life of the woman he declined

[3] Matthew Arnold, *Essays in Criticism*, 1864 ('Functions of Criticism at the Present Time').

to love. The opaque story also forces recognition on his selfish, dim imagination, stirring it into action. It is he and no one else who knows the full story, of the 'Painful Case', for whom the case is too particular to be so called, for whom the pain is acute and complicated. The title expands, as in 'Two Gallants' and 'The Sisters', to take in Duffy's painful case as well as Emily Sinico's.

The process is briefly told but it is slow and complex. The sordid story shocks him into revulsion:

> What an end! The whole narrative of her death revolted him and it revolted him to think that he had ever spoken to her of what he held sacred. The threadbare phrases, the inane expressions of sympathy, the cautious words of a reporter won over to conceal the details of a commonplace vulgar death attacked his stomach. Not merely had she degraded herself; she had degraded him. He saw the squalid tract of her vice, miserable and malodorous.
>
> ('A Painful Case')

He looks back at the past in the light of the long police narrative and reinterprets her outburst, which had led him to put an end to their association, 'in a harsher sense'. He feels justified. But then personal memory, irrational and physical, starts to work. He feels the imagined touch of a hand, he feels that painful process by which people become memories. Touched by memory, he looks back again, further and deeper. The police report had ended with the coroner's verdict that 'No blame attached to anyone', and Mr Duffy begins to be brought into the orbit of the irony felt by the reader as the realization of death brings uneasy remorse and an understanding both of her loneliness and his own. His expanded sensibility goes ahead to his future as a memory, 'if anyone remembered him'. She is nearer in memory than when she was alive because he is at last able to understand or at least to question what happened to them both, 'Why had he withheld life from her?'. Memory is powerful, sounding her name's syllables in the railway engine's drone. But the story ends with memory already going, physical imagery of touching hand and speaking voice both vanish, fading with the engine. He begins to doubt the memory and the story moves into silence, having been most thoroughly told. Mr Duffy is initially the most inert of Joyce's imaginative Dubliners but has a capacity for tragically sharp hindsight.

Like 'A Painful Case' and 'The Sisters', the last story, 'The Dead' also moves from mystery into narration and then into silence. The reticence, secrecy and final release are most dramatically present in 'The Dead' where the story is told to one human being by another. It is told first against another story, in the finest example of that warring of narratives which Joyce activates so finely. In *Dubliners* the whole history of a life is frequently contrasted with the inadequacies and superficialities of gossip, the vagueness of dream, the outlines of cheap literature, the baldness of report and public moralizing. In this story it is told against the story made up by Gabriel, in fantasy and memory. 'A Painful Case' was about the creation of a memory. 'The Dead' is about a most painful uncreation, of memory. What Gabriel Conroy loses is not only his fantasy and desire for the future—an immediate future of one passionate night and a general revival of passion, but the whole past. In seeing that the past has never existed, he sees the self who has created other people as convenient objects and counters, and in so seeing his imagination changes, to admit with difficulty the pang of difference and take in the intransigent personages that people the outside world. In all the stories the characters are deeply affected by story, their sensibility dinted and changes sometimes brought about. But in most there is at least a sense of a temporary inroad. Little Chandler and Maria have a moment of fury or dream but life will go on as before. But for the boy in the first stories and for Eveline and Mr Duffy, there is a change. In 'The Dead' the change is a marked one. While Gabriel is the life and soul of his aunts' party, despite the few small but ominous hitches and the reminders of the snow falling outside, he is all the time telling himself that continuous narrative which is the story of our life, the autobiography we make up, act from, touch up for others, think of implicitly or explicitly, and use as a moral base. Like Mr Duffy's, Gabriel's narrative of the self has been made possible by sequestration of the self, though unlike Duffy he is generous, entertaining, ambitious, cultivated and probably passionate. His is a portrait of an artist, and his complex web of story, weaving back into past and forward into present, is by no means entirely selfish, since it is composed of intense desire, strong affection, and the intention of being a better husband. What he anticipates in the amorous night ahead after he and his wife Gretta leave the party is not simply going to bed but telling her a story, their story, the most intimate story 'of their life together, that no one knew of or would ever know of'. He is hoping to tell the most profound, secret and binding story of the lovers' privacy and their shared memory. It is this most loving expectation which he plays over in his mind, forming for himself the anticipation of this shared memory which will 'make her forget the years of their dull existence together and remember only their moments of ecstasy'. What so shocks Gabriel is that this celebration of memory is outdone and undone by the memory which he has not shared, of her love for Michael. Her secret story is told simply and steadily, to destroy not only the sexual desire that has been kindled by 'so many memories' but the life of memory itself. He thinks that perhaps her thoughts 'had been running with his' and finds that not only were they running far away but that they ran to a secret place he had not known existed:

—What was he? asked Gabriel, still ironically.
—He was in the gasworks, she said.
Gabriel felt humiliated by the failure of his irony and by the evocation of this figure from the dead, a boy in the gasworks. While he had been full of memories of their secret life together, full of tenderness and joy and desire, she had been comparing him in her mind with another. A shameful consciousness of his own person assailed him. He saw himself as a ludicrous figure, acting as a pennyboy for his aunts, a nervous well-meaning sentimentalist, orating to vulgarians and idealising his own clownish lusts...

('The Dead')

Mr Duffy is forced to see, to feel and to accept responsibility for, the story he had not known. Gabriel is forced to see and to feel the story of his wife's life and what has been shut off from it. From her point of view, too, the story is finely revealed. Like his desire, her memory is stirred by the song, 'The Lass of Aughrim'. The past unfolds in her mind, like one of Proust's Japanese flowers, until the substance of its passionate regret is forced upon Gabriel.

When she sleeps, not, as he has imagined, after their embrace but after the storm of nostalgia, his feelings change. He revives her story, seeing it as a romance, 'a man had died for her sake'. He revises their past together, 'it hardly pained him now to think how poor a part he, her husband, had played in her life'. He compares past and present as he feels with 'a strange friendly pity' how she must have changed, and —in a thought characteristic of Joyce, 'perhaps she had not told him all the story'.

Hearing her story has been cathartic. What happens to Gabriel is the quieting of his riot of emotion, his contemplation of his aunt Julia's death and, at last, the recognition of a passion outside him and beyond him:

> He thought of how she who lay beside him had locked in her heart for so many years that image of her lover's eyes when he had told her that he did not wish to live.
>
> Generous tears filled Gabriel's eyes. He had never felt like that himself towards any woman but he knew that such a feeling must be love. The tears gathered more thickly in his eyes and in the partial darkness he imagined he saw the form of a young man standing under a dripping tree. (ibid.)

'The Dead' is about our common mortality, and what Richard Ellmann has called the sense of mutuality. It is also about a movement of imagination, hitherto impossible to Gabriel Conroy's mind, which takes him in past and future out of his personal limits. The movement into detachment, understanding, self-abnegation and sympathy is reminiscent of the ways in which King Lear, Adam Bede, Pip and Marlow move from the telling of their story the way they want to the recognition that there are other stories which they must listen to, and incorporate with their own.

Character, plot and the prevailing themes of imagination and sympathy, all depend on the inner narrative. It is as crucial as metaphor, as conspicuous as symbolism. It plays a special part in that art of compression and implication on which the short story depends. The story curled up within the story like the Babushka or Chinese puzzle, permits intensity, resonance and enlargement. It is a source of economy and compression. Michael Furey, Father Flynn and Emily Sinico live in the stories within the stories. Their lives enter the life of the short story to take up a very small space but to have immense effect.

Within the short story is contained also the response to story. *Dubliners* proclaims an act of faith in the narrative imagination. It shows how we tell each other stories in a request to be heard with understanding, sympathy and love. We accede to this request in a difficult action of patient self-denial which may be called imaginative. We attend. If we have listened properly, we then return to the auto-biography we are all engaged in making, to see it afresh, to revise and unmake it, incorporating the stories of other people's lives. Joyce was disinclined to make sublime or even loud claims for such request, compliance and change. Like Virgil, Milton and Shakespeare, he shows bluntly the misuses as well as the uses of narrative, the refusals to ask, tell, listen, the lies, ill-wishing, aggressions, jealousy and gossip. Gabriel Conroy's imaginative incorporation of his wife's life-story, before and after her telling, is an extreme case of the imaginative mind's capacity for distortion and recognition, and of its predatoriness and generosity. Our capacity for love and self-revision is demonstrable in the response to other people's stories, a response which requires negative capability and the temporary halting and permanent amendment of our personal narrative. When Joyce claimed to have written a chapter of the moral history of his country it was not in order to satirize and condemn but to take 'the first step towards spiritual liberation'.[4] What he called 'the genial illusion', which served him as a candlestick during the writing of the book, was a belief that he was energetically and truthfully telling a story which, listened to properly, could change lives. Like all great works of art, *Dubliners* is about itself. Its stories are about telling, listening, and responding to stories.

II. A PORTRAIT OF THE ARTIST AS A YOUNG MAN

In order to write *Dubliners*, Joyce had to withdraw the dramatized presence of his own imagination. In the first stories of childhood, he is there as the watching, reading, listening and ultimately self-reflecting boy. The stories he listens to, reads and fabricates in 'The Sisters', 'An Encounter' and 'Araby' cause him to enlarge and alter the story of himself to take in other people's telling. The narrative imagination of the boy makes way for the unadorned presence of that telling in all its simplicity and sluggishness. Nevertheless, every tale, however scrupulously its meanness is rendered, has some spark of energy, in foresight, desire, dream or memory. Joyce is implicitly refusing to show the average or less than average man as different in kind from himself. The average mind's powers over past and present may be feeble, falsifying and hard to rouse, but they are powers. *Dubliners* looks ahead to the refusal of *Ulysses* to draw a dividing line between the imagination of Leopold and Molly Bloom and the imagination of Stephen Dedalus.

[4] Letter to Grant Richards, 20 May 1906 (*Letters of James Joyce*, i, ed. Stuart Gilbert, London, 1957).

Between *Dubliners* and *Ulysses* arches the necessary bridge of *A Portrait of the Artist as a Young Man*. Joyce draws the portrait of an artist's imagination too young, too disturbed, too egocentric and too constrained to write *Dubliners*. But he is going to write it, to achieve its mastery of sincerity and accuracy, its scrupulous and skilful man-oeuvres between the Scylla and Charybdis of satire and sentimentality. At the beginning of the novel Stephen Dedalus is a listener but not a passive one. He is the child whose viewpoint needs to question, define and possess, drawing its small circle round experience. We begin with an imagination too young to create anything but already on the move, in leaps and bounds, transforming people, stories and language for its own purposes, taking in and giving out. The novel is a portrait of that imaginative egocentricity which had to be lost before *Dubliners* could be written, but which could have produced some of Joyce's poems. *Stephen Hero*, the second version of *A Portrait of the Artist as a Young Man*,[5] was a huge and various saga encompassing the world of family, college, Ireland and church, as even its fragments show, and it had to be shrunk into the smaller compass of Stephen's contracted but growing mind. In *A Portrait of the Artist as a Young Man* the rest of the world impinges but does no more and the narrative of its impingement avoids history, character and action in order simply to serve Stephen's purposes. Stephen's mind, however, is like the nutshell in which we may be bounded yet count ourselves as kings of infinite space. The book was written by the mature artist, is accordingly aware of its own contraction and able to offer rich compensation. Its re-tricted compass is necessary for a study of the growth of imagination, more ambitious than the attempts of other writers of *Künstlerromane* in its presentation and analysis of each stage of the process. It discusses the theory of that growth and offers actual evidence of the products of its own narrative imagination, its failures, successes, notes and sketches. If *Dubliners* resembles the *Lyrical Ballads*, *A Portrait of the Artist as a Young Man* is Joyce's *Prelude*, for in it he shows the early stages of imagination, before it has done more than imagine its own capacity for impersonalizing, purifying and reprojecting personal experience. Stephen does reach that stage of imagining imagination and

---

[5] The first version was the fictionalized essay or discursive story called 'A Portrait of the Artist'. It is printed in *The Workshop of Daedalus*, ed. R. Scholes and R. Kain (Evanston, 1965) and discussed by Richard Ellmann in his *James Joyce* (London, 1959).

provides a full and detailed account of its programme, as Thomas Mann does in *Doctor Faustus*. Mann was obviously unable to illustrate Adrian Leverkühn's music within his narrative, though he does his best. Other writers facing the seemingly easier question of literary evidence within the story of a writer have held back, preferring not to attempt the illustrations of immaturity, shying away from the pride of mature self-analysis, usually letting the work speak for itself. Goethe does provide poems within *Wilhelm Meister* but not to illustrate Wilhelm's art. Dickens tells about David Copperfield's story-telling in the dark and his success as a novelist but the only example of his narrative powers is the autobiography we are reading. Proust discusses the arts and crafts of memory and points most subtly to the timing and placing of Marcel's memories but *A la recherche du temps perdu* is ultimately as self-illustrative as *David Copperfield*. Joyce braves the difficulties, technical and psychological, to show his hero's powers, not only in his discussion of aesthetics and literature but in two poems, one bad and one better, and in the prose of the journal whose pages are the last pages of his author's novel.

The theory is there to draw our attention to what art can be and to what this art is trying to be. It helps also, eventually, to signal the method of self-analysis which is so cleverly but so mutedly imitative that it has often confounded its readers. If *Dubliners* has sometimes been taken for satiric caricature, *A Portrait of the Artist as a Young Man* has often been taken for satiric irony, though its ironies have sometimes passed unnoticed. Joyce uses language to express and dissociate himself from Stephen's narrative effort. The dangerous rocks here are those of parody and neutrality of style. He detaches himself from Stephen but does not reject him, using the free indirect style more ambitiously than it was ever used before, to present baby-talk, schoolboy slang, or a stiff literary nineteenth-century prose, as a narrative medium for the presentation and analysis of Stephen's sensibility, taste and imagination; his imitations are so careful, precise, and muted, that they merge disconcertingly but effectively into a neutral style. For instance, a romantic reverie is in the style of contemporary English translations of Dumas:

> Outside Blackrock, on the road that led to the mountains, stood a small whitewashed house in the garden of which grew many rosebushes: and in this house, he told himself, another

Mercedes[6] lived. Both on the outward and on the homeward journey he measured distance by this landmark: and in his imagination he lived through a long train of adventures, marvellous as those in the book itself, towards the close of which there appeared an image of himself, grown older and sadder, standing in a moonlit garden with Mercedes who had so many years before slighted his love, and with a sadly proud gesture of refusal, saying:

—Madam, I never eat muscatel grapes. (pt. ii)

It is a parody in an earlier sense of the word, not implying denigration or satire. The free indirect style, here as elsewhere, marks influences and stages in Stephen's style, and also in his narrative imagination. For most of the novel, the medium is that of story-telling, within and also outside literature. The first story is the most familiar kind, told by a parent to a child, the last is the invocation of epic, but within a journal, remembering, revising and forecasting in a familiar way. Joyce performs special and specialized feats of narrative imagination, summoning up the forms and languages of fairy-stories, boys' ghost-stories, schoolboy jokes and riddles, Dumas, the Elizabethans, Greek epic. In his enthusiasm for the Elizabethans and his taste for the poetry of the eighteen-nineties, Stephen's interest is relevant to narrative through the element of story which is present even in lyric, and also through the attempt to distinguish the lyric, epic and narrative stages set out in his theory of literary development. The more literary forms of narrative, as distinguished from the common, unpublished forms, are sufficiently asserted and also sufficiently subdued, by being made a part of the novel's narrative medium. 'Araby', 'An Encounter' and 'A Little Cloud' made full use of the traditional meeting of romance and reality basic to *Don Quixote* and all its descendants, including *Northanger Abbey*, *Madame Bovary* and *The Adventures of Huckleberry Finn*, but most of the stories in *Dubliners* used the literary narrative as a very muted strain, if at all. Although *A Portrait of the Artist as a Young Man* describes the development of a professionally literary imagination, which is partly formed through responses to literature, it is still

---

[6] The anglicized spelling of the heroine's name may stand as a small but significant example of the adaptation. The refusal of the grapes is comically authentic: Edouard Dantès refuses in order to be free to continue his revenge, and Joyce grafts his refusal to eat in his enemy's house on to Stephen's sad, proud, coldness, just as he shifts the very different circumstances of the parting of Dantès and Mercédès to Stephen's romantic fantasy of slighted love.

concerned with the theme of *Dubliners*, the common working narrative of everyday life, though perhaps for slightly different reasons. Joyce is always apparently anxious to show the relation of the artist's imagination to other imaginations, in a denial of artistic prerogative, but this anxiety is important in *A Portrait of the Artist as a Young Man* because he is showing how the artist's expressive powers develop out of a common imaginative experience. Stephen's childhood is like Joyce's childhood, it is an artist's childhood but it is also everyone's childhood despite its local colours. Stephen's growth is shown as a process of familiar learning through fantasy, memory, dream and reverie.

The fragment we have of *Stephen Hero* contains some excellent stories which do not appear in *A Portrait of the Artist as a Young Man* and they are permitted by the fullness and expansiveness of the earlier version. There are very few examples of public story-telling in *A Portrait of the Artist as a Young Man* and the most conspicuous, John Casey's story of his great Parnellite spit, is part of an unusually full rendering of the exchange and tensions of family and society. The Irishness, the anti-clericalism, the dislocation of family harmony and the loyalty to Parnell are all highly relevant to the gradual emergence of Stephen. Joyce's special interest in the aggressions of narrative also creates its spirit and power. But the anecdote at the Christmas dinner is really accounted for by the part it plays in Stephen's memory. It is told after he has dreamt about Parnell's funeral in which he has represented Dante as solitary and dignified in green and red, and the dream took its materials from his puzzled reverie about the family, politics and religion. The story of the spit is in its turn absorbed into the stream of Stephen's memory, which forms a chief part of the medium of Joyce's novel, mediated, however, through the author's narration, told in the author's voice. Although it is not a first-person novel, nearly all its events pass through a process of remembering and re-remembering, as in Proust. Stephen's response to the story of the spit is related to his earlier experience and to his later memories, is part of the continuous process of his learning, acceptance, questioning and rejection. Which side should one be on? Which colour? The social drama is there to create those aspects of Stephen's history which will be, that is, which have been, remembered. This is a novel of memory where everything remembered and re-remembered is remembered for a purpose, in different times and places, with different feelings and sensations. The unusual appearance of the narrative set-piece so common in *Dubliners*, *Ulysses* and *Finnegan's Wake* draws attention to the concentrated and introspective form of this novel which spares little room for anecdote.

The first story in the novel is told at the very beginning, its first words doing double duty as the beginning of Joyce's story and the beginning of the story told to Stephen by his father. The overlapping, sharing and duplication draws attention to the central theme of narrative. There is division into two functions, one for the author and one for the character:

> Once upon a time and a very good time it was there was a moocow coming down along the road and this moocow that was coming down along the road met a nicens little boy named baby tuckoo...
>
> His father told him that story: his father looked at him through a glass: he had a hairy face.
>
> He was baby tuckoo. The moocow came down the road where Betty Byrne lived: she sold lemon platt.
>
> > O, the wild rose blossoms
> > On the little green place.
>
> He sang that song. That was his song.
>
> > O, the green wothe botheth. (pt. i)

The traditional formula of 'Once upon a time' joins the little story with the larger novel and relates them to the ancient ritual of story-telling to which both belong. There is that sense of all stories being one story which is to be prominent in *Ulysses* and insistent in *Finnegan's Wake*. There is identity as well as division, because the novel begins with the first thing that Stephen remembers which is the beginning of the childhood story. It registers the time of its telling, the time of the novel's beginning and the comforting, glamorous remoteness of fiction. But the time is qualified, for the novel is to discuss time with scrupulous qualifications. 'And a very good time it was' belongs to the jocular, affectionate, paternal variations of the story, made up by the father for his child but using a traditional form and frame. It also belongs to the time of childhood, everyone's lost world which Joyce evokes with a nostalgic recognition of its comfort, protection and pastness. Stories were easy to tell and easy to listen to in that very good time. Stephen remembers and Joyce begins his novel, taking care to make that beginning look ahead to the end. It is about the past which is to be renounced and invoked in the last pages. It is about the family which is to be left behind but invoked also. It is about story, which is to return in the form of another ancient tale, the story of Daedalus. It also shows at once the assertive creativity of the child's mind which makes everything its own. The first memory of this artist is significantly a memory of a story. It is not a recollection of a passive listening but of something active, for the child has his stake in the story, lovingly provided by the special rhetoric and characterization, 'a nicens little boy' and happily asserted by the listener, 'He was baby tuckoo'. The story is given a local habitation in the road where Betty Byrne lived. Like story, song is claimed as 'his song' and immediately transformed into his language, a lisping prophecy of the dislocations of *Finnegan's Wake*, though after the model of the story's baby-talk, 'nicens'. The response to story and song are parts of a learning process. They help him to get his bearings in place, to seize his identity. They start him off on the speculations about what imagination seizes as beauty to propose truths: 'but you could not have a green rose' he thinks when white and red roses are on his mind at school and 'but perhaps somewhere in the world you could'. You can, three pages back, in the shufflings of memory, whose web is not woven randomly as it endows the wild rose with the greenness of its place and looks forward beyond the white and the red to the red and the green.

Language, rhythm and story grow together and through them Stephen constructs the world. He constantly halts words to look at them and constantly turns them into rhythm, meditating on meaning and pattern. 'Apologize' becomes an incantation and is part of a story. Words like 'hot', 'cold', 'suck', 'belt' and 'nice' recur, sometimes to be noted by Stephen, always to be insisted on by Joyce. The language of sensation is primary but is joined by the more difficult language of feeling. Attentiveness to language is always a part of a larger attentiveness and the nuances of 'nice' and 'belt' are only appreciated in narrative forms, which educate Stephen in the problems of permutation. His growth in language and imagination is everyone's growth, though it is of course recorded rhythmically and purposively in the chronicle of this individual style and sensibility. As he responds, he reflects, and as he reflects, he learns. Joyce's method is to show a stage of response, often part of a stage of conscious reflection, and then to incorporate the learning so that we see how it has become implicit in Stephen's use of words and forms:

That was not a nice expression. His mother had told him not to speak with the rough boys in the college. Nice mother! The first day in the hall of the castle when she had said goodbye she had put up her veil double to her nose to kiss him: and her nose and eyes were red. But he had pretended not to see that she was going to cry. She was a nice mother but she was not so nice when she cried.

(pt. i)

Joyce continues with the assimilation of the word 'nice': 'It was nice and warm to see the lights in the castle'. But there is more to learn about niceness, and a little later, during the Christmas holidays, when Dante comments bitterly on the story of the great spit, 'very nice!' Stephen is puzzled and thinks, 'It was not nice about the spit in the woman's eye', having still some way to go in his lessons of that irony so essential even in his early portrait. Meditations on the word are not isolated; they involve the narrative imagination which remembers and imagines the contexts of story.

Colour is at first simple sensation, though confused in memory, and later realized as metaphor with its part to play in the past and present of Ireland's story. The imagination of story also grows, using memory but taking off from it:

But they were very holy peasants. They breathed behind him on his neck and sighed as they prayed. They lived in Clane, a fellow said: there were little cottages there and he had seen a woman standing at the half-door of a cottage with a child in her arms as the cars had come past from Sallins. It would be lovely to sleep for one night in that cottage before the fire of smoking turf, in the dark lit by the fire, in the warm dark, breathing the smell of the peasants, air and rain and turf and corduroy. But O, the road there between the trees was dark! You would be lost in the dark! It made him afraid to think of how it was. (pt. i)

Joyce fuses responses, memories and meditations to show growth and continuity. 'Belt' and 'nice' are easily and naturally slipped into the stream of association, but Stephen's experiences of learning the complexities of language and meaning are bracketed so as to reinforce the pattern for reader and character. The reveries about the peasant woman and the night fuse with the ghost story and the dream of Parnell's funeral. Sensations of heat and cold provoke meditations on the language that describes them. Sexual speculations first appear as questions about words like 'suck' or 'thigh' and are related in their turn to other experiences, like water going down the plug-hole or the softness, wetness and sound of kissing. Gradually he connects and compares feelings, as in the movement from 'it would be lovely to sleep for one night' to fear in 'O, the road there between the trees was dark!' He soon moves away from the comfort of 'a very good time' to the disorder of the boys' ghost-story, which Stephen remembers and re-makes. The fear of the dark is covertly related to the fear of hell, 'he had to undress... and be in bed before the gas was lowered so that he might not go to hell when he died', and the ghost-story and his nightmare are rooted in fever, but also in the familiar surroundings. His dream is inventive and the sources of invention are made clear, together with the creative process of inspiration and respiration:

> The prefect's shoes went away. Where? Down the staircase and along the corridors or to his room at the end? He saw the dark. Was it true about the black dog that walked there at night with eyes as big as carriage-lamps? They said it was the ghost of a murderer. A long shiver of fear flowed over his body. He saw the dark entrance hall of the castle. Old servants in old dress were in the ironing-room above the staircase. It was long ago. The old servants were quiet. There was a fire there, but the hall was still dark. A figure came up the staircase from the hall. He wore the white cloak of a marshal; his face was pale and strange; he held his hand pressed to his side. He looked out of strange eyes at the old servants. They looked at him and saw their master's face and cloak and knew that he had received his death-wound. But only the dark was where they looked: only dark silent air. Their master had received his death-wound on the battlefield of Prague far away over the sea. He was standing on the field; his hand was pressed to his side; his face was pale and strange and he wore the white cloak of a marshal.
>
> O how cold and strange it was to think of that! All the dark was cold and strange. There were pale strange faces there, great eyes like carriage-lamps. They were the ghosts of murderers, the figures of marshals who had received their death-wound on battlefields far away over the sea. What did they wish to say that their faces were so strange? (pt. i)

There are many obvious links for Stephen and the reader, joining the themes and the feelings of the stories he tells. His early fantasy of the peasants' cottages is linked with Davin's story and his own sexual reveries. His thoughts of Mercedes, the heroine of *The Count of Monte Cristo*, with his sexual fantasy. His nightmare is linked with the dream of Parnell's funeral and with the dream-sketch in the journal. His familiar fantasy of pride and pity, 'They'll be sorry when I'm dead', is linked with his later fantasies of hell and sexual guilt. The stories that are never told are his 'monstrous' sexual reveries which torment him until guilt vanishes in the vision of the wading girl, his secularized and venereal Virgin.

Just as important as these links is the development and continuity of Stephen's narratives. Creation starts with his identification with baby tuckoo and his location of the cow in the nearby road, and is present in the opposite process of defamiliarizing the dark corridor outside the dormitory in order to imagine the far-stretching and more terrifying darkness of the distant road and the haunted castle. The development of narrative fantasy is a two-way process; what is outside is made internal, its forms, ideas and images used to express the personal feelings of fear and love. The word 'nice' is used to explore the nuances of language and the nuances of filial feeling about a mother's niceness and not-so-niceness. The ghost-story which is heard and re-invented is used to colour the fantasy of death:

> He might die before his mother came. Then he would have a dead mass in the chapel like the way the fellows had told him it was when Little had died. All the fellows would be at the mass, dressed in black, all with sad faces. Wells too would be there but no fellow would look at him. The rector would be there in a cope of black and gold and there would be tall yellow candles on the altar and round the catafalque. And they would carry the coffin out of the chapel slowly and he would be buried in the little graveyard of the community off the main avenue of limes. And Wells would be sorry then for what he had done. And the bell would toll slowly. (pt. i)

And what is inside is, in its turn, projected to understand and imagine what is outside, remote, foreign or mysterious, like the death of Parnell which derives colour, imagery and feeling from his dream:

> He saw the sea of waves, long dark waves rising and falling, dark under the moonless night. A tiny light twinkled at the pierhead

where the ship was entering: and he saw a multitude of people gathered by the waters' edge to see the ship that was entering their harbour. A tall man stood on the deck, looking out towards the flat dark land: and by the light at the pierhead he saw his face, the sorrowful face of Brother Michael.

He saw him lift his hand towards the people and heard him say in a loud voice of sorrow over the waters:

—He is dead. We saw him lying upon the catafalque.

A wail of sorrow went up from the people.

—Parnell! Parnell! He is dead!

They fell upon their knees, moaning in sorrow.

And he saw Dante in a maroon velvet dress and with a green velvet mantle hanging from her shoulders walking proudly and silently past the people who knelt by the water's edge. (pt. i)

That fantasy occurs just after the personal fantasy of death and is obviously linked with it. The linkings in this section are sometimes made feverishly, jerkily and violently by Stephen's delirium.

Joyce embeds each fantasy in the immediate surroundings and sensations of the infirmary. The fantasy of death emerges from the images of cold sunlight outside the window, the longing for his mother and self-pity. The delirious vision of Parnell's funeral comes out of the paler light at the window, the sounds of the fire, voices like waves breaking and the thoughts of a book about Holland with pictures of strange cities and ships. Moreover, each of the three early morbid fantasies is related to its causes and its effects in a mixture of emotional response, the first being 'cold and strange', the second 'beautiful and sad' and the third moving from 'it made you feel so happy' to the people 'moaning in sorrow'. Joyce uses the delirium to make plain the motions of Stephen's imagination but they are the same processes that we find throughout the book, the emphasis being placed on the interplay of fantasy with memory. Unlike most characters in novels, Stephen is shown remembering his memories. The medium of narrative is at times a double act of memory, as when he remembers what Heron once said while narrating a later incident. Both are linked with the early incident of the apology and his own 'monstrous reveries'. When he goes to Cork with his father, he suffers a paralysis of memory as a reaction to his father's sentimental reminiscences. His father's memory leaves him cold but a sudden vivid reconstruction of the past students is triggered by the word 'foetus' carved in the desk, to alarm and sicken him:

> He listened without sympathy to his father's evocation of Cork and of scenes of his youth, a tale broken by sighs or draughts from his pocket flask whenever the image of some dead friend appeared in it or whenever the evoker remembered suddenly the purpose of his actual visit. Stephen heard but could feel no pity. The images of the dead were all strangers to him save that of uncle Charles, an image which had lately been fading out of memory. He knew, however, that his father's property was going to be sold by auction, and in the manner of his own dispossession he felt the world give the lie rudely to his phantasy. (pt. ii)

He is stricken and oppressed by his fantasies which make him feel incapable of any response to the outside world, unless it is to something reflecting his own state of mind, like the word 'foetus' which he finds instead of his father's initials. The guilt and obsession replace his father's nostalgia for the 'fine decent fellows' of the past and Stephen suffers an imaginative blindness, finding words on shop signs unreadable, nothing being vivid except what echoes 'the infuriated cries within him'. His attitude to these reveries is like his attitude to the company of ghosts in the nightmare and the last dream of the cave of images, for he wonders about their origin, asking 'from what den of monstrous images' they come. Joyce knows what Stephen does not know, that sexual fantasies, like the child's ghost-story, are evidence of the energetic imagination. Stephen cannot trust his fantasy until he rejects the religious basis of his guilt and is faced by the Muse, his wading girl.

At this stage he suffers a paralysis of memory which Joyce represents by recalling two episodes from the early childhood, first, the boy's game of identity in which Stephen Dedalus, of the Class of Elements, Clongowes, was placed in the Universe:

> He could scarcely recognize his own thoughts, and repeated slowly to himself:
> —I am Stephen Dedalus. I am walking beside my father whose name is Simon Dedalus. We are in Cork, in Ireland. Cork is a city. Our room is in the Victoria Hotel. Victoria and Stephen and Simon. Simon and Stephen and Victoria. Names. (pt. ii)

Secondly, like David Copperfield, he sees his past image as he meditates on the death of Parnell and the 'fading' of the little boy that he once was. This crisis of memory is the opposite of Proust's involuntary recall of feeling. Proust's was a creative impulse, Stephen's an ineffective, cold, willed summons which can evoke only names and images, which we recognize as key images like the dream, the death of Parnell, and the belt:

> The memory of his childhood suddenly grew dim. He tried to call forth some of its vivid moments but could not. He recalled only names. Dante, Parnell, Clane, Clongowes. A little boy had been taught geography by an old woman who kept two brushes in her wardrobe. Then he had been sent away from home to a college, he had made his first communion and eaten slim jim out of his cricket cap and watched the firelight leaping and dancing on the wall of a little bedroom in the infirmary and dreamed of being dead, of mass being said for him by the rector in a black and gold cope, of being buried then in the little graveyard of the community off the main avenue of limes. But he had not died then. Parnell had died. There had been no mass for the dead in the chapel and no procession. He had not died but he had faded out like a film in the sun. He had been lost or had wandered out of existence for he no longer existed. How strange to think of him passing out of existence in such a way, not by death but by fading out in the sun or by being lost and forgotten somewhere in the universe! It was strange to see his small body appear again for a moment: a little boy in a grey belted suit. His hands were in his side-pockets and his trousers were tucked in at the knees by elastic bands. (pt. ii)

Like Defoe, Joyce presents us with two versions, for even the first one was a recollection. The second is dead, killed by the warring of sentimental nostalgia and sexual guilt, neither of which can tolerate the full and felt memory of childhood, love and innocence. Stephen suffers a disease of the narrative imagination, an affliction of religious guilt and of intolerable sexual frustration, and it is this guilt which has to be lost before he can remember with feeling and imagine with freedom, as the novelist and the free man must imagine. But even in this trauma of memory, his story-telling replaces and responds to the stories he hears.

Stephen's nightmare of a lecher's hell is stimulated by the rector's sermon which it appropriates and outdoes. It dwells on those feelings and imagery which are proper to Stephen's guilty imagination. Joyce does more than simply present the horrors of excrement, goats and weeds as the right afflictions for the disturbed senses and conscience. He is always aware of the psychic sources of Stephen's fantasies and the monstrous landscape goes back a long way beyond the rector's rhetoric to Stephen's boyish adventures. At Blackrock the rocks were shaggy and weed-grown, the odours were stale with rank seawrack and the smell of the dung had sickened him at the farm at Carrickmines. The boy's play was preparing images for the revulsions of reverie. Joyce knows the matrix of his hero's images, his portrait of artistry includes a devious and half-invisible analysis of the sources of Stephen's fantasies. The result is psychic accuracy, as he weaves the web of fantasy, memory and forgetfulness. It is also a way of achieving continuity. We recognize the transmutation of the past with a pang, as pastime and play rot into nightmarish guilts. Joyce endows his hero not only with voluntary and involuntary memory but with the unconscious recall of the past. Davin confides to Stephen a private memory, Irish, romantic and sexual. It invokes a national fantasy which Stephen has to take in and reject and, like the rector's sermon, it speaks with a special eloquence to his memories as well as to his fantasies. Davin's confidences are called up by Stephen's stinging use of that 'violent or luxurious language' into which he escapes from 'the cold silence of intellectual revolt'. He tells his story of the peasant woman who asks him to stay the night and the story becomes fused in Stephen's mind with the boyhood memory and memory of memories of the peasants at Clane:

> The last words of Davin's story sang in his memory and the figure of the woman in the story stood forth reflected in other figures of the peasant women whom he had seen standing in the doorways at Clane as the college cars drove by, as a type of her race and of his own, a bat-like soul waking to the consciousness of itself in darkness and secrecy and loneliness and, through the eyes and voice and gesture of a woman without guile, calling the stranger to her bed.
>
> (pt. v)

Immediately after this memory, Davin's story colours the actual encounter with the flower-girl, whose coarse and hoydenish appearance is made into a romantic image, guileless and blue-eyed, though only for a moment:

> The blue flowers which she lifted towards him and her young blue eyes seemed to him at that instant images of guilelessness, and he halted till the image had vanished and he saw only her ragged dress and damp coarse hair and hoydenish face. (pt. v)

And the image of the bat-like soul is later attached to E.C., thought of as 'a figure of the womanhood of her country'.

Stephen's fantasy of being a Jesuit is given motive, feeling, and form by the rector's account of the vocation:

> He listened in reverent silence now to the priest's appeal and through the words he heard even more distinctly a voice bidding him approach, offering him secret knowledge and secret power. He would know then what was the sin of Simon Magus and what the sin against the Holy Ghost for which there was no forgiveness. He would know obscure things, hidden from others, from those who were conceived and born children of wrath. He would know the sins, the sinful longings and sinful thoughts and sinful acts, of others, hearing them murmured into his ears in the confessional under the shame of a darkened chapel... (pt. iv)

Stephen's is the novelist's temptation of curiosity. He longs to hear other people's stories. But if he is tempted by the narrative imagination, he is saved by its power to forsee. He imagines the daily life of the community, looks up at a room which might be his and, while imagining intensely and particularly, he checks the fantasy for plausibility and finds it lacking. Fantasy is controlled by memory which recalls a sense of his own nature, the unhealthy air of Clongowes and imposes the rational test of probability:

> Some instinct, waking at these memories, stronger than education or piety, quickened within him at every near approach to that life, an instinct subtle and hostile, and armed him against acquiescence. The chill and order of the life repelled him. He saw himself rising in the cold of the morning and filing down with the others to early mass and tying vainly to struggle with his prayers against the fainting sickness of his stomach. He saw himself sitting at dinner with the community of a college. What, then, had become of that

deep-rooted shyness of his which had made him loth to eat or drink
under a strange roof? What had come of the pride of his spirit which
had always made him conceive himself as a being apart in every
order?

The Reverend Stephen Dedalus, s.j.

His name in that new life leaped into characters before his eyes
and to it there followed a mental sensation of an undefined face or
colour of a face. (pt. iv)

He is saved too by his ability to analyse his fantasies:

He was passing at that moment before the jesuit house in Gardiner
Street and wondered vaguely which window would be his if he ever
joined the order. Then he wondered at the vagueness of his wonder,
at the remoteness of his own soul from what he had hitherto imagined
her sanctuary... (pt. iv)

The vision of the wading girl is initiated by the play on the greekness
of his name, as 'Dedalus', 'Bous Stephanoumenos'. The image of the
hawk-like man, like the ghost-story and the sexual reverie, is solicited
for meaning, 'What did it mean?' It is recognized ecstatically and
fearfully as 'the call of life to his soul'. The wading girl is a substantial
image, a Muse made by the new transubstantiation of religion into
sexuality, not only permissible but praiseworthy as inspiration. This
fantasy marks the end of guilt and the acceptance of the artist's secular
mission, 'a wild angel... the angel of mortal youth and beauty, an
envoy from the fair courts of life...'[7]. The symbol is not pressed for
meaning because, like the others, the meaning is radiantly plain. The
vision is human, the resulting ecstasy is a sexual dream, enjoyed and
celebrated. The wading girl seems to bear a resemblance to Venus, as
she appears to Aeneas in the first book of the *Aeneid*, for she is also
wearing a kilted skirt, appears by the sea, is youthful and radiant,
urges on the hero, and at last reveals her divinity.

> There, from the heart of the woodland, his mother
> came to meet him
> Guised as a maiden in face and dress, with a
> girl's weapons—

[7] The association of the envoy from life with a prostitute makes the point
more clearly in the early draft, 'A Portrait of the Artist'.

A Spartan girl, as it might be, or Thracian
        Harpalyce,
Outpacer of horses, swift outrunner of running
        rivers.
In huntress wise she had handily slung her bow
        from her shoulder,
And her hair was free to blow in the wind, and
        she went bare-kneed
With the flowing folds of her dress kilted up and
        securely knotted.

The vision has to be incorporated with the facts of everyday life, squalidly present in the pawn tickets, the breakfast table and his mother querulously (but, as he observes, pleasurably) washing his neck, the folds of his ears and the wings of his nose. This return of 'the dull gross voice of the world of duties and despair' in part five is followed by another experience of imaginative paralysis. It is a literary trauma with a sexual cause, for he remembers telling his secrets to Cranly:

> Stephen, remembering swiftly how he had told Cranly of all the tumults and unrest and longings in his soul, day after day and night by night, only to be answered by his friend's listening silence, would have told himself that it was the face of a guilty priest who heard confessions of those whom he had not power to absolve but that he felt again in memory the gaze of its dark womanish eyes.
>
> (pt. v)

The image of Cranly invokes a strange dark cavern of speculation[8] he doesn't want to enter and he is left feeling 'the nightshade of his friend's listlessness'. Once more, words die, the shop-signs are emptied of meaning, the involuntary rhymes of 'The ivy whines' torment him and are violently expelled from the mind. But once more there is resilience and recovery, and he summons enough energy to approve the one good phrase, 'yellow ivy', and by association and learned word-play his brain 'shines' and moves into a meditation on ivory, which evokes a distaste for Irishness, confirmed by Thomas Moore's statue and leading straight into the story-telling of Davin.

After the meaningless jingle, the poem of listlessness, comes the

[8] It seems to have homosexual suggestions.

villanelle. The lyric creation is an essential part of the analysis of narrative imagination because it is a stage in Stephen's development, working in the way that poetry does work, distilling its passions from happenings and using only enough image and action for intelligibility so that the line of feeling is free and uncluttered. It also does what Joyce did to *Stephen Hero*, cutting out those actions extraneous to the development of the artist, creating what Joyce called in the fragment 'Portrait of the Artist', the portrait which 'is not an identificative paper but rather the curve of an emotion'. *A Portrait of the Artist as a Young Man* may be a lyrical novel but it is a novel. Joyce was a better novelist than he was a poet. And he tells the story of the writing of the *villanelle*; its sources, its proceeding and its effect. The poetic composition is related to the conversations and happenings of the day before, his meeting with E.C., his jealousy of her friendship with the priest, Father Moran, a joke about ellipsoidal balls, a phrase from Galvani, 'the enchantment of the heart', and the night's sexual dream. All the images and events and feelings are combined, sublimated or secularized, to write a poem about the process itself. The secularization precedes the poem: 'In the virgin womb of the imagination the word was made flesh. Gabriel the seraph had come to the virgin's chamber'.

We move step by step from the poet's awakening through the slow and interrupted making of the *villanelle*. Its first lines suggest the raying out of rhyme, rays being the rhyme not used in the poem which images succinctly its form and feeling. The poem draws on the matrix of imagery established in the novel, the fall, the seraphim, enchantment, temptation, and the images that occur in the mind, from literature, from the immediate surroundings, from dream and daybreak, permuted through the order of the *villanelle* to order and sieve the events of the previous day. This artist is to move from the lyric to the prose story and Joyce makes us see that the *villanelle* in fact tells a story, like most lyrics. It is about the forsaking of ardent ways, about a temptation, even about the awakening from a sexual dream and a revived sexual feeling, 'a glow of desire kindled again his soul and fired and fulfilled all his body'. It is about E.C. and her priest. Even the moment when he can't write any more provides the image of 'broken cries'. Not only is the curve of emotion and the imagery related to its source but the poem's history is followed into the mundane world where it might be read at breakfast amid the tapping of egg shells. It is like his prose journal in its secularization and sublimation, in its imagery, even in its feelings, but it is a rejection of the old ardent ways, of all that he had thought he thought and felt he felt. It is a poetic rendering of the journal's blunt advice, 'give it up, old chap!' It makes room for the world of breakfast and egg shells, and the cigarette packet on which it is written. It is a poetic valediction to E.C. and a proof of the secular and sexual inspiration of art. The vision of the wading girl stimulated one sexual dream, this dream inspires a poem. The action of imagination still works in two directions, from the outside to the inside and back again.

Stephen stops writing poems, which are love-poems, as he tells E.C., recording their conversation in that other remarkable illustration of his working imagination, the journal at the end of the novel. We now move, technically, from the third person to the first person, reversing the process of 'Turpin Hero', though to move into a reflexiveness which is a preliminary to the process of purification and impersonalization. He has found his name and nature, has cleared away the sexual guilt and religious lures which inhibited and distorted his imagination. The journal brings together every narrative mode in the book. Stephen's journal draws on the matrix of narrative forms and feelings provided by the novel, in dream, anecdote, prose-poem, mundane reminiscence, visionary fantasy and literature. At last, the faint but pervasive play of irony on the grand styles finds new company, an honest, blunt, self-critical ability which checks the grandiose and allows it—briefly—to be grand. The dream-figures in the long curving gallery look to the future, but go back to the beginning, peering, questioning, and producing the shadowy answer in their suggestions of undifferentiated stuff for the novelist's imagination to work on: 'Their hands are folded upon their knees in token of weariness and their eyes are darkened for the errors of men go up before them for ever as dark vapours... They peer at me and their eyes seem to ask me something. They do not speak'. The fragmentary stream of consciousness in the entry for April 5 salutes life, 'O life!' and looks forward in many ways to *Ulysses*: 'Dark stream of swirling bogwater on which apple-trees have cast down their delicate flowers. Eyes of girls among the leaves. Girls demure and romping'. The strictly prosaic account of the farewell to E.C., clinched by the reference to Cranly's succession, is reinforced by the memory of Lynch's comment that women are obsessed with memory, a comment disappointingly lacking in irony for such a novel. Just as the endings of many Victorian novels assemble characters and fates, so this novel brings together the images and forms of Stephen's imagination. It dismisses memory, but as a journal depends on it and will preserve it. It is constantly self-critical, objecting to the phrase 'into Nile mud' and to the 'vague words for a vague emotion' in the prose-poem of the entry for April 10, one of the several that come from Joyce's recorded dreams. Its romantic fluidity looks ahead and questions, 'to what journey's end—what heart?—bearing what tidings?' The novel in which fantasy and memory have fought so vigorously celebrates the future and rejects Yeats's celebration of the past, 'I desire to press in my arms the loveliness which has not yet come into the world'. He tells with mockery and respect Mulrennan's story of his visit to the west of Ireland and makes it, too, his own. He fears the red-rimmed eyes of the old man, an Irish Ancient Mariner who is an ominous warning for a traveller, not only in his insistent Irishness but in the image of the 'terrible queer creatures at the latter end of the world'. He is a grisly stay-at-home Ancient Mariner, but Stephen's hostility to him significantly drops off and the image of the struggle ends, 'I mean no harm'.

The shift from aggressiveness to benevolence is implicit in the record of his last encounter with E.C., where he comments ironically on his own refrigerating irony. He responds to her good wishes, 'I call that friendly', and 'I liked her and it seems a new feeling to me'. It is a new feeling to the reader of the novel too and a new way of telling the story of his passionate problems. The journal marks a significant movement away from the unanalysed ironies of the literary parody and *erlebte Rede* of the main narrative into a frank and open reflection on event, narrative and style. Tensions and pretensions are scrupulously recorded and regarded. The modes of memory and fantasy are changed. The unpretentious relaxation of 'give it up, old chap!' permits the final intensity of the images of distant roads, with the challenge or promise of their 'tale of distant nations'. His mother's equivocal blessing is followed by the equivocal invocation of Daedalus. The novel ends, as it began, with fatherhood and story. The last story, like the first, is traditional and its invocation provides a role and a recognition for Stephen. He was once 'baby tuckoo', and he is now Daedalus, perhaps also Icarus. The last story is a caveat to sons, fathers, inventors, travellers, exiles and refugees. It is a story of murder and failure, enterprise and imagination, fall and flight.

He has inserted himself into a story, flexibly, warily, but for good, a fiction within his own fiction, his life imitating his art. The final flourish of an invocation comes as part of the tentative series of journal entries. Their stories have been informal and provisional, checked by each other. Their responses have been impromptu, relaxed and readily directed towards the presences of other people. Stephen frequently says he is free and the insistence is suspect, especially in a novel which has trained us to be suspicious of styles and stories, and has shown the hero's progress through the dangerous solicitations of language and literature. In a sense he is free, or freer, at the end, because he admits the provisional nature of his visions and the inevitability of revisions. Stephen's journal is an admission of his arrival, or at least of his departure, since it marks a beginning in an informal form. For the novelist, it is the end of parody, the beginning of a serious commitment to the personal narrative. The artist has arrived at the point of using mutually controlling styles and forms which fluctuate between intensity and informality, allowing for preciser forms for preciser feeling. Narrative can include the prose-poem, the anecdote and the dream, and can also include the broken, revised and analysed version of his days and nights. Each entry is set down quickly for immediate scrutiny, to be inspected, contemplated and criticized. This broken and provisional narrative expresses a professional wariness, a respect for the form and for the feeling it embodies, but also self-respect, confidence and determination. The form of the journal is a perfect medium for such decisions and revisions. The novelist is at least preparing for the later stages where self is re-projected, perhaps even purified. If his clothes are new, they are second-hand. He leaves home but still has mother to do the packing. He goes to forge the 'uncreated conscience' of his race 'for the millionth time'. He may be getting ready to write *Dubliners*.

III. ULYSSES

Ulysses contains and extends the self-analysis of the narrative imagination in *Dubliners* and *A Portrait of the Artist as a Young Man*. It continues the weavings and un-weavings of memory and fantasy, the exaltation and extinction of public story-telling, the coincidence and counterpoint of private stories. Like *Dubliners*, it inspects and sets to work the minds of people who are not artists and shows the business and busyness of their narrative constructions. Like *A Portrait of the Artist as a Young Man*, it shows the processes of imaginative procreation as its story-tellers listen to other people's stories and their telling is changed by their listening. In all this it emphasizes what Stephen tried to deny, the strengths of memory.

Ulysses is a novel of memory, in the long tradition which includes the science and humour of Sterne, the evolutionary analysis of Wordsworth and George Eliot, and Dickens's movement from the nostalgia of *David Copperfield* to the ironic, experienced understanding of *Great Expectations*. It is startlingly unlike these ancestors in its time-span. The short span of the short story is transferred to the novel. Its people have only a day in which to remember. The apparent disadvantage is an immense advantage, showing the synchronizing of mental adventures, the presence of past in present, the constant shuttling between what was, what is and what may be. All three of the main characters remember intensely and persistently. Stephen Dedalus is still writing love-poems. He has written some epiphanies but he has not yet written anything like Joyce's *Dubliners*. He is haunted by memories which circle around his refusal to serve religion and mother, by remorse or *agenbite of inwit*, the Anglo-Saxon term which in its pedantic esotericism gives Stephen's conscience a code name and an impersonal dignity. Leopold Bloom moves freely and actively through his diurnal round, but constantly turns back from the defects of the present to earlier, better times, to the old days of courtship, early marriage and the love-making that was never the same after Rudy's death. The ghostly fantasy of unacted possibilities, which shadows the memories of what actually was, accompanies him but does not pervert his imagination. He remembers the child dead and can conjure him up as the boy he might have become, but he can shake off sentimentality, remorse and even jealous curiosity. Molly shares Bloom's life-in-memory but has her own secrecy and privacy. She also shares his remarkably strong acceptance of past and present.

Stephen's powers of invention are still alive and the Proteus and Ithaca episodes show his imagination working in poetic and narrative forms. In *A Portrait of the Artist as a Young Man*, his savouring of the word was conspicuous but his learning to use and relish language was invariably seen as a narrative activity. The word lived as part of a story. When it went dead, it partook of the larger demise of memory and reverie. In *Ulysses* also, we see a sensuous and intellectual response to experience which expresses and constructs. Stephen has thrown off the religious inhibitions but has found the new inhibition of remorse.

He was confident about casting off memory at the end of *A Portrait of the Artist as a Young Man* where he spoke with contempt of the backward glance as female and archaic, but in *Ulysses* his imagination looks back constantly. Stephen begins with the memory of a dream of his mother, 'in a dream she had come to him after death'. He sees the dream image while he looks at the fraying coat-sleeve of the punctilious mourning which he shares with Hamlet. Like his poetry, his remorseful imaginings inhabit the ordinary world. Over his sleeve he can see the sea which Buck Mulligan has just described as 'our great sweet mother', but the encircled bay with its green waters invokes the china bowl which held his mother's vomited bile. The links and affinities are perceived by imagination but its action is obsessive. Like Hamlet, he has returned home from his studies for a funeral; like Hamlet, he needs but flouts his companions; like Hamlet, he wears mourning and, like Hamlet, he can only remember. He broods on Buck Mulligan's words about his mother being 'beastly dead', and Mulligan reproves him in the mocking quotation from Yeats, 'And no more turn aside and brood', to present Stephen with a convenient motif which turns out to be yet another reminder of his mother's death-bed, for 'she wanted to hear my music'. The dream is repeated, accompanied by his attempt to imagine his mother's early memories. Although Stephen cannot escape the remorseful memory, he is for the first time imagining someone else's memory, her secrets put away with her sacred objects, 'muskperfumed'. There follows a chain of painful, involuntary memories which 'beset his brooding brain', the drink of water before mass, a roast apple and 'her shapely fingernails reddened by the blood of squashed lice'. Stephen's uncertainties and inhibitions are defined as well as provoked by Mulligan's verses and stories about old mother Grogan and Mary Ann, his esoteric joke about the collector of pre-puces, which addresses itself to his fellows over the old milk-woman's head, the mocking 'Heart of my heart' and the ballad of Joking Jesus. Stephen responds gloomily, though he later shows his own prowess in flouting narrative with the shaggy-dog story of the three ladies who climbed Nelson's pillar, his 'Pisgahsight of Palestine or The Parable of the Plums', which he uses to deride Nelson, 'the one-armed adulterer' and all Dublin viewed from the column.

His theory of *Hamlet*, composed of a re-telling of the play and some biographical speculation is also a self-undermined performance, an ironic and throwaway story. Joyce's analysis of mourning, melancholy and companionship on the Martello tower harps on *Hamlet*, and Stephen's *Hamlet* analysis still harps on his mother. It also invokes Hamlet's doubts about the reliability of the ghost's image in its sense of paternity's uncertainty—'Amor matris, subjective and objective genitive' seeming the 'only true thing in life'. It is appropriate that Stephen should brood on Hamlet's brooding in this backward-looking phase.

It is also appropriate that he should brood on history. The flexible efforts of his imagination are evident in his biographical and narrative essays in literary criticism, and in his teaching. When he is helping Cyril Sargent to do his sums after school, he broods on Mrs Sargent's mother-love and once more a personal obsession leads away from self. He is genuinely asking about somebody else's life:

> Ugly and futile: lean neck and tangled hair and a stain of ink, a snail's bed. Yet someone had loved him, borne him in her arms and in her heart. But for her the race of the world would have trampled him under foot, a squashed boneless snail. ('Nestor')

He overcomes his revulsion by compassion; he has regard for someone else and self-pity gives way to sympathy. He reverts to his earlier question: 'Was that then real? The only true thing in life?' but thinks about Sargent's story, gives him help beyond the call of duty, speaks to him kindly, and sees their common life and their common privacy. Here too, imagination is inseparable from memory:

> Like him was I, these sloping shoulders, this gracelessness. My childhood bends beside me. Too far for me to lay a hand there once or lightly. Mine is far and his secret as our eyes. Secrets, silent, stony sit in the dark palaces of both our hearts: secrets weary of their tyranny: tyrants willing to be dethroned. (ibid.)

Stephen reflects on history, considering Blake's view that it is fabled 'by the daughters of memory', and meditating on the necessity of fable, 'And yet it was in some way if not as memory fabled it'. He rejects an Irish view that 'history was a tale like any other too often heard, their land a pawnshop'. He struggles with concepts of history and the sense of history because it has become imperative for him to imagine the past. Remorse has moved him beyond the simple future-worship of the end of *A Portrait of the Artist as a Young Man*, where he disagreed with Yeats's Michael Robartes. Now he takes mood, motif and motto from Yeats's Fergus, but his personal obsession with the past has a larger dimension and a more generalized brooding. He realizes that historical events like the deaths of Pyrrhus or Caesar[9] 'are not to be thought away' since 'Time has branded them and fettered they are lodged in the room of the infinite possibilities they have ousted'. The meditation moves beyond narrative to consider problems of possibility, Stephen's thinking having become more agile in speculation than when we saw it last. But he is still a narrator and his abstract thinking is concerned with historical narration. His interest in history is alerted by the obsessions of memory, the bitter brooding having encouraged a new attitude towards past as well as present. And Joyce is writing a novel where myth and analogy encourage a new attitude towards past as well as present. The boys ask Stephen for a ghost story and he keeps telling other ghost stories to himself and others, the story of Hamlet, and the story of his mother's wraith. Joyce is also telling a ghost story and *Ulysses* is haunted by many ghosts, Mrs Dedalus, Parnell, Rudy, Rudolf Virag, Telemachus, Penelope and Ulysses. Stephen's specializations in narrative are like those of his novelist in this novel; he is backward-looking but he recoils in order to leap forward.

When he mimics what Joyce does in historical narrative and biographical surmise Stephen too marks coincidences, relates himself to another son because they both had mothers, imagines the toppling masonry and shattered glass of Asculum as if it were present, 'I hear the ruin of all space', and later on makes it present indeed when he breaks the lamp-chimney in the brothel. Joyce brings together Stephen's imagination, still that of the artist as a young man, and his own maturer imagination. Stephen's imagination works like his author's, joining disparities, especially disparities of time and space. There are occasions in the novel when he almost seems to be writing his own story, especially in the Proteus section where events are thought through his mind and seen through his eyes. Among his memories, anticipations and fantasies, comes an actual experience of writing; he imitates Hamlet's use of his tablets as he bends to scribble part of a poem on the blank end of Mr Deasy's letter. The poem contains the image of 'mouth to her kiss' which he rewrites more glueily as 'mouth to her mouth's kiss'. He adds in reflection, and not on paper, 'who ever anywhere will read these written words?' At this moment his writing

[9] Hamlet also broods on these deaths.

is assimilated to Joyce's as the reader of *Ulysses* reads and therefore answers his question.

There are some things in Stephen's imagination which he shares with Bloom. Amongst these coincidences is the image of the kiss and its appropriate expression. On Bloom's first appearance the gluey kiss turns up in Bloom's equally good poetry, 'lips kissed, kissing kissed. Full gluey woman's lips'. This image copulates with another like love with death. Stephen and Bloom adopt the Odyssey's recurring image of the journeying sun. Stephen's version follows the sun west towards its overthrow by night:

> Across the sands of all the world, followed by the sun's flaming sword, to the west, trekking to evening lands. She trudges, schlepps, trains, drags, trascines her load. A tide westering, moondrawn, in her wake. Tides, myriadislanded, within her, blood not mine, *oinopa ponton*, a winedark sea. Behold the handmaid of the moon. In sleep the wet sign calls her hour, bids her rise. Bridebed, childbed, bed of death, ghostcandled. *Omnis caro ad te veniet.* He comes, pale vampire, through storm his eyes... ('Proteus')

Bloom's mind traces the pattern from lips to the orient sun, countering Stephen's westering by his eastering:

> Somewhere in the east: early morning: set off at dawn, travel round in front of the sun, steal a day's march on him. Keep it up for ever never grow a day older technically. Walk along a strand, strange land, come to city gate, sentry there, old ranker too, old Tweedy's big moustaches leaning on a long kind of a spear. Wander through awned streets. Turbaned faces going by. Dark caves of carpet shops, big man, Turko the terrible, seated crosslegged smoking a coiled pipe. Cries of sellers in the streets. Drink water scented with fennel, sherbet. Wander all day. Might meet a robber or two. Well, meet him. ('Calypso')

Again, each has his own style; Stephen's is elegantly cadenced, flowing and exotically imaged; Bloom's is less euphonious but lit with humour: 'steal a day's march', punctuated by courageous resignation: 'Well, meet him', and rattled off in his own brand of telegraphese which may have derived from Dickens's Jingle in *Pickwick Papers* to answer perfectly his very different individual needs. (Jingle was the fast-talking con-man, blinding his victims with words and narrative. Bloom's rapid movement is the notation and the proof of his agile sympathies.) The joining of two minds, subliminally and secretly, helps on the feeling that Stephen's relationship to the novel Joyce is writing is peculiarly reflexive. It also impels expectation towards the juncture of Stephen and Bloom, and comes to create the sense of subliminal affinity. But Stephen's imagination is not only linked with Bloom's. When Bloom and Molly are in bed, making love after a fashion and telling stories, like Odysseus and Penelope, he tells her about Stephen, who immediately becomes part of her fantasy-life too. Like Stephen and Bloom, Molly and Bloom also share certain stories and the sharing testifies to their compatibility and curious constancy. They are both active in imagination and both loyally appreciative of each other's mental qualities. But their loyalty takes many forms.

Molly comes to give an almost free rein to her fantasy about having an affair with Stephen. Her sexual narration falls into two parts, the memory and the fantasy, both heated by her afternoon in bed with Boylan. Despite the powers of local physical stimulus, her mind comes back home from the excursions of both memory and anticipation. She weaves a web of promiscuous memory and fantasy, to unweave it and return to Bloom. The image of weaving is Homeric, Joycean, and just right for Molly's shapely acts of remembering. Her monologue is anything but random in its processes and the last brilliant spurt of memory is carefully placed within another memory. What passes through her mind is what passed through it sixteen years ago when Bloom proposed to her. As she remembers his proposal we are suspended for a page while she tells her memory of all those memories that delayed her answer:

I gave him all the pleasure I could leading him on till he asked me to say yes and I wouldnt answer first only looked out over the sea and the sky I was thinking of so many things he didnt know of Mulvey and Mr Stanhope and Hester and father and old captain Groves and the sailors playing all birds fly and I say stoop and washing up dishes they called it on the pier and the sentry in front of the governors house with the thing round his white helmet poor devil half roasted and the Spanish girls laughing in their shawls and their tall combs and the auctions in the morning the Greeks and the jews and the Arabs and the devil knows who else from all the ends of Europe and Duke street and the fowl market all clucking outside Larby Sharons and the poor donkeys slipping half asleep and the vague fellows in the cloaks asleep in the shade on the steps and the big wheels of the carts of the bulls and the old castle thousands of years old yes and those handsome Moors all in white and turbans like kings asking you to sit down in their little bit of a shop and Ronda with the old windows of the posadas glancing eyes a lattice hid for her lover to kiss the iron and the wineshops half open at night and the castanets and the night we missed the boat at Algeciras the watchman going about serene with his lamp and O that awful deepdown torrent O and the sea the sea crimson sometimes like fire and the glorious sunsets and the figtrees in the Alameda gardens yes and all the queer little streets and pink and blue and yellow houses and the rosegardens and the jessamine and geraniums and cactuses and Gibraltar as a girl where I was a Flower of the mountain yes when I put the rose in my hair like the Andalusian girls used or shall I wear a red yes and how he kissed me under the Moorish wall... ('Penelope')

The suspension is syntactically clear and controlled, beginning with 'I wouldnt answer first only looked out over the sea and the sky I was thinking of so many things he didnt know of Mulvey and Mr Stanhope...'. The many objects of 'I was thinking' follow in a stream of memory as superficially disordered and as fundamentally orderly as the garrulous narrative flow of Miss Bates in *Emma*. The last memory is reached as she remembers how 'he kissed me under the Moorish wall'. The internal memories end, to return to the primary memory of Bloom, the governing subject of which she has never lost sight:

and I thought well as well him as another and then I asked him with my eyes to ask again yes and then he asked me would I yes to say yes my mountain flower and first I put my arms around him yes and drew him down to me so he could feel my breasts all perfume yes and his heart was going like mad and yes I said yes I will Yes. (ibid.)

The memory of memory so elegantly managed in *A Portrait of the Artist as a Young Man* is here used to suggest misleadingly a random flow but actually to lead and direct that flow. Molly's memories crowd upon each other but she is not confused or distracted. She directs them, and they are, after all, distinctly memories of memories. She may not punctuate but she manages an elaborate periodic style and its control is significant. She remembers Bloom first and last and only through him does she remember Mulvey. If Molly's memories are controlled, so is her fantasy which is romantically made and realistically unmade:

Ill read and study all I can find or learn a bit off by heart if I knew who he likes so he wont think me stupid if he thinks all women are the same and I can teach him the other part Ill make him feel all over him till he half faints under me then hell write about me lover and mistress publicly too with our 2 photographs in all the papers when he becomes famous O but then what am I going to do about him though. . . (ibid.)

To recognize Molly's pattern of memory and fantasy is to appreciate the care Joyce takes not to sentimentalize her imagination. At times her mental narratives sway about. She moves from 'O thanks be to the great God I got somebody to give me what I badly wanted' to 'I wish somebody would write me a love letter his wasn't much'. She remembers Mulvey's penis but isn't too sure of his Christian name. Her memory of Boylan sometimes rouses her aggressiveness towards Bloom and she sometimes lumps all her men together in superiority and hostility. But her memory and fantasy invariably give way to the appreciative recall of Bloom's intelligence and delicacy, a recall of qualities which the reader shares, for he has experienced them too. If it were not so, Molly's memory would be sentimental but its curious fidelities are justified, appreciated as appreciative of a real present. She is never merely nostalgic. Her fantasy may move more quickly, more erratically and more roughly than Bloom's sympathetic but terse story-telling, but it is nearly as fertile, nearly as sympathetic and just as faithful. Grounded in matter-of-factness, humour, craft and loyalty, her memory is a Penelope.

The Blooms' jingling bed, in which Molly does all her story-telling and listening, is Joyce's mutation of the deeply-rooted marriage bed[10] built by Odysseus. Though significantly different in kind and use, the bed plays a part in Joyce very like that of its more stable ancestor in the *Odyssey*. The same is true of the story-telling of the hero, though not so straightforwardly. Homer's Odysseus is one of the best inventors in history or literature and his imagination, like Bloom's, is scientific (occupied with technical constructions) and literary (occupied with verbal constructions). Odysseus is a great liar, surpassing Huckleberry

[10] It is also related to the second-best bed bequeathed by Shakespeare to Anne Hathaway.

Finn and Beckett's story-tellers, but, like them, telling his stories in order to survive. His lies, so opprobious to Dante, were as necessary for his survival as his wooden horse and equally concerned with materials, methods and reception. He talks and tells his way back home from Calypso's cave and his stories are inspired by the artist's sense of purpose, plausibility, performance and audience. Each of his lies is effective because he has one eye for disguise and impersonation, which he greatly enjoys, and one for his listener, whether it is Calypso, Circe, Menelaus, Helen or Nausicaa and her parents. Only once does he lose his head, to be carried away by his inventive history, when he tells the superfluous lie to Pallas Athene,[11] in an episode of some importance to feminist chroniclers of narrative imagination.

Perhaps the only close parallel between Odysseus and Bloom as narrators is the story each tells to his wife. It is the common, necessary and sometimes loving spousal tale of what has happened since they last met, of particular value to stay-at-home wives[12] like Penelope and Molly. It is not a story that can be told completely and candidly and Bloom leaves out several details and adds others:

> With what modifications did the narrator reply to this interrogation? Negative: he omitted to mention the clandestine correspondence between Martha Clifford and Henry Flower, the public altercation at, in and in the vicinity of the licensed premises of Bernard Kiernan and Co, Limited, 8, 9 and 10 Little Britain street, the erotic provocation and response thereto caused by the exhibitionism of Gertrude (Gerty), surname unknown. ('Ithaca')

Joyce makes it plain that his story is carefully shaped and by its most recent and most important incident, for the salient character emerges as 'Stephen Dedalus, professor and author'. Molly interrogates her husband when he wakes her up by kissing her behind. We are told that the narration was intermittent 'and increasingly more laconic', and that during its course listener and narrator reflected on their history of 'limitations of activity and inhibitions of conjugal right'. This is the story of a man's day. It is Joyce's version of Odysseus's homecoming history of his nineteen years' absence, which also involved

---

[11] See above p. 14.

[12] Molly also introduces a happy variation on the ancient theme of the listening woman, for though she is a stay-at-home, like Calypso, Circe, Dido and Desdemona, her bedroom has its adventures and her memory has the last word.

a foreclosure of conjugal rights, and was also to be told during the reunions of the night:

> But Odysseus and Penelope, after their love had taken its sweet course, turned to the fresh delights of talk, and interchanged their news. He heard this noble wife tell of all she had put up with in his home, watching that gang of wreckers at their work, of all the cattle and fat sheep that they had slaughtered for her sake, of all the vessels they had emptied of their wine. And in his turn, royal Odysseus told her of all the discomfiture he had inflicted on his foes and all the miseries which he himself had undergone. She listened spellbound, and her eyelids never closed in sleep till the whole tale was finished. (*Odyssey*, bk. xxiii)

Odysseus's narrative imagination would have translated easily into Irish blarney or Jewish story-telling. Such translation was perhaps too obvious to appeal to Joyce, who is in any case not sympathetic to garrulousness. Joyce's talking Irishmen (Lenehan, Corley, Gallaher and Murphy) are often dishonest, alcoholic and on the make, and in *A Portrait of the Artist as a Young Man* Stephen's memory is drained of sentiment by his father's sentimental reminiscences. It is one of Joyce's most brilliant feats of invention to make his Ulysses a silent man, though perhaps it would be more accurate to say that Bloom is relatively silent. He is certainly not taciturn and on some occasions would like to say more than he actually does. On the way to Paddy Dignam's funeral, for instance, Martin Cunningham, who headed the narrative pecking order in 'Grace', returns to rebuke Bloom's genius. Bloom tries to tell an eager and ingratiating story, chiefly to cover an awkward moment ('That's an awfully good one that's going the rounds about Reuben J. and the son'), but first Simon Dedalus interrupts him several times before he can even get started and then, after three attempts to tell the story, he is 'thwarted...rudely' by Martin Cunningham. Bloom does not excel at public story-telling, being frequently ill at ease in society, subdued by other men's talents, embarrassed, preoccupied and solitary. He is a great story-teller nonetheless, though the stories he tells are not in the least Homeric. Joyce endows him with a private energy of narrative imagination very different from Odysseus's assured, authoritative and manipulative performances, which are designed to impress, command, win, survive and get back home.

But Bloom also gets through his day, and his life, by telling stories, chiefly to the excellent audience of himself.

His story-telling is circumambient and fetching. If love was the word Joyce disliked to say aloud, he shows its power and direction in Bloom's imagination. Despite the jostling and ousting of his narrative, he is indebted to Martin Cunningham who knows the story of Rudolph Virag's suicide and talks tactfully and tolerantly on the subject. Bloom follows his grateful but silent recognition by imagining the story of the private life of the successful public man. Martin Cunningham's story is rehearsed in Bloom's characteristic telegraphese, which conveys a quick, vibrant, energetic survey of the essentials of another man's life:

And that awful drunkard of a wife of his. Setting up house for her time after time and then pawning the furniture on him every Saturday almost. Leading him the life of the damned. Wear the heart out of a stone, that. Monday morning start afresh. Shoulder to the wheel. Lord, she must have looked a sight that night, Dedalus told me he was in there. Drunk about the place and capering with Martin's umbrella. ('Hades')

Like is quick to know like and Cunningham recognizes John O'Connell, the cemetery-keeper, as a good sort when he tells his story of the two drunks looking for Mulcahy's grave:

—They tell the story, he said, that two drunks came out here one foggy evening to look for the grave of a friend of theirs. They asked for Mulcahy from the Coombe and were told where he was buried. After traipsing about in the fog they found the grave, sure enough. One of the drunks spelt out the name: Terence Mulcahy. The other drunk was blinking up at a statue of our Saviour the widow had got put up.

The caretaker blinked up at one of the sepulchres they passed. He resumed:

—And, after blinking up at the sacred figure, *Not a bloody bit like the man*, says he. *That's not Mulcahy*, says he, *whoever done it.*

Rewarded by smiles he fell back and spoke with Corny Kelleher, accepting the dockets given him, turning them over and scanning them as he walked.

—That's all done with a purpose, Martin Cunningham explained to Hynes.

—I know, Hynes said, I know that.

—To cheer a fellow up, Martin Cunningham said. It's pure good-heartedness: damn the thing else. (ibid.)

Bloom also appreciates this Dublin Dis, but his appreciation takes the narrative form of a good-tempered comic fantasy:

> Fancy being his wife. Wonder how he had the gumption to propose to any girl. Come out and live in the graveyard. Dangle that before her. It might thrill her first. Courting death... Shades of night hovering here with all the dead stretched about. The shadows of the tombs when churchyards yawn and Daniel O'Connell must be a descendant I suppose who is this used to say he was queer breedy man great catholic all the same like a big giant in the dark. Will o' the wisp. Gas of graves. Want to keep her mind off it to conceive at all. Women especially are so touchy. Tell her a ghost story in bed to make her sleep. Have you ever seen a ghost? Well, I have. It was a pitchdark night. (ibid.)

Like his author's, his story is about story-telling. This is Bloom's narrative style, adaptable to all occasions. He reminds himself in the quick run-through of the stories of his acquaintances and offers the same fast but attentive response to strangers and people he scarcely knows, such as the slavey in the butcher's shop. The tale he outlines is shrewdly speculative, laconically picking on essentials:

> He stood by the nextdoor girl at the counter. Would she buy it too, calling the items from a slip in her hand. Chapped: washing-soda. And a pound and a half of Denny's sausages. His eyes rested on her vigorous hips. Woods his name is. Wonder what he does. Wife is oldish. New blood. No followers allowed. Strong pair of arms. Whacking a carpet on the clothesline. She does whack it, by George. The way her crooked skirt swings at each whack. ('Calypso')

Bloom's thousand and one stories are not usually sentimental; they are often matter-of-fact or even ruthless. He is capable of sufficient detachment, imagining what it is like to be a priest, or a chemist, quickly telling himself the likely story of a life. Waiting for his prescription, he shadows forth a biography of the chemist:

> The chemist turned back page after page. Sandy shrivelled smell he seems to have. Shrunken skull. And old. Quest for the philosopher's

stone. The alchemists. Drugs age you after mental excitement. Lethargy then. Why? Reaction. A lifetime in a night. Gradually changes your character. Living all the day among herbs, ointments, disinfectants. All his alabaster lilypots. Mortar and pestle. Aq. Dist. Fol. Laur. Te Virid. Smell almost cure you like the dentist's doorbell. Doctor whack. He ought to physic himself a bit. Electuary or emulsion. The first fellow that picked an herb to cure himself had a bit of pluck. Simples. Want to be careful. Enough stuff here to chloroform you. Test: turns blue litmus paper red. Chloroform.

('Lotus Eaters')

His characteristic mode of speculative biography can run a more difficult course. When he sees the blind man across the road, his consciousness both of his telling and the other's silence is sympathetic. But there are limits to sympathy and limits to listening. Bloom imagines the other life, but returns to his own reverie, and is certainly not sentimental about the blind man:

Look at all the things they can learn to do. Read with their fingers. Tune pianos. Or we are surprised they have any brains. Why we think a deformed person or a hunchback clever if he says something we might say. Of course the other senses are more. Embroider. Plait baskets. People ought to help. Work basket I could buy Molly's birthday. Hates sewing. Might take an objection. Dark men they call them.

Sense of smell must be stronger too. Smells on all sides bunched together. Each person too. Then the spring, the summer: smells. Tastes. They say you can't taste wines with your eyes shut or a cold in the head. Also smoke in the dark they say get no pleasure.

And with a woman, for instance. More shameless not seeing. That girl passing the Stewart institution, head in the air. Look at me. I have them all on. Must be strange not to see her. Kind of a form in his mind's eye. The voice temperature when he touches her with fingers must almost see the lines, the curves. His hands on her hair, for instance. Say it was black for instance. Good. We call it black. Then passing over her white skin. Different feel perhaps. Feeling of white.

Postoffice. Must answer. Fag today. Send her a postal order two shillings half a crown.

...

Poor fellow! Quite a boy. Terrible. Really terrible. What dreams would he have, not seeing? Life a dream for him. Where is the justice being born that way? All those women and children excursion beanfeast burned and drowned in New York. Holocaust. Karma they call that transmigration for sins you did in a past life the reincarnation met him pikehoses. Dear, dear, dear. Pity of course: but somehow you can't cotton on to them someway.

(‘Lestrygonians’)

The imagining of other people's lives is detailed, amused, irreverent, racy, never in any danger of excessive empathy. Bloom goes in and out of his own story with speed and agility, imagination on tap, sympathy at the ready. Negative capability never runs away with him. He stops short before imagination leads him into a debilitating pity for the blind or the dead. He even checks his depressed and depressing fantasy of the cities of the plain which a clouded sun has encouraged:

A barren land, bare waste. Vulcanic lake, the dead sea: no fish, weedless, sunk deep in the earth. No wind would lift those waves, grey metal, poisonous foggy waters. Brimstone they called it raining down: the cities of the plain: Sodom, Gomorrah, Edom. All dead names. A dead sea in a dead land, grey and old. Old now. It bore the oldest, the first race. A bent hag crossed from Cassidy's clutching a noggin bottle by the neck. The oldest people. Wandered far away over all the earth, captivity to captivity, multiplying, dying, being born everywhere. It lay there now. Now it could bear no more. Dead: an old woman's: the grey sunken cunt of the world.

(‘Calypso’)

His ability to live in the present is remarkable. It is made possible by his imaginative and scientific self-knowledge. Joyce knows that the cloud over the sun impelled his fantasy of social and sexual death. Bloom knows that his depression is related to his somatic state (‘Morning mouth bad images’) and can be controlled. He plans to take exercise (‘On the hands down’) and warms himself with the memory and anticipation of Molly's ample bedwarmed flesh.

He is impressively alert to the story of cattle going to be slaughtered, seagulls, billboard men, women in childbed and the hungry Dedalus girls, but he is also sufficiently and impressively self-centred. He reflects dispassionately that the ‘noisy, self-willed man’ Mr Dedalus is right to be 'full of' his son but moves passionately to his own sonless state and the soul of fantasy, the might-have-been. The fantasy too is preserved from nostalgia and self-pity by its amused and solid matter-of-factness:

> If little Rudy had lived. See him grow up. Hear his voice in the house. Walking beside Molly in an Eton suit. My son. Me in his eyes. Strange feeling it would be. From me. Just a chance. Must have been that morning in Raymond terrace she was at the window, watching the two dogs at it by the wall of the cease to do evil. And the sergeant grinning up. She had that cream gown on with the rip she never stitched. Give us a touch, Poldy, God, I'm dying for it. How life begins.
>
> Got big then. Had to refuse the Greystones concert. My son inside her. I could have helped him on in life. I could. Make him independent. Learn German too. ('Hades')

Like Molly's, his fantasies and memories are active but grounded by common sense, like that shared fantasy of stealing a march on the sun or his plan for investing in olive-groves or oranges north of Jaffa, which is gravely read and contemplated, then turned down, 'Nothing doing. Still an idea behind it'. As he walks, shops, reads, sees, smells, talks, observes, defecates, masturbates and urinates, his imagination invents, plans, speculates, fancies and remembers. Its benevolence of imagination is like that of Hardy's story-tellers, shrewd, tolerant, but capable of optimism, pity and imaginative self-denial, at least for a while. His inventiveness is technological, quickly stimulated to story by the thought of all the dead bodies in the cemetery,[13] by buildings, food, weather, animals and objects. As for most fervent minds, much in the present is unwelcome, yet the present is accepted and praised for its liveliness. His stoutness and tenderness of memory is significant, reminding us of that return which is literal and metaphorical, a homing of love:

> Silvered powdered olivetrees. Quiet long days: pruning ripening. Olives are packed in jars, eh? I have a few left from Andrews. Molly spitting them out. Knows the taste of them now. Oranges in tissue paper packed in crates. Citrons too. Wonder is poor Citron

---

[13] Like Homer and Hamlet.

still alive in Saint Kevin's parade. And Mastiansky with the old cither. Pleasant evenings we had then. Molly in Citron's basketchair.

('Calypso')

Who has the organ here I wonder? Old Glynn he knew how to make that instrument talk, the *vibrato*: fifty pounds a year they say he had in Gardiner street. Molly was in fine voice that day, the *Stabat Mater* of Rossini. Father Bernard Vaughan's sermon first, Christ or Pilate? Christ, but don't keep us all night over it. Music they wanted. Footdrill stopped. Could hear a pin drop. I told her to pitch her voice against that corner. I could feel the thrill in the air, the full, the people looking up:

Quis est homo!

('Lotus Eaters')

Nostalgia, like fantasy and pity, is solidly based on the sensations and things of the real world, in present time, and the thrill of love and music is permitted by irreverent humour, 'Christ, but don't keep us all night over it'.

His inventiveness is practical; it includes ideas for ads, such as the caption 'On the track of the sun', and the scheme for the transparent show cart with smart girls inside to replace Hely's sandwich-men as promoters of good stationery. If pity is seasoned with humour and practicality, it keeps him in mind of the pathetic walking alphabet, 'Three bob a day, walking along the gutters, street after street. Just keep skin and bone together', then reverts to business, concluding that the sandwich-men, however ill-paid, are commercially hopeless. He loves to listen but is alert to persuasions, confidence tricks and lies. But he is not superior and is not averse to making the most of Paddy Dignam's death when Mrs Breen's 'O dear me' encourages him to reflect, 'May as well get her sympathy'.

His creativity and his lovingness are casually, undemandingly, briefly and shyly registered in his stories. His openness is restricted by fear and jealousy. There is the recurring story of his cuckoldry, told behind his back and constantly repressed, which can only be told in the uninhibited narratives of dreams. In Nighttown he hears and tells those most private fantasies we are afraid to tell or hear and yet wish to tell or hear. But his reticence is not always characterized by jealousy or sexual inhibition. It aspires to decorum and a sensitive prudence.

As Stephen and Bloom exchanges stories and silences in the Ithaca episode, Stephen outlines a story in the curt style of the prose-poems, dreams and epiphanies.[14] It seems to be suggested by the image of a girl writing by Bloom's idea for the advertising stunt of girls writing in a transparent cart:

> Which example did he adduce to induce Stephen to deduce that originality, though producing its own reward, does not invariably conduce to success?
>
> His own ideated and rejected project of an illuminated showcart, drawn by a beast of burden, in which two smartly dressed girls were to be seated engaged in writing.
>
> What suggested scene was then constructed by Stephen?
>
> Solitary hotel in mountain pass. Autumn. Twilight. Fire lit. In dark corner young man seated. Young woman enters. Restless. Solitary. She sits. She goes to window. She stands. She sits. Twilight. She thinks. On solitary hotel paper she writes. She thinks. She writes. She sighs. Wheels and hoofs. She hurries out. He comes from his dark corner. He seizes solitary paper. He holds it towards fire. Twilight. He reads. Solitary.
>
> What?
>
> In sloping, upright and backhands: Queen's hotel, Queen's hotel, Queen's Ho... ('Ithaca')

Bloom at once responds to Queen's Hotel because his father committed suicide in the Queen's Hotel, Ennis, County Clare, and unlike the other subterranean coincidences of which the characters are unaware, this one is raised conspicuously by the author:

> Did he attribute this homonymity to information or coincidence or intuition?
>
> Coincidence.

---

[14] A good example of Joyce's terse narrative is in a letter to Stanislaus Joyce (10 Jan. 1907):

No more at present: rushing off to WORK. Scene: draughty little stone-flagged room, chest of drawers to left, on which are the remains of lunch, in the centre, a small table on which are *writing materials* (*He* never forgot them) and a saltcellar: in the background, small-sized bed. A young man with snivelling nose sits at the little table: on the bed sit a madonna and plaintive infant. It is a January day. Title of above: *The Anarchist.*' (*Letters of James Joyce*, ii, ed. Richard Ellmann, London, 1966.)

Did he depict the scene verbally for his guest to see?

He preferred himself to see another's face and listen to another's words by which potential narration was realised and kinetic temperament relieved. (ibid.)

This is one of those moments in the novel when the novelist asserts artifice. We know that Bloom's explanation will not do. Like Diderot's Jacques, he is fictional and determined. The homonymity is not caused by coincidence but by collusion. It is created by Joyce. A moving moment in Bloom's imaginative encounter is made ironic as Joyce at once divulges and explains away his artifice. But the declaration is itself a shy one. No great claim is made for the junction of stories, coming, as it does, within a story about reserve. Bloom's shyness is not undermined but joined by Joyce's reticence.

IV. FINNEGANS WAKE

Encyclopaedic about so much, *Finnegans Wake* surveys narrative forms and themes. In this 'claybook' or 'allaphbed' we 'rede...its world', which is 'the same told of all'. In this world all conceivable variants of telling and listening are cast—though only just—in the form of a novel. Its ranging confusions make the perfect medium for the analysis of the narrative forms which create most books and all lives. Joyce's other novels are like other novels; their analysis of narrative imagination draws a line round narrative and publishes it as literature, while making it plain that the frame and form do not create an exclusive aesthetic category.[15] *Dubliners* and *Ulysses* insist on the continuity of life-stories and literature's stories but *Finnegans Wake* goes further, refusing to parade art at the expense of nature. Joyce's last novel not only discusses every imaginable form of unliterary and literary narrative, exhaustively and profoundly, but argues for the openness of literary narrative by conflating artistic and natural tellings and listenings. It shows the continuity and ubiquity of narrative through the power and economy of a brilliant work of narrative art.

After some of the eloquent silences of Leopold Bloom, *Finnegans*

[15] Compare Stanley E. Fish's observation: 'literature is language . . . but it is language around which we have drawn a frame, a frame that indicates a decision to regard with a particular self-consciousness the resources language has always possessed' ('How Ordinary is Ordinary Language?' *New Literary History*, vol. 5, no. 1, Autumn 1973).

Wake clamours and gabbles deafeningly, invoking a medley of sounds to make the noisiest novel ever written. Babble is one of its important effects. Though babble is from time to time found in poetry—in Smart's '*Jubilate Agno*', Hopkins's 'Spelt from Sibyl's Leaves', and in certain refrains—it rarely appears in novels. Northrop Frye believes that the form of *Finnegans Wake* is 'the one traditionally associated with scripture and sacred books, and treats life in terms of the fall and awakening of the human soul and the creation and apocalypse of nature'.[16] Joyce's last novel may be a Bible but it is even more clearly and certainly a Babel. It unifies and invokes linguistic confusion in order to attack the divisive propensities of the Old Testament God. The Tower of Babel's attempt at a vast and ambitious building was a pre-national enterprise which alarmed Jehovah. Threatened, he cleverly confounded language and frustrated architecture, observing 'Behold, the people is one, and they have all one language; and this they have begun to do: and now nothing will be restrained from them, which they have imagined to do' (Genesis II. 6). Joyce dislikes autocracy, so makes his own myth of rising after fall. Countering destruction with construction, division with unity, he erects a second Babel, international and high-rising. *Finnegans Wake* joins the scattered languages together again in a new humane attempt to make a unity and a name 'lest we be scattered abroad upon the face of the whole earth'. Unlike the Babel-builders, Joyce is fully aware of disintegration and cunningly admits its principle into his construction. But its aim is oneness. Its babble divides and unites.

The silences of narrative art are hard to render. The poem and the play, which may be designed to be spoken aloud, can assert stops, rests and quiet, but the novel can only express wordlessness through wordiness. Its compulsive talkativeness cannot even surround verbality with silence and it can only retail silence, never incorporate it. We might have supposed that it would be just as difficult for the novel to be noisy. A deafening sound that stops telling and listening resists the plain and referential trends of prose. But *Finnegans Wake* mocks our sense of limits by creating a new language and a new form. It takes narrative imagination round yet another unturned corner to include deafening and incoherent chatter, drunken slurring, stammering, dreamy incoherence, thunderclaps, white noise and radio interference. Don Quixote asked Sancho for a story in order to endure the frightful

[16] *The Anatomy of Criticism* (Princeton, New Jersey, 1957), p. 314.

noise and we often tell each other stories to keep noise or silence at bay. Cervantes keeps his din off the page but Joyce brings it on, admitting and even exploiting its obliterative power. We have to read this novel very slowly and over and over again, often finding it more legible when we read aloud. Many novelists have composed the stylized and elegant choruses that represent the crowd's good and bad gossip but only Joyce deafens us with its barrage. There are times when the thunderwords help us to listen; they punctuate the narrative with their peremptory cacophony. They are never mere sounds but eloquent reminders of the constructions of Babel or babble, concatenating words for thunder in a polyglot sesquipedalianism.

Joyce's patiently erected Babel is built out of many stories as well as many languages. His conflations of narrative are as startling as his confusions of the word. All novels join the story of individual lives with the story of life in general. The stories of Jacques the Fatalist, Lord Jim and Lucky Jim tell the stories of their heroes and the stories that their heroes tell and hear. Through these stories and stories about stories the novelist offers his account of what it is like to be human. He may also remember earlier versions of his story. Artists do not stand on each other's shoulders in the way that scientists and scholars do but they often show an inclination to rub elbows with their predecessors, in fellow-feeling, praise, deference, imitation, expostulation, criticism or revolt. The recognition of authority has a long history. Longinus calls for a study of the best models and Swift imagines *The Battle of the Books* in order to plead for the way of the Ancients. Fielding and Twain imitate Cervantes, Diderot praises Sterne, Jane Austen improves on Mrs Radcliffe, George Eliot summons Fielding, Dickens invokes the eighteenth-century novels and the *Arabian Nights*, Proust incorporates Anatole France, Thomas Mann revives Goethe, and Beckett mimes Joyce.[17] These are familiar acknowledgements to helpers, teachers, sponsors and begetters.

The act of salutation often produces mutations in the language and structure of the salutation. But Joyce's final account of humanity seems particularly to need not only to make the traditional bow to muses and masters but to join and collaborate with them most intimately. Throughout his novels the acknowledgements are humble, assertive, self-deprecatory, ambitious, grateful and a little mocking.

[17] 'A Wet Night', *More Pricks Than Kicks* (London, 1934).

He invokes the past in order not just to define and place but to create the activity of the present. Beginning as both a demonstration and an analysis of sources in *A Portrait of the Artist as a Young Man* and then moving into a multiple imitation in *Ulysses*, Joyce's homages give scaffolding and styles to his central story. He weaves analogy and allusion into his own fabric but is still writing novels which visibly set his individual text in a larger tradition and context. In *A Portrait of the Artist as a Young Man* the style and form of the schoolboy, Dumas' translator or the Elizabethans infect the style of Joyce, but the story told is clearly the story of Stephen's growing powers, as he assumes, assimilates and discards other men's styles and forms. In *Ulysses* the parallels of the *Odyssey* and *Hamlet* help to bring out the significances of the relationships of the three main characters but Penelope and Gertrude cast a faint shadow compared with Molly Bloom, Hamlet echoes thinly behind Stephen and Odysseus is less vivid than Leopold Bloom. Past stories make plain the changing or unchanging ways of heroism and love but there is no ambiguity about the ground-effect in the novel. Homer, Shakespeare, Dante and Mozart are in the background, felt as literary analogies and ancestries lying behind the present's particularity. To remember their yawning graves and reproachful ghosts is to assert the stronger presences of the dead and living in the cemetery in Dublin.

In *Finnegans Wake* Joyce has gone further. Salutation of the past has become constant re-creation; every utterance and incident is shaped and shadowed by models and precedents. The past jostles the present, alternative styles and stories[18] are part of the particularity of the book. This means, of course, that its particularity is a very odd one. There is no space between past and present or allusion and action. The novel tells the most past-haunted of all Joyce's ghost-stories, the most riddling of his beloved riddles which yearn for the answer 'Guess', the most curiously speculative of all his surmises, the most taciturn of his secrets. Analogy accompanies instead of staying in the background. The invoked words and forms now interfere with lucid reception of an individual language and story, like that crossing or jamming of radio waves felt in *Finnegans Wake*, an inspiration as well as an interference. Allusiveness makes the reader work—and perhaps also play—harder than he has ever done before, except in the speculations and exchanges of his own everyday life. Joyce's multiplied myths

[18] See particularly James S. Atherton. *The Books at the Wake* (London, 1959).

are codified explanations of human life. His own explanations seem to need the company of other explanations, just as Stephen and Bloom, however ineffectually, inhibitedly or transiently, rely on each other, as characters in fiction and as imitations of characters in life. Joyce blurs and blends his style and his stories with other actual and possible versions, thus re-erecting Babel's communal aspiration. When Shaun's exaggeratedly deferential audience begs him to tell an 'Aesiop's fable' in his 'own sweet way with words of style to your very and most obsequient', he introduces his story, 'The Ondt and the Gracehoper', with the comment, 'Well it is partly my own, isn't it'. Joyce may be more like Shem the artist than Shaun the operator but he is also trying to tell a story which is partly, but only partly, his own, and in a language ('slanguage' or 'Big Language') which is also only partly his.

Finnegans Wake creates a style out of punning and its narrative form is also a kind of pun. Particulars are obscured, references meet on equal terms, allusions and analogies are warmly welcomed. All that fall and rise again, the rivers, the sun, Finn, Finnegan, HCE, Humpty-Dumpty, Alice, Adam, Christ, the Phoenix, the phallus, Anna Livia, Shem and Shaun, Wellington, the White Knight, Dick Whittington and others, rise and fall and rise in unison. Babel rose and fell and Joyce makes it rise again. Rising and falling merge in puns like 'Phall if you will, rise you must', 'Finnegan' and 'Wake'. Many of the puns and neologisms suggest the common nature of narrative: 'the leaves of the living in the boke of the deeds', 'tolled', 'taling', 'wrongstoryshortener', 're-membore', 'bagateller', 'thumbnail reveries', 'sustained innerman monophone', 'nonday diary', 'allnightsnewseryreel', 'rintrospection', 'gabgutmemoirs', 'tattlepage', and many others. Puns, jammings, portmanteaux and wordladders generalize the particular as soon as it is formed, neighbouring it with precedents, surrounding it with fellow-myths. Allusion and expansion are so apt, witty and amusing that they create a particularity and keep abstractions fresh. This is after all mostly Joyce's story and no one else has managed to subdue particulars just like this, in narrative and verbal conflation which so remarkably summons community. There is a price and a risk, to be sure, and the demand for such hard work loses many readers. Those who hang on long enough to get something may or may not call it a bargain but can scarcely complain of short measure.

Joyce joins stories and tongues in order to show that all tongues tend to join in a common telling of need and nature. Joyce's is one story and one story only, the story of sex and death, rising and falling, beginnings and ends. He creates a recirculating narrative form in order to demonstrate his meaning. To programme such a motion simply to make the point would be a brilliant frivolity, a game played with imitative form, a flouting of readers. Joyce's much quoted comment that he expected us to spend our whole lives on the book seems reasonably imaginative and modest if we take it as a hint about his tale-in-mouth form—a form with many precedents in jokes, tales and songs. If we read this book to look for one thing or follow one thread we inevitably observe others out of the corner of our attention and are likely to start again, to re-focus and re-collect, turning back pages to link the last fragment with the first: 'A way a lone a last a loved a long the' (p. 628) . . . 'riverrun, past Eve and Adam's, from swerve of shore to bend of bay, brings us by a commodius vicus of recirculation back to Howth Castle and Environs' (p. 3).[19] The form of the novel enacts the cycle, refuses the arbitrary sense of both ending and beginning and admits the impossibility of ordinary broad scanning. It offers a new experience of re-reading, scarcely exhaustible in a lifetime, but unlikely to engross that lifetime.

A central myth in *Finnegans Wake* is summed up in 'every telling has its taling and that's the he and the she of it'. 'Taling' is a pun which gathers together story, death and coupling to declare more economically and piercingly than T. S. Eliot ('birth, copulation and death') that ends and beginnings are inseparable, adding that all life-stories turn on birth and death. The rise and fall constitute the elementary story of all recorded cultures. Joyce's style is polyglot, erudite and colloquial, in order to remind us of the commonness and ordinariness of story-telling. Each birth and death is a crucial event in the individual life but it has to be narrated and not experienced, since the protagonist, out of hearing when he is born as when he dies, can neither observe nor tell the major events of his own life. Joyce uses his novel to say something ancient and simple about the human story. His key to mythologies is as uncasaubonlike as possible for he insists that it is a key which pedants cannot turn. In *Middlemarch*, Casaubon draws the line at the story of Cupid and Psyche, which is not to be reckoned as a genuine mythical product. George Eliot reserves her sympathy for the Nazarene sculptor, Adolf Naumann,

[19] (London, 1934). All references are to this edition.

one of those chief renovators of Christian art, one of those who had not only revived but expanded that grand conception of supreme events as mysteries at which the successive ages were spectators, and in relation to which the great souls of all periods became as it were contemporaries. (bk. ii, ch. xxii)

Like George Eliot, Joyce contributes to the persistent renovation of art. The originality of *Finnegans Wake* lies in its generous eclecticism. It is dense and puzzling in order to get everything in.

Joyce's generalization in *Finnegans Wake* sometimes insists on the barest, least literary and most familiar form of narration, which outlines event to answer our deepest needs by its very absence of particulars. But the announcement of myth is complex and devious. The novel turns from one mode of familiar narrative to another, invoking all the forms of literary and unliterary experience to insist that there is one story which we start hearing in childhood and go on hearing and telling as long as we live:

> The fall (bababadalgharaghtakamminarronnkonnbronntonner-ronntuonnthunntrovarrhounawnskawn toohoohoordenenthurnuk!) of a once wallstrait oldparr is retaled early in bed and later on life down through all christian minstrelsy. (p. 3)

To start in one's childhood is not enough. The beginning of the novel denies beginnings. The first word 'riverrun' with its 'vicus of recirculation' declaims the principle of recirculation, typographically (by its lower case 'r'), structurally (by joining with the last word on the last page), philosophically (by incorporating Vico into the language and vulgarizing his proper name), symbolically (through the truths about rivers) and historically (by taking us from the Creation, un-assumingly present as a local pub, to the here and now of Howth and environs). Tristram is as penisolate as Tristram Shandy and Tristan and joins with Tom Sawyer, Shem and Shaun, the Bible and Swift to insist on the community of story-telling. The third paragraph insists on the lifescale and the historical scale of narrative, as it joins the story of childhood to the story of literature: 'early in bed and later on life down through all christian minstrelsy'. Such assimilation of story to story constantly accompanies the invocation of past story-tellers, including the once and always dedal Joyce:

The answer, to do all the diddies in one dedal, would sound: from pulling himself on his most flavoured canal the huge chesthouse of his elders (the *Popapreta*, and some navico, navvies!) he had flickered up and flinnered down into a drug and drunkery addict, growing megalomane of a loose past. This explains the litany of septuncial lettertrumpets honorific, highpitched, erudite, neoclassical which he so loved as patricianly to manuscribe after his name. It would have diverted if ever seen the shuddersome spectacle of this semidemented zany amid the inspissated grime of his glaucous den making believe to read his usylessly unreadable Blue Book of Eccles, *édition de ténèbres* ... (p. 179)

Just as *Ulysses* contains the characters of *Dubliners* in a reminder of reality and art, so *Finnegans Wake* contains references to all Joyce's earlier works and is haunted by some of their characters. It also contains the well-known instances of a snatch of accidental conversation with Beckett[20] and a jibe at Stanislaus's jibes about *Finnegans Wake*. The most abstract of novels makes a point of accidentals. This admission of the accident insists on the incorrigibility of narrative, opening cracks in the frail wall of literature. At one extreme of the novel's narrative range are the myths and fables and at the other are the fragments of narrative *trouvé*. The first sentence describes both the principle of narrative recirculation and the narrative range.

We are throughout not only in the presence of a huge number of books and authors but a huge number of unbookish stories and tellers. The literary, historical, philosophical and scientific narrative is linked to the narratives of ordinary life, the private and the social narrative, oral and written. There are epics, romances, fables, poems, novels, novelettes, stories, riddles, word-games and the sly narratives of mathematical calculations and lessons. There are dreams, speculations, prayers, testimonies, judicial summaries, confessions, rumours, detractions, surmises, tattling and tale-telling, secrets, codes, gossip, reminiscences, correspondence, stammerings, incoherences, babble, foreign languages and the attempt at overcoming foreignness through pidgin English, Esperanto and Volapük. There are the narratives of the public media, the post, lecture, learned treatise, magazine, newspaper, radio, television, cinema, gossip column and interview. The novel establishes not only vast area but continuity. We are throughout in the presence of

[20] Richard Ellmann, *James Joyce*, p. 662.

all the narrative forms that mark and have marked human culture. Joyce is not just mapping mythologies. He is interested in indicating the difficulty of telling and listening, so needs both to blur the comprehensible and affirm the incomprehensible.

The novel is filled with urgent listeners and desperate tellers. The reader's needs and frustrations are reflected and so are the novelist's. But Joyce goes far beyond literature. He makes up an artificial language of his own which reveals and tries to overcome general problems of discourse. As he puts in bits and pieces of language which he knew well or not very well and sometimes got up for the purpose of the novel, so he also puts in as many modes of narrative as possible. What may look like a wilful experiment seems to be impelled by a desire to imagine all possible forms of listening and telling and to appreciate their successes and failures.

The most conspicuous narrative form in *Finnegans Wake* is probably the dream, which symbolizes, justifies and subsumes the difficulties of telling and listening: 'the action of *Ulysses* was chiefly in the daytime, and the action of my new work takes place at night. It's natural things should not be so clear at night, isn't it now?'[21] The fragmentariness and confusions of dream structures and language is no naïve imitation, for the surrealist fallacy which supposes that the wakeful reason can tap the language of the unconscious mind does not appeal to Joyce. He had used *erlebte Rede* (the free indirect style) in his previous writing and the lived form, like the lived language, of *Finnegans Wake* represents a compromise between first-person dreaming and the third-person story of a dream. The dream is a decorous form for the uncertainties and difficulties of telling and imagining. Joyce knew of Freud's interest in the puns and witticisms of dream-work, if indeed he needed Freud to draw his attention to them. The dream presents the perfect excuse for continuous punning. It is also a dream dreamt in many languages, polyglot and playful. The dream also makes a good medium for telling uncertain stories, about the Phoenix Park mystery, the crime of HCE and the goings-on of Anna Livia. It is right that such an inaudible novel should be filled with demands and prayers for intelligibility, that it should contain confessions of incoherence, rude and courteous requests for enlightenment and admissions of defeat. It is indeed misleading to stress the obscurity of nocturnal narration. Much of *Finnegans Wake* is eagerly communicative in the most

[21] Ellmann, *James Joyce*, p. 603.

familiar way. The best instances of bad and good gossip are here.
There is the rumour that blackens and travesties HCE:

> Hung Chung Egglyfella now speak he tell numptywumpty top-
> sawys belongahim pidgin. Secret things other persons place there
> covered not. How you fell from story to story like a sagasand to lie.
> Enfilmung infirmity. On the because alleging to having a finger a
> fudding in pudding and pie. And here's the witnesses. Glue on to
> him, Greevy! Bottom anker, Noordeece! And kick kick killykick
> for the house that juke built! Wait till they send you to sleep,
> scowpow! By jurors' cruces! Then old Hunphy-dunphyville'll be
> blasted to bumboards by the youthful heralds who would once you
> were. (pp. 374–5)

> and he was so sorry, he was really, because he left the bootybutton
> in the handsome cab and now, tell the truth, unfriends never, (she
> was his first messes dogess and it was a very pretty peltry and there
> were faults on both sides) well, he attempted (or so they say) ah,
> now, forget and forgive (don't we all?) and, sure, he was only
> funning with his andrewmartins and his old age coming over
> him...(pp. 391–2)

There is the banal off-the-cuff public response of the opinion poll
or the pundit's interview:

> Sylvia Silence, the girl detective (*Meminerva*, but by now one hears
> turtlings all over Doveland!) when supplied with informations as to
> the several facets of the case in her cozy-dozy bachelure's flat, quite
> overlooking John a'Dream's mews, leaned back in her really truly
> easy chair to query restfully through her vowelthreaded syllabelles:
> Have you evew thought, wepowtew, that sheew gweatness was his
> twadgedy? (p. 61)

There is the gossips' gossip about 'giddgaddy, grannyma, gossipace-
ous Anna Livia':

O

tell me all about
Anna Livia! I want to hear all

> about Anna Livia. Well, you know Anna Livia? Yes, of course,
> we all know Anna Livia. Tell me all. Tell me now. You'll die
> when you hear. (p. 196)

Onon! Onon! tell me more. Tell me every tiny teign. I want to know every single ingul. Down to what made the potters fly into jagsthole. And why were the vesles vet. That homa fever's winning me wome...
How many aleveens had she in tool? I can't rightly rede you that.
(p. 201)

Describe her! Hustle along, why can't you? Spitz on the iern while it's hot. I wouldn't miss her for irthing on nerthe. Not for the lucre of lomba strait. Oceans of Gaud, I mosel hear that!

...

Bon a ventura? Malagassy? What had she on, the liddel oud oddity? How much did she scallop, harness and weights? Here she is, Amnisty Ann! Call her calamity electrifies man.
No electress at all but old Moppa Necessity, angin mother of injons. I'll tell you a test. But you must sit still. Will you hold your peace and listen well to what I am going to say now? (p. 207)

The novel balances social and personal narrative, malignant, loving, scurrilous, tolerant, brilliant and banal.
Finnegans Wake is also speculative biography, trying to piece together facts, fictions, rumours, documents, interviews, traditions, slanders, hints, clues, confessions, revelations, admissions and secrets. Dream and gossip are probing, provisional and speculative, and so is the investigation of biographer, journalist, informer, spy, judge and jury. All narrative forms make stabs at meaning, are fascinated by secrets and confessions. Secrecy is often about death and sex, as the telling keeps its promise to be about the 'taling' and the 'he and she'. Joyce deprives us of the particulars which the novelist usually supplies but has an eye to the deprivations and restrictions of telling and listening which are the rule in life outside novels. The satisfactions of narrative are realized in the anatomy of curiosity and gossiping but they are also withheld from the reader, facts left shadowy, truth untold. The telling of the novel is as obscure and unreliable as dream and also as a wide-awake narrative. Speculation, memory, rumour and eye-witness reports are untrustworthy, though they are often all we have. The most trivial game or joke, like the three-page bibliography of Anna Livia's 'mamafesta' (pp. 104-7), and the most solemn summons to literary precedent, like the invocations of obituary and fable, combine to force the novel into its most elastic form, compressed and stretched.

Joyce turns the tables on the Old Testament God in flouting 'broken heaventalk', for his iconopoeic novel builds its new Babel in the most unpromising political and linguistic conditions. Its ambitiousness is ancient and its stories admit as much, as they assemble the most exhaustive anatomy of the narrative imagination, modestly, tentatively, evasively and even vaguely.

Index

This index is restricted to authors (including critics) referred to by name or by work in the text. Anonymous works are listed according to their title. Italic type indicates substantial discussion.